MORALITY WITHIN THE
LIMITS OF REASON

MORALITY
within the
» LIMITS «
of
REASON

Russell Hardin

THE UNIVERSITY OF CHICAGO PRESS

Chicago and London

RUSSELL HARDIN is the Mellon Foundation Professor of
Political Science, Philosophy, and Public Policy Studies at
the University of Chicago. He is the editor of *Ethics: An
International Journal of Social, Political, and Legal Philosophy*
and coeditor of *Nuclear Deterrence: Ethics and Strategy*, both
published by the University of Chicago Press.

The University of Chicago Press, Chicago 60637
The University of Chicago Press, Ltd., London

97 96 95 94 93 92 91 90 89 88   5 4 3 2 1

Library of Congress Cataloging-in-Publication Data

Hardin, Russell, 1940–
   Morality within the limits of reason.

   Bibliography: p.
   Includes index.
   1. Ethics.   2. Social ethics.   3. Utilitarianism.
   I. Title.
BJ1012.H285   1988   171'.5   88-1172
ISBN 0-226-31618-1

FOR JOAN AND JOSH
who have borne with the limits of my reason

Contents

Preface

In what follows I wish to reconstruct utilitarianism on the basis of two
fundamentally important classes of considerations that bear on the
problem of choosing in social life: these are the limits of reason that
prevent us from even approaching ideal conditions and the pervasive
problem of strategic interaction in bringing about good results. Another major class of considerations is difficulties in the value theory of
utilitarianism. I will address this class of difficulties at some length, but
I will not pretend to offer a constructive resolution of these difficulties.
One may read much of this as critical of utilitarianism, especially if one
has a firm view of what utilitarianism must be and if that sense is not
subject to reconstruction. I think the core of utilitarianism is commitment to welfare as the good to be promoted. This will remain true even
as our understanding of the nature of welfare changes, as it has changed
over the past two centuries.

Often we can see that recognition of relevant limits of reason in
moral choice yields understandings of the structure and even content of
a general theory of moral choice. Indeed, virtually all of the standard
problems and practices—such as promising, beneficent action, generalization, protection of rights, distributive justice, paternalism, and
collective responsibility—of moral and political theory can be seen
more clearly against the backdrop of an account of relevant limits of our
reason. It is, however, an irony implicit in the view that we suffer from
limits of reason that the general task of explicating consequentialist
moral theory—or any moral theory that is sufficiently articulated as to
be worthy of extensive discussion—demands more grasp of more issues and even of whole intellectual disciplines than anyone is likely to

muster. The fracturing of intellectual discourse into disciplines both reflects and exacerbates the difficulty of our enterprise.

A modest stance toward any ethical theory of long standing with articulate contributions by many critics and defenders is incumbent on any genuinely philosophical person. The best criticisms should perhaps typically be seen as contributions to clarity rather than as refutations. Surprisingly much of modern moral theory takes the form of dramatic refutations of whole schools of thought. Most of the refutations turn on quick intuitions, and many turn on neat paradoxes. A common argument from quick substantive intuitions against utilitarianism is, not to caricature excessively, as follows. Utilitarianism permits us to override the norm of promise keeping in order to enhance welfare. But we know that it is immoral to break a promise. Q.E.D., utilitarianism is an immoral theory. Arguments from paradox often take the form of demonstrating that it would not be utilitarian to try to be utilitarian.

It is common to canvass problems with one's own program and almost as common to treat them very cursorily before implicitly supposing that they must be resolvable or not troubling. In moral theory there are massive, troubling difficulties with all programs, many of which are fundamentally conceptual. These difficulties in utilitarianism are in its value theory and in the nature of the person who is valued. In action-based theories they are in the nature of action and agency (as discussed in §15) and, again, in the value theory. In rationalist theories they are typically in the failure of the rational deductions to persuade many evidently intelligent people. The best way to make progress in one's own and in our collective understanding is to acknowledge the difficulties and to make their character and significance as clear as possible in order that we might deal with them. It is not inconceivable that the chief difference between certain apparently quite different moral theories is primarily a reflection of different misunderstandings rather than of different understandings. As we struggle with the enterprise of moral and political theory, honesty coupled with any understanding of the complexity of the problems frequently recommends modesty in asserting conclusions.

In this work I will primarily address what I think are the easy issues in utilitarianism. These are the structural issues of getting problems straight and understanding all of the relevant causal relations that go into our consequentialist judgments. Many of these are readily resolvable if limits of reason are taken adequately into account. I will leave for last and least the major problem of utilitarianism as it stands now: its value theory or the theory of human welfare. I think that argument on these two classes of issues is often separable, so that we may get structural issues straight even without succeeding in first getting the welfare theory clear. Indeed, I think that discussion generally profits from holding these issues apart as far as possible. I will therefore present structural issues and see how far they can be resolved with the least demanding value theory assumptions. Then I will bring in more demanding value theory considerations to see how much further we can go with a richer value theory. Virtually everyone interested in moral and political theory, whether utilitarian or not, should want to master such issues, which are central to the main arguments of both critics and proponents of utilitarianism as well as of most moral theorists more generally. I hope at the least that I have made some of them clear enough that critics and proponents alike can more readily agree on what it is they are rejecting or defending.

Readers have noted many shortcomings of my struggle in this work that I can acknowledge but not repair. For example, I will not attempt to answer the question, "Why be moral?" I will not assess the meaning or function of moral discourse in the context of my own discussions. And I will not attempt to give full critical responses to many alternative theories or even to previous utilitarian accounts of all or parts of my concerns here. In particular, I will not deal with Kant's far more extensive treatment of reason and its limits. I regret that my title suggests affinities with Kant,[1] as though I were presenting a rationalist account and trying to deduce what is good from pure reason as well as trying to deduce how to achieve it. My 'reason' is concerned in a sense with means rather than ends.[2] One reader has therefore strongly recommended another title, such as "Information. Strategy, and Morality." Among the limits of reason that sometimes confuse moral discourse are the misleading resonances we get from words that have manifold meanings. Few or no words can be appropriated to such widely diverse uses as reason while continuing to have a positive aura.

1. Immanuel Kant's *Religion innerhalb der Grenzen der blossen Vernunft* has been translated into English as *Religion within the Sphere of Naked Reason, Religion within the Boundary of Pure Reason,* and, under the title by which it is perhaps most familiar to contemporary English speakers, *Religion within the Limits of Reason Alone* (New York: Harper, 1960; trans. by Theodore M. Greene and Hoyt H. Hudson; trans. first published 1934; German original first published 1793). (See the "Translators' Preface," pp. cxxxv–cxxxvii, in ibid.) None of these is entirely felicitous.

2. Kant remarks that "it is one of the inescapable limitations of man and of his faculty of practical reason . . . to have regard, in every action, to the consequences thereof" (ibid., p. 6). Utilitarianism might therefore be dismissively characterized as merely an inescapable limitation of practical reason. May we at least live well by our practical reason.

Acknowledgments

It is a pleasure no less than a duty to acknowledge assistance from many people and a couple of institutions in the writing of this book. It got its initial start toward being a book rather than an odd collection of papers with the support of the Earhart Foundation in the spring of 1983. It survived the subsequent four years while I served as chair of the Committee on Public Policy Studies at the University of Chicago only because there were wonderful people on the staff of the committee who made life possible: Adèle Pardee, Steven Wheatley, Carol Hendrickson, Steven Loevy, Diane Brady, Diane Hall, Doug Sell, Francis Billingsley, Beth Boland, and Annette Barrett. This book should appear as that committee matures into a school. The book has had the able research assistance of Paul Bullen throughout. It has benefited from careful readings and extensive written commentaries by several colleagues here and elsewhere: Sissela Bok, David Braybrooke, Michael Cain, Thomas Christiano, Alan Gewirth, Bernard Grofman, Don Herzog, Margaret Levi, Richard A. Posner, Bart Schultz, Amartya Sen, and an anonymous reviewer for the University of Chicago Press. Most of its various parts have benefited from exposure to my informal Tuesday evening seminar in contemporary moral and political theory at the University of Chicago and to colloquia in many other institutions. That it exists at all is due in large part to David Gauthier and Brian Barry, who invited me to present initial variants of Chapters 2 and 3 to conferences and who imposed severe deadlines, a device that anyone who has an instinctive understanding of weakness of will (§35) must well appreciate. One could write an academic author's variant of Mill's observation: "As civilization advances, every person becomes dependent, for more and more of what most nearly concerns him, not upon his own exertions, but upon the general arrangements of society" (see Chap. 4, §27). If I had ever doubted such arguments, I have had ample opportunity to be tutored of their truth these past four years.

Parts of Chapters 3 and 2 of this book have been published in somewhat different form in *Ethics* (October 1986) as "The Utilitarian Logic of Liberalism" and in *Social Justice Research* (April 1987) as "Social Justice in the Large and Small." Parts of the paper, "Collective Rights" (*The Restraint of Liberty* [1985], vol. 7 of the *Bowling Green Studies in Applied Philosophy*) have also been borrowed for scattered parts of the present book. I thank the University of Chicago Press, Plenum Publishers, and the Department of Philosophy, Bowling Green State University, for permission to republish this material here.

Introduction

Utilitarianism is the moral theory that judges the goodness of outcomes—and therefore the rightness of actions insofar as they affect
outcomes—by the degree to which they secure the greatest benefit to
all concerned. In its simplest version, utilitarianism has been based on
the supposition that the benefits or utilities to all concerned could simply be added. If this were possible, we could decide among a collection
of alternative outcomes by simply picking that which yielded the greatest sum of benefits. This simplistic value theory is no longer given
credence by sophisticated philosophers—nor for that matter by economists or other social theorists. The reason it is generally rejected
is primarily that we doubt the exactitude, perhaps even the epistemological possibility, of interpersonal comparisons of utility,
welfare, or benefits that such a theory requires. The degree to which we
can make interpersonal comparisons will substantially affect the degree
to which we can make claims of fairness or justice.

Most social scientists interested in social justice seem to be utilitarian
in large part, at least insofar as one can assign a general moral theory to
those who are not typically articulate about their underlying moral
assumptions. Against this near consensus among social scientists,
many, perhaps most, contemporary philosophers who contribute to
moral theory argue against utilitarianism. A chief objection to utilitarianism is that it supposedly violates our sense of distributive justice.
Even if one wished to reject utilitarianism, however, an investigation of
the game theoretic structures of the interactions that interest us and of
the limits of our reason in dealing with them is enlightening for the
clarity it gives to issues in social justice as well as to other moral
problems.

Utilitarian moral theory has two major elements. One is the concern with consequences in the form of human welfare. The other is the nature of human welfare, the value theory of utilitarianism. We can say a great deal about the first concern while leaving the second somewhat open. It is characteristic of the literature on utilitarianism that it generally focuses on problems arising from the concern with consequences per se and that it commonly takes the issue of the value theory of utilitarianism for granted. (Critics of utilitarianism often make their task easy by assuming an implausible value theory and directing criticism at the implications of their value theory rather than at its assumptions. They draw some license for this uninstructive enterprise from the fact that utilitarians, such as Bentham, have sometimes adopted an implausible value theory.)

Oddly, that emphasis is just backward. In what follows I hope to show that the utilitarian program is on strong footing in its consequentialism. Its greatest difficulties are in its value theory, which, as is true also of other value theories, such as that of economics, has come to seem increasingly problematic as it has been increasingly investigated and understood. The most demanding enterprise for utilitarians—as for all moral theorists—is in articulating a credible value theory, which for utilitarians must be a theory of human welfare.[1] Most of my effort here will be expended on establishing the structural footing for utilitarianism while leaving the value theory open. In Chapter 5, I will canvass several of the most important problems for a utilitarian theory of human welfare.

§1 An Overview

The constructive argument of this book will be presented in Chapters 1–4. These deal with limits of reason in moral and political decisions and with the resolution of moral and political problems in the light of these limits. This discussion is undertaken on the assumption that much of the specific content of our value theory of human welfare is left undefined. Chapter 5 then takes up the nature of major problems inherent in a theory of human welfare. Throughout the earlier chapters conclusions vary depending on the richness of the value theory claims we can make.

Chapter 1 considers the limits of reason that burden moral choice and that underlie all the further discussions. These are the usual cog-

---

1. One may wish to go further and include some other beings in the larger assessment of welfare effects of our actions. This is not an issue I will address.

nitive and structural limits to good decision making, which are well understood by philosophers and, especially, social scientists in various fields. These include limits on mental ability, limits on time available for deciding, limits on information, and limits on relevant theory. Another major limit of moral reason that is not usually discussed in this context is the inability of a single individual to determine an outcome independently of the actions of others. This is the problem of strategic interaction, the understanding of which has been greatly advanced by its game theoretic representation. Given various limits of reason, we can recast much of the debate over utilitarianism as floundering efforts to deal with difficulties in making good decisions to determine good outcomes, as in the debate over act- versus rule-utilitarianism. And we can grasp why certain forms of essentially a priori argument do not yield compelling conclusions.

Chapter 2 presents a strategic analysis of the range of interactions we face, both individually and socially. These are divisible into those that involve small numbers of people, even dyads, and those that involve large numbers of people, even whole societies. On another dimension, they are divisible into those that involve pure conflict, those that involve pure coordination, and those that involve a mixture of both conflict and coordination. From an understanding of the strategic structures of these categories of problems, we can already deduce a great deal about the way to handle them and about how to judge outcomes from the relevant interactions. If we wish to push judgment of outcomes very far, however, we must be able to make strong claims from our value theory.

Chapter 3 takes up some elementary problems in the institutional resolution of interactions. Many institutions, such as legal rights, are easily seen as responses to limits of reason. They are devices of institutional protection or intervention to achieve better outcomes than could be achieved by individuals acting without constraint. Often, as is typically assumed in procedural theories of justice, institutional constraints on action have effects that are essentially liberating or enabling in their larger impact. We can reach initially strong conclusions about the form of certain institutional arrangements even from the exceedingly limited welfare theory that assumes interpersonal comparisons are not possible or not meaningful. If we push very far, however, we find, as in Chapter 2, that we require stronger value theory assumptions to resolve our problems. Indeed, the prima facie conclusions we can reach about certain kinds of interactions even from the most limited value theory do not stand up when we combine them into a general set of institutional arrangements, as in Chapter 4.

Chapter 4 explores institutional issues further by focusing on problems that cannot, even prima facie, be treated as though they could be addressed without interpersonal comparisons of welfare. Any reasonably extensive institutional structure for regulating social interactions can be justified only from a relatively rich value theory that assumes at least some degree of interpersonal comparisons of welfare. This is patently true for issues of distributive justice, a notion that makes little sense without interpersonal comparisons of welfare. But it also follows for many institutional interventions that seem to benefit almost everyone. Given a welfare theory that supports modest interpersonal comparisons, however, we can make utilitarian sense of many interventions that are often criticized as paternalistic. Indeed, we can make substantially clearer sense of the whole notion of paternalism when we bring it under an institutional utilitarian theory.

Finally, Chapter 5 takes up several difficult issues in utilitarian value theory. The most articulate and sophisticated approach to such a theory so far has been the utility theory developed in modern economics from Smith to the present day. Alas, this theory is not a single, coherent theory but is several strains that do not fit well together. If we had a coherent structure for utilitarian value theory, we would still need to give it substantive content before we could apply it to our choices. Relevant content is often assumed by direct intuition. Unfortunately, such intuition is inherently fraught with problems, especially the problem that Bentham labeled *ipse dixitism,* which is the failure to give any kind of justification. Moreover, the substantive content of a theory of human welfare must depend on the nature of the human person. If the welfare theory is subjective, as it seems it must be, this fact raises questions about the strength of subjective identification with the self over time and perhaps even in any given moment. Moreover, a welfare theory that is based in subjective valuations raises difficult issues of the origin of the valuations and the autonomy of the individual who makes them.

If we are to devise a utilitarian or other moral theory that is compelling, it must finally deal with all of the structural issues of Chapters 1 through 4 and the value theory issues of Chapter 5. Much of the criticism of utilitarianism has been directed at supposed contradictions in its handling of structural problems. I think such criticism has generally been misguided. If there is a major problem in the articulation of utilitarianism, that flaw is the difficulties that still stand in the way of its being given an adequate value theory. In this, utilitarianism is remarkably at one with all moral theory.

In this book I generally wish to leave the question of the relevant value theory open while discussing structural, informational, strategic, and other constraints on our utilitarian evaluations. We can then bring in value theories of varying strengths to see how far we can go with our moral prescriptions. Rather than speak of utility, I will generally speak of 'welfare,' which is a less well-defined term and is therefore less fraught with specific associations (see further, chap. 5, especially §33). I will generally start from the least demanding value theory, one that requires no interpersonal comparisons and no cardinal measures, and then bring in stronger assumptions. This way we may see how compelling our utilitarian conclusions are even in the face of serious doubts about the more demanding value theories. Surprisingly often, we can derive substantial conclusions from minimalist assumptions, at least prima facie, as in Chapter 3. When we bring very many of these conclusions together, their interaction may suggest that we need stronger value theory assumptions to reach the whole *set* of conclusions (see especially §§25 and 26).

Sometimes, as discussed especially in Chapters 2 and 3, we can reach substantial utilitarian conclusions on a welfare theory that allows no interpersonal comparisons. Sometimes, as discussed in Chapters 2 (especially §12) and 4, we would require substantial comparisons to make utilitarian prescriptions for action or for the design of institutions. I think it is reasonable to suppose that we can make limited comparisons of welfare between individuals in many contexts. For example, it is easy to imagine contexts in which no reasonable person would disagree with the claim that my mosquito bite is less harmful to my welfare than your broken hip is to yours. Presumably *you* would not disagree with such a claim—and that is a start on generalizing to the evaluation of every reasonable person.

A difficulty in presenting the theses here is that each has its importance and even its meaning to some extent only in conjunction with others. One cannot successfully discuss any of them in isolation. But one can only present them more or less serially a page at a time. As a result, it may often happen that the reader can make better sense of an early argument after reading later arguments. Two necessary devices for coping with this difficulty are to take up some issues in a preliminary way early on and then to address them more fully later and to bring up some problems to which the analyses apply in each of several contexts in order to help tie them together. I use the former device for the central issue of value theory. It is important throughout to keep clear whether interpersonal comparisons are assumed and, if they are, whether they are ordinal or additive. If they are additive, we can simply add welfare changes from each of various possible actions or policies and conclude in favor of that with the largest sum. Generally, however, we cannot assume additive interpersonal measures of welfare.

I use the second device of addressing the same practical problem in the context of several analytical issues for such problems as promise keeping and for a tale proposed by William James for the purpose of undercutting utilitarian recommendations that run against egalitarian distributions. I think promise keeping is not an issue of major moral significance despite the role it has played in a remarkably large number of books and articles on moral theory in the twentieth century.[2] It is only in the context of the informational, value theoretic, and strategic issues discussed here that it is clear why it is not a major issue in moral theory (see §§10, 11, 13, 27). James's tale supposes that we are offered the possibility of bliss for the millions at the cost of lonely torture for one poor soul. The tale has many elements typical of nifty examples that are used to undercut whole schools of thought—a dramatic device that is especially common in moral theory. It assumes many things that, on the account of limits of reason discussed here, are generally dubious: radical factual knowledge far beyond the capacities of a pragmatist (§7), a facile value theory (§27), and extraordinary confidence in odd intuitions (§34). It is instructive to see how many odd assumptions come into such an example.

2. A recent bibliography includes over 600 references (see Eddie Yeghiayan, "Promises: A Bibliography," *Philosophy Research Archives* 7 [1981]: 1055–1092).

1

Limits of Reason in
Moral Theory

One of the first lessons of any serious attention to the problem of
rationality is that a complete account of everything involved in one's
significant decisions is not possible. If this is true of one's choices of
means to ends in general it is also true of one's choices of means to moral
ends. Any moral theory that is concerned with the ends of actions must
therefore be incomplete in its recommendations unless it includes a
theory of the contingent decision-making abilities and behavior of people. All versions of utilitarianism, and consequentialist moral theories
or principles in general, are of course concerned with what ends result
from actions—hence G. E. M. Anscombe's appellation "consequentialism."[1]

The fact of our limited rationality and lack of information has often
been noted in discussions in ethics, especially of utilitarianism. But I
want to argue that these and other limits are more fundamentally
important than is generally recognized and that to take them into account at the outset, rather than as a marginal corrective to specific
conclusions, often drastically alters the conclusions one reaches. I think
many of our most important moral arrangements and norms result
from these limits. Hence, it would be perverse to construct our theory
as though these limits do not matter. Many arguments and conclusions
in the debates over utilitarianism are greatly clarified and, I think, even
resolved by viewing the issue as one of choosing well rather than as one
of positing first principles. Among the problems that the focus on

1. G. E. M. Anscombe, "Modern Moral Philosophy," in Anscombe, *Ethics, Religion
and Politics,* vol. 3 of *Collected Philosophical Papers* (Minneapolis: University of Minnesota
Press, 1981), pp. 26–42. Also see C. D. Broad, "The Doctrine of Consequences in
Ethics," *International Journal of Ethics* 24 (April 1914): 293–320.

rational limits to decision making helps to resolve are the issues of autonomy and liberalism as principles supposedly in conflict with utility or welfare, differences in utilitarian recommendations in policy and in personal realms, conflicts between rights and consequential considerations more broadly, the significance of the distinction between so-called act- and rule–utilitarianisms, collective responsibility, paternalism, generalization in ethics, and the strategic significance of coordination and convention in moral choosing.

There are three large classes of limits of reason that I wish to discuss. The first, which will be discussed in this chapter, includes various limits of cognitive ability. This class of limits of reason is generally well recognized and even moderately well understood, so that discussion of it can be brief here. The second class of limits, which is the focus of the next chapter, comprises the difficulties inherent in the fact that consequences of great interest are seldom the result of one individual's actions alone but are the product of strategic interaction with others. The third class, which will be outlined in Chapter 5, involves limits of the power of our value theory.

In what follows in the present chapter, I will lay out briefly the range of cognitive limits of reason (§2). Then I will very briefly discuss the role of game theoretic reasoning in consequentialist moral theory and the strategic limits on individual achievement of outcomes that game theory well represents (§3)—this topic will be pursued at length in Chapter 2. I will then relate these to the unfortunate separation of moral and political theory in much of twentieth-century philosophy (§4) and to the debate on act–utilitarianism versus rule–utilitarianism and the argument of David Lyons that certain forms of rule–utilitarianism are extensionally equivalent to act-utilitarianism (§5). Then, to clear the ground of certain objections to the nature of utilitarianism, I will briefly rehearse the utilitarian program as historically represented in its major strains (§6). This is largely an account of variously sophisticated recognitions of the role of particular limits of reason in the project of achieving utilitarian outcomes. Finally, I will turn to the difficult problem of testing ethical claims by applying them to generally imaginary examples (§7), which sorely try the limits of our reason.

§2 Limits of Reason

A conspicuous quality of any consequentialist moral theory is that it turns on relationships of means to ends. Hence, insofar as it is concerned with individual agents, it must be based on an understanding of the rational capacities of choosers. The literature on utilitarianism, whether arguing for it or against it, often makes assumptions about human decision making that are egregiously simplistic. Theorists of organizational decision making and of individual choice recognize significant limits to our ability to make holistically rational choices in complex social situations. Given reasonable assumptions about the rational limits to decision making, one must reach conclusions concerning the actual implications of a consequentialist moral principle that are often substantially different from those in the debates over utilitarianism and moral theory more generally.

Much of the discussion of moral choice involves issues that have come to be better understood by social theorists than by philosophers, not least because social scientists are concerned with a much broader range of issues to which they might apply their analyses. This is especially true of decision making in general, of limits to our information, and of the strategic implications of choices and actions. To some extent it is even true, perhaps surprisingly, of value theory, which one might suppose to be of more urgent concern to philosophers. Each of these topics is the subject of a vast theoretical literature that abstracts from particular problems to reach general conclusions. The most important conclusion is that in typical decision contexts we could not possibly be rational in the demanding, holistic sense implied by excessively pristine common notions of rationality, pristine notions that pervade moral philosophy.

It is common to argue against utilitarianism that it does too much. Its greatest weakness, on the contrary, is one it shares intuitionism and every other moral theory: it cannot do enough. The urge to have it do more than it can has led to the weakest and most easily refuted claims of utilitarians from at least Bentham forward. One might claim that this has been the central urge of utilitarians: to achieve synoptic completeness on Cartesian deductive bases. But this is not a distinctively moral impulse, and it need not be treated as though it were. The moral impulse of utilitarianism is to define the right as good consequences and to motivate people to achieve these. Hence, the utilitarian dictates for action are contingent, not a priori. Among other things, they depend on the perceived facts of the case and on the particular moral actor's mental equipment. Because utilitarianism is about general consequences of actions, it fundamentally involves the rationality of calculating such consequences.

Clearly, utilitarian conclusions will turn on correct application of rational principles. But utilitarianism is not a theory of rationality and insofar as any assertion by a utilitarian violates considerations of rationality the assertion should be corrected. F. A. Hayek argues that

"the trouble with the whole utilitarian approach" is that "it completely
eliminates the factor which makes rules necessary, namely our ignorance."[2] He is right that ignorance often makes rules necessary, but
neither recognition nor failure of recognition of our ignorance is inherently a part of utilitarianism. Sidgwick understands this issue better: he
forcefully argues that ethics does not include science, as for example the
science of navigation.[3] If we develop a better system for determining
relevant causal relations so that we are able to choose actions that better
produce our intended ends, it does not follow that we then must change
our ethics. The moral impulse of utilitarianism is constant, but our
decisions under it are contingent on our knowledge and scientific understanding. In a similar way, to be rationally self-interested is to seek
one's own benefit. An improved understanding of how to do that does
not require a revised understanding of what that means.

One of the cuter charges against utilitarianism is that it is irrational in
the following sense. If I take the time to calculate the consequences of
various courses of action before me, then I will ipso facto have chosen
the course of action to take, namely, to sit and calculate, because while I
am calculating the other courses of action will cease to be open to me. It
should embarrass philosophers that they have ever taken this objection
seriously. Parallel considerations in other realms are dismissed with
eminently good sense. Lord Devlin notes, "If the reasonable man
'worked to rule' by perusing to the point of comprehension every form
he was handed, the commercial and administrative life of the country
would creep to a standstill."[4] James March and Herbert Simon escape
the quandary of unending calculation by noting that often we satisfice,
we do not maximize: we stop calculating and considering when we find
a merely adequate choice or action.[5] When, in principle, one cannot
know what is the best choice, one can nevertheless be sure that sitting
and calculating is *not* the best choice. But, one may ask, How do you
know that another ten minutes of calculation would not have produced
a better choice? And one can only answer, You do not. At some point
the quarrel begins to sound adolescent. It is ironic that the point of the
quarrel is almost never at issue in practice (as Devlin implies, we are
almost all too reasonable in practice to bring the world to a standstill)
but only in the principled discussions of academics.

    2. F. A. Hayek, *The Mirage of Social Justice*, vol. 2 of *Law, Legislation, and Liberty*
(Chicago: University of Chicago Press, 1976), pp. 17–23, quote on p. 20.
    3. Henry Sidgwick, *Methods of Ethics*, 7th ed. (London: Macmillan, 1907), pp. 15–16.
    4. Patrick Devlin, *The Enforcement of Morals* (Oxford: Oxford University Press,
1965), p. 49.
    5. James G. March and Herbert Simon, *Organizations* (New York: Wiley, 1958),
chap. 6.

The practical conclusion of March and Simon is that terms such as 'best' and 'maximum' are in principle often useless in our context. But such terms seem to set the tone of almost all discussions of utilitarianism. One of the most parodied definitions of the good is G. E. Moore's supposedly utilitarian dictum that "the assertion 'I am morally bound to perform this action' is identical with the assertion 'This action will produce the greatest possible amount of good in the universe.' "[6] Oddly, Moore very well grasped the practical impossibility of this dictum in the sense that he knew one could not plausibly predict all the consequences of one's actions and hence could not plausibly compare total implications of various alternative actions for the amount of good they would produce in the universe. He therefore fell back on common sense judgments of the probable efficacity of following established moral rules.[7]

In sum, the extent to which we can calculate the consequences of actions is sharply limited. This is not to say that we cannot calculate anything but only that we cannot calculate everything. Hitler's father may once have dallied in the cheerful company of a beer hall and may have fretted whether he would therefore be too tired to work well the next day. It is implausible that he would have fretted whether his dalliance would lead later in the week to the conception of a transhistorical monster. But it is plausible that his dalliance did contribute to the conception of Adolf rather than of a lovable buffoon. It is in the nature of our very limited understanding of causal relations that whether my wife and I attempt to conceive a child tonight rather than later in the week cannot generally be a matter of moral concern even in the most rigorously consequentialist ethics.

If our judgment of actions turns on both their rationality and their consequences, we may expect people with different capacities to achieve different results. Our concern with consequences may bring us to pass moral judgment on someone for being stupid or ignorant. My stupidity or ignorance might have morally horrifying consequences even when I am not culpable for the stupidity or ignorance. It might then be a misjudgment to blame me morally. But we may not easily be sure because we may find it difficult in fact to separate judgments of stupidity and ignorance from judgments of moral weakness or turpitude. The data are often inherently run together.

So much for the first broad class of limits of reason and their significance for moral argument. Turn now to the third large class of

6. G. E. Moore, *Principia Ethica* (Cambridge: At the University Press, 1903), p. 147.
7. Ibid., pp. 154–158.

limits: limits of our value theory. Two of the most important limits of individual reason in consequentialist ethics are limits for which the recognition of their significance is very much an outgrowth of the utilitarian program and its child, welfare economics. These are the limit on one's ability accurately to assess the utility to oneself of various consumptions and the limit on one person's ability to decide what is good for another or, more generally, on our ability to make strict interpersonal comparisons of utility. On the first, R. Duncan Luce and Howard Raiffa discuss the fact that people rarely categorize a single dimension into more than seven or so distinct levels. Hence, "discrete categorization of preferences may be the basic case to study."[8] If we cannot accurately measure our own utility and we cannot accurately make comparisons across people, then we cannot accurately aggregate the utility to a group or society by simple addition of the utilities to the relevant individuals. However, one can exaggerate the difficulty of making such comparisons, as do many economists who may be captivated by pristine logic.

This is an issue that will arise repeatedly in what follows and whose significance to our utilitarian understanding will become clearer in later contexts. Let me simply stipulate for the moment that additive utility across people is not a valid notion unless it is extremely fuzzy. Much of the moral content of various utilitarianisms can carry through with little more than ordinal utility with fuzzy comparisons (your broken hip is worse than my mosquito bite). An obvious difference between a utilitarianism based on fuzzy comparisons and one based on comparisons of strictly additive utilities is that the former will far more often be indecisive or indifferent in its rankings of alternatives.

As an example of how such a quasi-ordinalism of fuzzy comparisons applies, consider a problem to be discussed at greater length later (§13): the utility of promising. Most moral theorists would hold that the keeping of promises is not absolutely required in all circumstances— but they may not easily be broken either. If the best comparison of overall utilities I can make between keeping my promise to you to do x and breaking it to do y is very fuzzy, it will not be easy to conclude that breaking the promise is better unless y has sufficient advantages over x that y significantly outweighs the combination of x, your opportunity costs (if any) in your planning on the fulfillment of my promise, and the strategic costs of my breaking the promise (such as damage to my reputation for future promising). A utilitarian cognizant of the difficul-

---

8. R. Duncan Luce and Howard Raiffa, *Games and Decisions* (New York: Wiley, 1957), p. 37.

ties of summing utilities to different people would agree with Joel Feinberg that the "consequences of breaking a promise must be more than 'slightly better on the whole' than those of keeping the promise if the breach is to be permitted; they must be substantially better."[9]

Finally, let us turn to a problem that has been the subject of a highly sophisticated technical literature: How can I assess the utility of various states of affairs to myself? Historically, the crudest utilitarian answer would be that I break each state of affairs into its components, assess the utility of each component to me, and then sum my utilities over all components for the total utility of the state of affairs to me. That this involves a fundamental misunderstanding of the nature of value in many circumstances has long been recognized. It is a commonplace and it was a central principle of Moore's ethics that the *"value of a whole must not be assumed to be the same as the sum of the values of its parts."*[10] Why? Because the various components which make up a state of affairs may be complementary or redundant.

Moore's principle is presumably compelling for anyone who has pondered the problems of Weber's law in measuring sensations, anyone who is cognizant of modern utility theory in economics, or anyone who has read, say, C. I. Lewis's several page argument against simple addition of the values of parts (indeed, contemporary readers must find Lewis's discussion prolix).[11] Consideration of such problems in economic choice theory has led to the indifference curve utility theory which easily accommodates both complementarity and substitutability (if two goods are complementary, enjoyment of one enhances or detracts from the simultaneous enjoyment of the other; if two goods are perfectly substitutable one for the other, they can be as redundant as two of a kind).

Of course, if the utility to me of a state of affairs is not an additive function of the utilities to me of its components, there is little point in my conceiving of utility as a numerical, additive quantity. I will seldom if ever be concerned to assess the utility to me of my whole state of affairs. I will generally only want to assess the effects on me of alternatives to certain components of my whole state of affairs. That is to say, I will want to assess which of several alternatives—such as entrées on tonight's menu—will add most to my overall utility. Hence, my concern will be to determine *at most* an ordinal ranking of the contribu-

9. Joel Feinberg, "The Forms and Limits of Utilitarianism," *Philosophical Review* 76 (July 1967): 368–381, p. 379.

10. Moore, *Principia Ethica*, p. 28; emphasis in original.

11. C. I. Lewis, *An Analysis of Knowledge and Valuation* (La Salle, Ill.: Open Court, 1946), pp. 479–510.

tion each of the alternatives will make to my well-being. (Generally, I will not seriously care to make a complete ordinal ranking but only to select the best few alternatives for comparison or even only to select the one best alternative. Furthermore, I may merely satisfice and settle for finding a merely adequate alternative [see further, §33].) Since the contribution of any of the alternatives is a function of other aspects of my current state of affairs, then by Moore's principle it would be wrong-headed of me to assign an amount of utility *to that alternative*.

Now if the utility to me of various actions is so complex as all this seems, then it is unlikely that many others could assess the utilitarian consequences for me of certain of their actions. Of course, the force of this conclusion may vary substantially with the nature of those actions. Anyone who breaks my leg or gives me a thousand dollars may be fairly confident of the direction of the impact of those actions and, given relatively limited knowledge of my circumstances (for example, how rich or poor I am), may even be confident of some crude sense of the size of the impact on me of the action. But one would have to be dotty to hand out exquisite recordings of Bartók's quartets to random people on the street. Such an action, no matter how well-meant, could plausibly, I am sad to acknowledge, bring about a net reduction in welfare for everyone involved.

One must readily recognize that, inasmuch as one's own trade-off functions for various consumptions are relatively idiosyncratic and fuzzy, one cannot easily generalize to another's utility. Hence, what one must do to increase the welfare of another will not be easy to decide except insofar as one merely adds to the other's means. Of course, this is less true for one's close associates, such as family and friends, and overwhelmingly true for the unmet run of humanity. Hence, even Bentham's simplistic quantitative utility may be satisfactory for making many social choices if, for example, we may use money income as a surrogate measure for utility. This quantitative notion of utility will apply least in cases in which one knows most how to evaluate the good or bad effects of one's actions because one knows very well those who will be affected. Our theory of the good is thick in our immediate vicinity, but it thins quickly as we get farther away. At its thinnest, means may often stand proxy for ends.

In summary, there are at least three in-principle cognitive obstacles to our calculating the overall good of the consequences of our actions: (1) we lack the information required to carry out such calculations (this is a central claim in the work of Hayek and many contemporary economists), (2) we lack relevant causal theories of the implications of our actions, and (3) we could not do the necessary calculations in any case because our minds have limited capacity (Simon speaks of "bounded rationality").[12] There are also two difficulties in our value theory: pleasures, benefits, or whatever may not add, either for an individual or across individuals. These two classes of limits are partly interrelated. For example, the latter class of problems adds to the burden of the first insofar as nonadditivity of benefits means that we have to know more about one another to assess the utilitarian consequences of our actions. Similarly, one might say that if we had relevant causal theories nonadditivity would be less problematic.

There is still another class of limits to our own achievement through our own reason and action: we cannot alone bring about outcomes but must depend in part on the actions of others to bring these about. This problem of strategic interaction is fundamental to ethics because ethics is largely concerned with our effects on others. This limit to our abilities to control the goodness of outcomes will be the subject of the following section and then more fully of Chapter 2.

§3 Strategic Interaction and Moral Theory

One of the most important changes in the way we analyze moral choice is through the recent introduction of game theoretic reasoning and, more generally, economic reasoning. It is a characteristic of game theory that it highlights the relationship between actions (or choices of strategies) and outcomes. In this it is analogous to utilitarianism. Much—perhaps most—moral theory focuses on actions with at best occasional reference to outcomes. In such theory the subject of evaluation is actions per se. A fundamental assumption of a consequentialist moral theory is that the evaluation of actions must be derived from an evaluation of their implications. It takes little thought to realize that few generally definable actions can plausibly be seen as always good or always bad in their consequences (although there may often be modal tendencies). Actual consequences of an action often depend on complex causal relations. One of the most important causal considerations is the interaction of an agent's actions with the actions of other people.

Part of the resistance to utilitarianism as a moral theory may derive from the strategic nature of life: it is actions that we do, not outcomes or states of affairs. Hence, if we are to judge individuals, we may too readily incline to judge them by their actions. But, again, actions are not simply right or wrong independently of context and the actions of others.

12. March and Simon, *Organizations*, chap. 6.

If we make certain value theory assumptions, game theory yields a natural fit with utilitarian analysis of choices we face. Game theory in the hands of most social scientists has a simpler value theory: its principle of choice is the benefit of the individual player rather than the benefit of all. In most of its development, game theory has been based on a particularly simplistic assumption: an interpersonally additive conception of utility, benefit, or pleasure. This value theory is shared with the crudest variants of utilitarianism, in which my pleasures are added to your pleasures to get the sum of happiness, which is then to be maximized. In principle, game theory and utilitarianism can both be made intellectually more compelling as general theories of rational choice and of moral choice, respectively, if their value theory assumptions can be made more nearly credible.

There are two sometimes debatable characteristics of the usual value theory assumptions of game theory. First, its utility is interpersonally transferable or comparable, so that utility can be taken from one individual and given to another.[13] Second, its utility is cardinal, so that we can speak of specific numbers of units of utility to each individual. These assumptions are independent and, indeed, each can be varied in its strength. For example, we can have a utility theory that involves completely interpersonally comparable, cardinal utility with infinitely fine divisibility of the unit of utility. Or we can have a utility theory that involves only ordinal rankings of whole states of affairs for each individual with no comparisons whatever between two individuals. Between these relatively extreme variants we can have a theory that allows limited ordinal, but not cardinal, comparisons between individuals, all of whom can have (separate) cardinal scales of utility for themselves.

To do consequentialist moral theory well we will need more articulate developments of game theory based on variant value theories. In particular, we need a game theory based on ordinal utility with and without interpersonal comparisons. Unfortunately, such game theory is far less developed than the Neumann-Morgenstern game theory with transferable cardinal utility. Until we have such developments, the

13. Technically one should speak of "transferable utility," which, Luce and Raiffa note, "for all the world behaves like money" (Luce and Raiffa, *Games and Decisions*, p. 168). This is clearly what Neumann and Morgenstern intended: "We . . . assume that the aim of all participants in the economic system . . . is money, or equivalently a single monetary commodity. This is supposed to be unrestrictedly divisible and substitutable, freely transferable and identical, even in the quantitative sense, with whatever 'satisfaction' or 'utility' is desired by each participant" (John von Neumann and Oskar Morgenstern, *Theory of Games and Economic Behavior*, 3d ed. [Princeton: Princeton University Press, 1953; first ed. published 1944], p. 8).

chief role of game theory in moral theory may be quite different from that suggested by R. B. Braithwaite:[14] its role is not to yield solutions but to change the nature of the discussion, even to redefine some of the problems.

Finally, note that game theory is a formalization of one of Sidgwick's variants of moral theory: egoism. More properly, in Sidgwick's terms, one should call the Neumann-Morgenstern game theory quantitative egoistic hedonism because egoism, "if we merely understand by it a method that aims at Self-realization, seems to be a form into which almost any ethical system may be thrown without modifying its essential characteristics. And even when further defined as Egoistic Hedonism, it is still imperfectly distinguished from Intuitionism if quality of pleasures is admitted as a consideration distinct from and overruling quantity."[15] Intuitionism is the so-called method of reasoning from direct intuitions of moral truths as one might reason from direct intuitions of mathematical relationships. We could now as well call the moral theory of egoism the ethic of games. Insofar as we weigh moral choice against purely egoistic choice, we can use the game theoretic representation of *interests*, whether with additive utility across players or without, as a baseline against which to compare moral choice. That representation will provide the baselines in the discussions here. Hence, I will generally speak of moral choice as concerned with effects on others as well as on the self, so that moral choice will often conflict with egoistic choice.

§4 Moral and Political Theory

Although there are many reasons for institutional devices, among the most important is to deal with certain limits of reason and the complexities of strategic interaction. Institutions can help us achieve better results than we could hope to achieve through individual actions, even well-intentioned individual actions. Despite this strong connection between institutional arrangements and moral results, moral and political theory have been relatively separated. Perhaps this is a peculiar consequence of the division of academic discourse into so-called disciplines. Moral theory has become primarily the province of those who inhabit philosophy departments while political theory has become that of those who inhabit political science departments. This separation makes non-

14. R. B. Braithwaite, *Theory of Games as a Tool for the Moral Philosopher* (Cambridge: At the University Press, 1955).
15. Sidgwick, *The Methods of Ethics*, p. 95.

sense of many of the concerns of Athenian philosophy, of the Scottish Enlightenment, and of much that went between them. Any effort to grasp moral theory full must lead to concern with the nature of politics and of institutions for regulating human affairs. The term 'moral philosophy' once meant everything from what is now narrowly construed as ethics to political economy. One who writes of 'moral philosophy' now is apt to be read as concerned essentially with the much narrower problems of strictly individual choice and individual character.

Against the commonplace separation of moral and political theory, I wish to argue three theses more or less simultaneously throughout this book. Two of these are critical and one constructive. First, we often tend to think of moral philosophy in too narrow a way and to relegate larger concerns to political science, economics, and other disciplines. Second, we sometimes argue too casually from narrow to larger concerns. For example, we approach paternalism by treating face-to-face personal interactions and then generalizing to societal level principles as though the latter followed in a straightforward way without consideration of any additional complications of limits of reason. And third, constructively, both larger and narrower concerns are relevant to moral philosophy. But we must understand how they differ, often on variant grounds of limits of reason and variant complications of strategic interaction. Our understanding of either larger or narrower concerns will be enhanced by the effort to understand the other and to relate the two in a coherent effort.

Of all moral theories perhaps none has originated more clearly from a consideration of the fullest range of human interaction than utilitarianism, the theory that judges the rightness and wrongness of all actions according to their likely effect on human and perhaps animal welfare. Amartya Sen and Bernard Williams remark, "Utilitarianism has always been discussed . . . in two different roles: On the one hand as a theory of personal morality, and on the other as a theory of public choice."[16] Indeed, one may say that in utilitarianism morals and political and institutional arrangements are inextricably interwoven.[17] Utilitarianism provides both an individual and a social moral theory because the one is inherently incomplete without the other. To a large and sad extent, this view was lost in much of twentieth-century utilitar-

16. Amartya Sen and Bernard Williams, *Utilitarianism and Beyond* (Cambridge: Cambridge University Press, 1982), p. 1.

17. John Austin, a utilitarian institutionalist, sees it this way (Austin, *The Province of Jurisprudence Determined* [New York: Noonday, 1954; first published 1832], p. 66). As Rawls notes, early utilitarianism was political and institutional in its focus ("Two Concepts of Rules," *Philosophical Review* 64 [1955]: 3–32, esp. pp. 18–19n).

ianism, which, in the spirit of most twentieth-century moral theory of all philosophical varieties, has typically focused on essentially personal problems of choice in small-number interactions such as personal promising and face-to-face charity. With the work of John Rawls, especially his *A Theory of Justice,*[18] and the extraordinary response it has evoked this deplorable narrowing of moral theory has been reversed.

In the narrowing of its focus during most of the twentieth century utilitarianism took on more of the quality of traditional quotidian morality, which largely addresses small-number interactions. At its best, moral theory that is narrowly focused in this way has been increasingly broadened and generalized in other respects. "Thou shalt not kill" was not an absolute or even a general command—it applied only to the children of Israel, and not always to all of them, as is revealed by various Old Testament slayings that are presented as morally praiseworthy.[19] We have universalized the command by cutting it loose from the brutality of its tribal mooring. We have done so by bringing it under abstract reason. Yet there has been a considerable loss in this abstraction from the confining strictures of particular cultures and conventions because much of our moral life is dependent on the structure of our particular institutions. It is inherently contingent. What we must do to grasp the whole of the morality of life is to recognize relevant contingencies and to ignore irrelevant contingencies.

It is sometimes supposed that utilitarianism reduces to beneficence. There is a grain of truth in this supposition because utilitarians are generally concerned with the welfare of all, almost all of whom are, of course, others. To act for the welfare of others is to be beneficent. Against this simple reduction, however, most of us cannot actually do very much for the welfare of very many others. Individual acts of beneficence provide too limited a basis for achieving generally good results. The chief result of successful utilitarian actions over the long run, therefore, must be the creation of institutions that will take over the task of enhancing the general welfare. This means that the chief aim of utilitarianism in many contexts must be to reduce the need for individual beneficence and even to eliminate it in many contexts.

This is clearly the urge in utilitarian policy prescriptions that address

18. John Rawls, *A Theory of Justice* (Cambridge, Mass.: Harvard University Press, 1971).
19. Recall, for example, the tale of the man of Israel who took unto himself a Midianitish woman. "And when Phinehas, the son of Eleazar, the son of Aaron the priest, saw it, he rose up from among the congregation, and took a javelin in his hand; And he went after the man of Israel into the tent, and thrust both of them through, the man of Israel, and the woman through her belly" (Numbers 26: 7–8).

anything other than momentary emergencies and isolated momentary needs, for which simple beneficence may be the only possible policy. In many ongoing contexts, as in the two difficult policy issues discussed in §29, utilitarian prescriptions will be concerned with institutional arrangements to help individuals become independently capable of achieving their own well-being. But if this is the result that utilitarianism recommends, then it is a moral theory that is inherently also a political theory, as spelled out in Chapters 3 and 4. Hence, for a utilitarian a morality without a political theory must fall very far short in its possibilities of achieving moral outcomes.

§5 Rule-Utilitarianism and Act-Utilitarianism

An act-utilitarian is someone who decides which of available alternative actions to undertake by first deciding which will produce the greatest utility overall. As the best utilitarian theorists have recognized, it will often be difficult to determine overall utility because causal theories are deficient, the time for decision is short, and so forth. Moreover, one may have an understandable but nonetheless wrong tendency to see things too much from one's own vantage point and may therefore tend to take actions that serve one's own interests more than they serve the more general good. The answer to these problems is commonly thought to be some form of rule-utilitarianism, as in Moore's *Principia Ethica*,[20] in which one follows well-established moral rules (do not lie, do not break promises, etc.) in lieu of trying to calculate the overall good of one's actions in each specific case. To clarify the issues in such a system, let us briefly consider the position of a particular utilitarian theorist: F. A. Hayek.

Hayek's position is fully consequentialist. He takes it for granted that the "rules of morals are instrumental in the sense that they assist mainly in the achievement of other human values."[21] Hayek argues that in principle one *cannot* have the knowledge to judge the full consequences of acts, so that one cannot be act-utilitarian. He therefore opts for following rules. Of course, if one could in principle have the knowledge to judge a rule generally good, one might also in principle have the knowledge to judge an act good. Nevertheless, rules might be adopted as a satisficing device given that the costs (in decision time and delayed action) of deciding on each act individually may be expected commonly to outweigh the benefits. But Hayek's general argument obviously

20. Moore, *Principia Ethica,* esp. chap. 5.
21. F. A. Hayek, *The Constitution of Liberty* (Chicago: University of Chicago Press, 1960), p. 67.

implies that one can also not know whether following a rule will have net beneficial consequences. So how can he opt for rules? He opts only for those rules that have been adopted as part of a culture or a tradition, not for rules that have been justified by calculation of their benefits if consistently applied. He chooses, essentially on faith, to trust societally evolved rules (customs, mores) because they have been more severely tested in practice than any Cartesian rule-utilitarian's rules could be in principle.

Is Hayek then a rule-utilitarian? Contrary to his own claim,[22] it seems to me he is a straight act-utilitarian who understands the complexities of decision making and right choosing. In many contexts what it is rational to do is as indeterminate as what is utilitarian. Hayek's argument against act-utilitarianism is nothing more than his argument more generally against what he calls constructivist or Cartesian thinking, or synoptic deductivism, in social policy. An act-utilitarian can readily accept strictures such as Hayek's on decision making and therefore accept his socially chosen rules.[23] In this respect, moral rules are not unlike laws in a science. When George Washington was afflicted with fever, he was bled according to the canons of an ignorant but presumably well-meaning medical profession. A doctor who bled a patient in similar straits today would likely go to jail—justifiably, most of us would think. Often choices must be made in the absence of moral certainty about the consequences of every available option. The medical profession of Washington's day, dependent on an absurd theory, misjudged the consequences of their actions. Similarly, not so long ago, boys at Eton were punished for *not* "smoking." Lack of certainty about moral and other rules or laws resides in the necessity of things.

To the discussion of the limits to rationality in the previous section, one might respond in various ways in practice. Most obviously, one might simply look to immediate, relatively predictable consequences of actions. One might prefer, however, to use any socially developed response, as Hayek and many professed rule-utilitarians do. But clearly, following rules because, say, their existence recommends their utility is not a problem for a reasonable act-utilitarian. Because of limits of knowledge and reason, social acceptance of a rule could plausibly be counted as strong evidence for determining the utility of an act that falls under the rule.[24] Of course, one might conclude in the case of a particular rule that other evidence overrides the evidence of social evolution.

22. Hayek, *The Mirage of Social Justice,* pp. 17–23.

23. David Lyons argues this point convincingly in *The Forms and Limits of Utilitarianism* (Oxford: Oxford University Press, 1965), pp. 144–150, 178–182.

24. See further, Moore, *Principia Ethica,* p. 158.

After all, social evolution may produce bad as well as good practices. Quick recourse to the supposedly superior "wisdom" inherent in evolved practices and institutions is often the conservative's attempt to trump demands for changes, especially changes to achieve greater equality.

What then makes rule-utilitarianism different from act-utilitarianism? Only a more rigid adherence to rules than this account suggests. One might suppose that Moore was a rule-utilitarian in this strong sense. After his principled defense of utilitarianism, he resorts to "commonsense" morality as the best utilitarian guide to conduct. He asks whether one can ever be justified in breaking one of the commonsense moral rules. And he answers "that this question may be *definitely* answered in the negative."[25] But this answer is based on the view that social evolution of those rules is such forceful evidence of their utility that the probability that my calculations in a particular instance can *correctly* suggest overriding the rule on utilitarian grounds is too small for me to believe my calculations when they do suggest overriding one of the rules.[26] Again, such reasoning is simply utilitarian and, given Moore's claims about the limits to our powers of reasoning, it is act-utilitarian. If there is a difficulty with his positon, it is the difficulty of his odd epistemology that dictates that socially derived knowledge must *always* be superior to individually deduced knowledge with exceedingly high probability. Since this principle is not itself socially derived, one may wonder how Moore knows it so confidently.

Is there any rule-utilitarianism distinctively different from act-utilitarianism? Many philosophers have insisted there is. Generally, however, they seem simply to fail to grasp as clearly as Moore that their issue is one of the general limits of reason and therefore has little or nothing to do with the moral content of utilitarianism. Just as societies have "learned" that certain engineering, legal, farming, medical, and so forth, rules work, so they have learned that certain moral rules "work." There is inadequate scientific understanding to prove the general utility of many of these rules whether practical or moral. Social

25. Ibid., p. 162; emphasis added. Berkeley reaches a similar conclusion ("Passive Obedience: Upon the Principles of the Law of Nature," pp. 101–135 in Alexander Campbell Fraser, ed., *The Works of George Berkeley,* vol. 4 [Oxford: Clarendon Press, 1891; essay first published in 1712], pp. 107–108, 120).

26. Moore concludes against "the breaking of moral rules generally recognised and practised, and which, *therefore,* we may assume to be generally useful" (*Principia Ethica,* p. 163; emphasis added). This would presumably be Moore's answer to Anscombe's complaint that under a consequentialist ethics "you can exculpate yourself from the *actual* consequences of the most disgraceful actions, so long as you can make out a case for not having foreseen them" (Anscombe, "Modern Moral Theory," p. 35).

testing is often therefore a better guide for our action than is abstract deductive reasoning. As Whitehead remarks, "Civilization advances by extending the number of important operations which we can perform without thinking about them"—we do not have to think about them because others have done the practical thinking and testing before us.[27]

Lyons has argued on other grounds that act-utilitarianism and rule-utilitarianism are "extensionally equivalent."[28] Although his argument is of instructive interest, it is almost entirely beside the point for a practical moral theory. To establish their equivalence he assumes away the problem of limits of reason and presumes that we perform the calculations necessary to judge whether following a rule would yield results different from simply comparing the overall utilities that would result from alternative actions. His conclusion is essentially that a rule-utilitarian would have to qualify all the rules to meet particularities of various circumstances in which the rules are to be invoked. Hence, the highly articulated set of rules would yield the same results as simply comparing overall utilities. Alas, any argument that turns on perfect information, perfect calculation, and perfect theory is a house of cards. Both the act-utilitarian and the rule-utilitarian calculations Lyons discusses are in principle impossible in general, and the highly articulated set of rules he imagines is inconceivable. Any utilitarian who is persuaded to follow rules should be persuaded only on such grounds as persuaded Moore or on grounds that rules can often help to coordinate us in mutually beneficial ways when the lack of a rule would lead us to fail to coordinate. One of these latter rules might be inferior to others we could have if we were able to legislate a new rule, but without ability to legislate and change the rule it might still be better than not having a rule at all.[29] In the cases both of Moore's socially evolved rules and of rules for coordination, the rules will be radically less articulated than the rules Lyons imagines. Moore's commonsense moral rules are a response to ignorance of the kind that Lyons assumes away.

27. A. N. Whitehead, *Introduction to Mathematics* (London: Williams and Norgate, 1911), p. 61. What is true of civilization is true also of the individual. James remarks that each individual must turn over as much of the detail of daily life as possible to habit in order to free the mind for better work. "There is no more miserable human being than one in whom nothing is habitual but indecision, and for whom the lighting of every cigar, the drinking of every cup, the time of rising and going to bed every day, and the beginning of every bit of work, are subjects of express volitional deliberation" (William James, *The Principles of Psychology* [Cambridge, Mass.: Harvard University Press, 1981; first published 1890], p. 126).

28. Lyons, *Forms and Limits,* pp. 115–118.

29. David Braybrooke, "The Choice between Utilitarianisms," *American Philosophical Quarterly* 4 (1967): 28–38.

Coordination rules, especially if they are not ideal, are a response to the difficulty or cost of re-coordinating on a new rule.

§6 The Utilitarian Program

Although it has precursors in antiquity and in the work of many philosophers of the Renaissance and the Enlightenment, utilitarianism was extensively developed only by Hume, Bentham, Austin, Mill, and Sidgwick. As in any theory worked out over so long a time by so many hands, it is not surprising that its content varies considerably. Indeed, the content has continued to change in this century in the work of Moore, Rashdall, and contemporary writers. It would be more appropriate to call utilitarianism a movement than a theory. In this respect, utilitarianism is like natural rights theories, intuitionism, and even Kantianism: these are all movements within which there are large differences of detail. Some of the changes that have taken place in the utilitarian movement over time have resulted from greater understanding of complex issues as more intellectual effort was expended on them. Some of the changes reflect fundamentally different thrusts, sometimes so different as to cast doubt on their lineage, as in the ideal utilitarianism of Moore, in which the good has little relation to usual notions of human welfare.

Other than idiosyncratic elements such as Hume's assumption of sympathy and Austin's derivation of utilitarianism from god, the main contributions to the utilitarian program include the following. Hume specified the range of problems and placed individual and institutional problems in a coherent system that fits the strategic structures of the problems. The problems include benevolence, justice, and the choice of particular governmental arrangements. Although he did not invent it, Bentham is the chief advocate of the greatest happiness or greatest felicity principle. Austin gave a realistic assessment of the problems of rational decision making in moral contexts.[30] Mill emphasized the principle of universalization. Sidgwick acknowledged the intuitionist basis of the basic moral principle of utilitarianism and insisted on the practical nature of utilitarianism. With the possible exception of Bentham, all of these recognized the dualism of egoistic and universalistic motivations.[31] Moore grappled with the value theory of

---

30. Austin remarks, "Little of any man's knowledge is gotten by original research. It mostly consists of *results* gotten by the researches of others, and taken by himself upon *testimony*" (John Austin, *The Province of Jurisprudence Determined*, p. 62).

31. Moore's refutation of this duality is specious (*Principia Ethica*, §§60–61).

utilitarianism and contributed the notion of "organic wholes" (Mill speaks of "chemical combinations") or of the nonadditivity of values.[32] The early theorists, through Mill, were also interested in economics and law. Three of these initial contributions have not been subject to extensive further development; indeed, they have been generally neglected in subsequent accounts. These three are the limits of reason implied in Hume's strategic grasp of the range of moral problems, Austin's realization of the difficulties of rational choosing, and Moore's insight into the complexity of value theory. These are the central issues of this book. All three classes of issues pervade most discussions here, but the present chapter focuses especially on the difficulties in rational decision making in moral contexts, Chapter 2 lays out the strategic categories of moral problems, and Chapter 5 surveys conceptual and logical complexities of utilitarian value theory. Chapters 3 and 4 make more nearly positive contributions in constructing a utilitarian theory of the institutional devices for dealing with limits of reason.

One might sensibly claim that the greatest twentieth-century contributions to utilitarianism have come from economists, who have drifted away from social and political theory as philosophers understood it. Issues in value theory that confused Bentham, Mill, and Sidgwick have been clarified by Pareto and his followers in the development of contemporary utility theory.[33] The program is not yet finished—nor is it yet totally disqualified as Bernard Williams asserts.[34] Indeed, if one surveys the magnitude of the major unresolved issue—value theory— one might suppose that the program has only been crudely outlined; now the work may begin. That economists and, increasingly now, psychologists should have contributed so much to our understanding of the value theory of utilitarianism is not surprising: because utilitarianism is about what people value, its value theory is partly an empirical matter.

What of all this is the core of utilitarianism? The fundamentally moral impulse of utilitarianism is the concern with consequences for people in general. Hence, the core of utilitarianism is its consequentialism, its universality, and some kind of value that is value to individuals. The element here that is not fixed is the value theory, which can take diverse contents. The analytical structure, as opposed to the con-

32. Ibid., pp. 27–30.
33. Indeed, the early intellectual development of modern economics often parallels that of utilitarianism.
34. Bernard Williams, "A Critique of Utilitarianism," pp. 76–150 in J. J. C. Smart and Bernard Williams, *Utilitarianism: For and Against* (Cambridge: Cambridge University Press, 1973), p. 150.

tent or focus, of the value theory, however, is not so much a matter of choice as the diversity of claims might suggest. Rather, it is subject to logical constraints that have not always been well understood, constraints such as that recognized by Moore, that partial values may not be additive, and those recognized by economists over the long history of the development of utility theory, the value theory of economic choice. As these constraints become better understood, utilitarianism should become more refined. This part of the theory is at least partly subject to scientific or conceptual advances whereas it would be odd to claim that the distinctively moral content of the theory is altered by such advances. Alan Ryan notes that "it is characteristic of utilitarian arguments that they are reversible in the face of altered factual suppositions."[35] One might similarly note that they are also changeable in the face of certain alterations in scientific understandings of the nature of welfare.

It is the core of at least consequentialism and a value theory of welfare for individuals that comes through fleeting remarks of many writers before Hume. In a famous phrase, Horace declared utility the mother of just and right. Descartes wrote to Elisabeth that in speaking of "the worth we ought to set on this life, one considers as good everything one finds there from which one can draw some convenience, and one calls evils anything from which one can receive inconvenience."[36] Locke, Beccaria, Helvetius, Paley, Berkeley, and others groped toward richer utilitarian conceptions. Their arguments often run afoul of their theological, epistemological, and psychological theories and of residues of natural rights theory. But there is a more or less steady development of utilitarian thinking from Locke forward. Not surprisingly, the development involved many confusions and even errors.[37]

Among the apparent errors of various contributions to the move-

---

35. Alan Ryan, *Property and Political Theory* (Oxford: Basil Blackwell, 1984), p. 91.

36. René Descartes, letter to Elizabeth, January 1646, pp. 632–637 in Descartes, *Oeuvres Philosophiques,* vol. 3, ed. Ferdinand Alquié, (Paris: Garnier Frères, 1973), quote at p. 635 (translation from John J. Blom, *Descartes: His Moral Philosophy and Psychology* [New York: New York University Press, 1978], p. 175). See also Descartes's comment on "the law which obliges us to do all in our power to secure the general welfare of mankind" (*Discourse on the Method,* pp. 111–151 in John Cottingham, Robert Stoothoff, and Dugald Murdoch, eds., *The Philosophical Works of Descartes* [Cambridge: Cambridge University Press, 1985; *Discourse* first published in 1637], part 6, p. 142).

37. Of earlier theories in economics, Pareto comments, "It would be a serious error to think that it would have been a good thing had these erroneous theories never seen the light of day. These or other similar ones were indispensable in order to arrive at better theories" (Vilfredo Pareto, *Manual of Political Economy* [New York: Kelley, 1971; trans. of 1927 French ed.], chap. 3, sec. 31, p. 111).

ment are some that are essentially errors of logic or consistency and some that are seemingly errors of practical understanding. Perhaps the most common error in practical understanding is the presumption (mentioned in §2) that, to be utilitarian, one must spend so much time calculating consequences as to fail to have any pleasure. It is supposed that, therefore, utilitarianism is incoherent because it requires calculation to the point of preventing the achievement of good while striving for the best. Ironically, utilitarians, such as Austin and Mill, are among the earliest theorists to recognize that rational decision making in many contexts requires sensible approximations and relevant shortcuts. To this claim of the incoherence of utilitarianism, Mill retorted, "Men really ought to leave off talking a kind of nonsense on this subject, which they would neither talk nor listen to on other matters of practical concernment."[38] His plaint is one with which philosophers in every field must often have sympathized. Hayek is not the only sophisticated contemporary writer who continues to assert this objection to the coherence of utilitarianism despite Mill's well-grounded, withering rejection of it more than a century ago.

One error of logic that similarly persists to this day is some variant of the dictum that utilitarianism is "the greatest good of the greatest number." This dictum appears in Hutcheson and Bentham.[39] (The dictum occasionally gains a third maximand: for the greatest time.) Unless this dictum is intended merely as a way of saying with a flourish that utilitarianism is the maximization of the aggregate good,[40] welfare, or pleasure, the dictum is a logical morass: in general, one cannot maximize over two functions at once. This last claim is one that any serious thinker should understand even without a firm grasp of calculus. Despite its illogicality, however, the dictum pervades popular conceptions of utilitarianism. In *The Duke's Children* Trollope has the liberal duke give his errantly conservative son "a somewhat lengthy

38. John Stuart Mill, *Utilitarianism*, pp. 203–259 in Mill, *Essays on Ethics, Religion and Society*, ed. J. M. Robson, vol. 10 of *Collected Works of John Stuart Mill* (Toronto: University of Toronto Press, 1969), chap. 2, p. 225.

39. Hutcheson says, "That action is best, which procures the greatest happiness for the greatest numbers" (Frances Hutcheson, *Inquiry into the Original of Our Ideas of Beauty and Virtue* [London, 1725], treatise 2, sec. 3, §8). D. D. Raphael remarks that this may be the first use of this formula (D. D. Raphael, *British Moralists, 1650–1800* [Oxford: Oxford University Press, 1969], 1:284n).

40. F. Y. Edgeworth puts the case well: "The principle of greatest happiness may have gained its popularity, but lost its meaning, by the addition '*of the greatest number*'" (Edgeworth, *Mathematical Psychics: An Essay on the Application of Mathematics to the Moral Sciences* [London: C. Kegan Paul, 1881], p. 118). Neumann and Morgenstern aptly call this double maximization principle a "pseudo-maximum" problem (Neumann and Morgenstern, *Theory of Games and Economic Behavior*, p. 11).

political lecture, which was intended to teach him that the greatest benefit of the greatest number was the object to which all political studies should tend."[41] (A true son and a true conservative, his son was not persuaded.)

Indeed, Lionel Robbins, renowned for his demolition of interpersonal comparisons in economic theory,[42] concluded an address on Bentham in 1964 with the hope that his audience "never cease to regard the greatest happiness of the greatest number as a worth-while objective of social policy."[43] Can an impossible objective be a worthwhile objective? Oddly, Robbins's previous paragraph asserts that Bentham would favor birth control, so that we might presume we should pursue the greater happiness of smaller numbers. The whole exercise recalls a mathematical theorem, reported by Gerald Dworkin, that utilitarianism is false. The elegant proof of the theorem is as follows: utilitarianism is the greatest good of the greatest number. As has long been known, there is no greatest number. Q.E.D.[44]

No philosopher should ever take the dictum of the greatest good for the greatest number seriously except as a subject in the history of thought—but it would be rash to suppose that woefully many will not continue to treat it as a live issue when it is merely an error. This is one of the pains of philosophical discourse: in it dead issues are never finally buried. Many arguments against utilitarianism have often and easily been shown to be fallacious. Nevertheless, they are regularly brought back as conclusive objections.

§7 Peculiar Examples and Ethical Argument

One of the inherent problems in all consequentialist moral reasoning is that the judgments are in principle comparative so that one may be challenged to dredge up relevant examples for comparison or even to invent relevant hypothetical examples. The use of hypothetical examples, especially peculiar examples, may be subject to various distortions. The pertinent issue here is that they overburden our limited

41. Anthony Trollope, *The Duke's Children* (Oxford: Oxford University Press, 1973; originally published 1879–1880), p. 57. I owe this and many other lovely references to my colleague, William H. Kruskal.

42. Lionel Robbins, *An Essay on the Nature and Significance of Economic Science* (London: Macmillan, 1937; first published 1932), esp. pp. 136–142.

43. Lionel Robbins, "Bentham in the Twentieth Century," pp. 73–84 in Robbins, *The Evolution of Modern Economic Theory and Other Papers on the History of Economic Thought* (Chicago: Aldine, 1970), p. 84.

44. Gerald Dworkin, "The Journal of Mathematical Ethics: A Proposal," *Philosophical Forum* 13 (Summer 1982): 413–415.

reasoning capacities, perhaps sufficiently to undercut any hope that we can draw relevant inferences from them. Because the invention of hypothetical examples may be both easier and more entertaining than finding real examples, it is not surprising that ethical theory is almost entirely hypothetical, perhaps especially when it is concerned with criticizing others' theories. Unfortunately, once the value of entertainment enters discussion, it too often drives out other values, especially reasonableness, relevance, and even understanding. Insofar as this latter value is the ostensible purpose of the use of examples, we should be particularly alert to its abuse. Any example that relies on essentially impossible assumptions or on relationships among beings that are radically un-human is prima facie suspect because we cannot know how to think through our issues in its context.

If our examples must be hypothetical, why not make them really beautiful? William James, child of a rhetorical age, has naturally given us one of the most beautiful examples of the sort that are put to the task of destroying utilitarianism once and for all. It is too beautiful a story not to restate it whole:

> . . . if the hypothesis were offered us of a world in which Messrs. Fourier's and Bellamy's and Morris's utopias should all be outdone, and millions kept permanently happy on the one simple condition that a certain lost soul on the far-off edge of things should lead a life of lonely torture, what except a specific and independent sort of emotion can it be which would make us immediately feel, even though an impulse arose within us to clutch at the happiness so offered, how hideous a thing would be its enjoyment when deliberately accepted as the fruit of such a bargain?[45]

Once the rush of entertainment has passed, one must sense the elemental lunacy of James's story. Could anyone be persuaded of anything by it after reflection? Too many of the hard cases used to test moral—especially utilitarian—theories involve interventions as if by god or satan into normal causal relations. Surely we should reject conclusions based only on such examples on simple grounds as that, say, James's bargain cannot be faced because there is no being out there capable of

---

45. William James, "The Moral Philosopher and the Moral Life," pp. 184–215 in James, *The Will to Believe* (London: Longmans, Green, 1897; reprint, New York: Dover Publications, 1956), p. 188. Against the sentiment of his wonderful example, in a letter of December 29, 1869, to Henry Bowditch, James wrote, "Now, I confidently expect that you will sit down and write me a long letter immediately on receiving this. . . . If you don't, 'twere better you had ne'er been born, for I'll cause you to die by tortures so lingering and horrible that the mind of man has not yet conceived of the like of them" (in Ralph Barton Perry, *The Thought and Character of William James* [Boston: Little, Brown, 1935], 1:321).

genuinely and credibly offering it.[46] Hence, it does not rely on any usual understandings we have about how to choose. No moral theory need prevail in the face of such examples. One cannot imagine objecting to a bridge design with the question: But what if satan says he will smash the bridge and all the people on it if we build it that way?

Manipulating causal relations in absurd ways may provide instructive thought experiments, but it is unlikely to produce definitive tests of a moral theory (or of any other theory embracing behavior). This may be especially true of a moral theory that takes as its standard the general state of affairs. One cannot sensibly have such a moral theory that is right independently of one's theory of causal relations. For example, if one believed the world to be involved in a Manichaean contest between the forces of good and evil with the minions of both sides occasionally entering the fray to manipulate outcomes, one could not take seriously much of Greek or of eighteenth- through twentieth-century Western philosophical ethics. If one held Heraclitus's flux-doctrine and took it to mean that "one could not say anything before the flux of things made it false,"[47] one could hardly take consequentialist ethical principles seriously.

That such test cases as James's have any respectability in the conclusions of moral theorists is an oddity, an aberration of intellectual fecundity. No moral theory can withstand the intuitionist implications of such tests absolutely, because a test case can be made strategically dependent on one's moral theory or principle. "If you do what follows from your principle, I, satan, will blow up the world. Now can you really defend your principle?" Must the rigid anticonsequentialist insist on principle and challenge satan to blow us up? If this sort of "test" rules out utilitarianism, it also rules out every moral theory that includes *any* consequentialist element. The test depends on the fact that a consequentialist is open to strategic manipulation, at least in one's fanciful imagination. But all *moral* theories must take consequences into account. Rawls asserts, "All ethical doctrines worth our attention take consequences into account in judging rightness. One which did not would simply be irrational, crazy."[48] Anscombe seems to disagree with the first judgment and, one presumes but can never be sure,

46. Of course it might just happen that I am wrong and that satan will stand before me the day after this has gone irrevocably into print. That would be a disappointment.

47. J. N. Findlay, *Plato and Platonism* (New York: Times Books, 1978), p. 7.

48. Rawls, *A Theory of Justice*, p. 30; also see pp. 159–162.

therefore with the second as well.[49] Most of us, however, would evidently agree with Rawls.

Against this account of the perversity of James's example, one might say that moral theory is a priori and must therefore apply to all conceivable cases. This was once the view of Alan Donagan, who wrote that moral theory "is, as Leibniz would say, true of all possible worlds."[50] A later Donagan defends "traditional morality" against the implications of such examples as that of James on the ground that they depend on manipulating causal relations in impossible ways. He says, "Whoever may maintain that there is such a possible system owes us some account of it."[51] Surely the later Donagan has the more compelling view. If we get a moral theory that is compelling for our own world, we should be delighted at the success and not worry whether it would be compelling in some fanciful alternative world.

James's example has elements that make it relevant to several points at issue here and later. The objection here is that in the example our fundamental concern with consequences is tricked up against us by intruding impossible causal relations that wreck our normal understanding of 'consequences'. James's tale introduces elements that pollute our reasoning. Given that our reasoning already faces severe limits, it is unwise to burden it unnecessarily with such hypothetical elements. The example will be recalled in later discussions. One of these deals with problems in value theory, in particular with the problem of interpersonal comparisons such as that implicit in James's story (§27). Another deals with the problem of the value of the supposed intuitions we can have about such a tale (§34).

It is part of the inherent logic of consequential considerations, however weak, that they are strategically open to impossible tests such as that implicit in James's story. If we find morality in consequential considerations, we should not be deterred by logical games, not even

49. Anscombe, "Modern Moral Philosophy."
50. Alan Donagan, "Is There a Credible Form of Utilitarianism," pp. 187–202 in Michael D. Bayles, ed., *Contemporary Utilitarianism* (Garden City, N.Y.: Doubleday, 1968), p. 188. He further states that "whether a moral theory is true or false depends on whether its implications for all possible worlds are true. Hence whether utilitarianism is true or false cannot depend on how the actual world is" (ibid., p. 194). One may wonder what is the point in talking about the "truth" of a moral theory.
51. Alan Donagan, *The Theory of Morality* (Chicago: University of Chicago Press, 1977), p. 36. Donagan cites the familiar example of Ivan Karamazov's challenge to his brother Alyosha in Dostoevsky's novel. Ivan asks whether Alyosha would consent to the torture of a little girl in order to make men happy in a state of peace and contentment. Alyosha, like James, was repelled by the prospect (Fyodor Dostoevsky, *The Brothers Karamazov* [Harmondsworth, Middlesex: Penguin, 1958], 2:287–288).

such entertaining ones as this. The relevant tests of our moral—as of our scientific and practical—principles is whether they would be good principles to follow in actual life, not in fanciful circumstances. Too many of the examples of moral theorists are so contrived and unrealistic with their deus ex machina devices that it is hard to draw any—pardon the word—morals from them.

In addition to arguing from fanciful examples, moral theorists often contrive whole worlds in which to test theories. For example, D. H. Hodgson's account of act-utilitarianism in a world of perfect information and perfect rationality is irrelevant to moral theory and, apparently, misleading to Hodgson himself: he rejects act-utilitarianism in that context and *therefore*, as though there were any implication, in real contexts. The assumption of perfect information and perfect rationality may be a useful simplification in parts of economic theory. It is not useful in deciding what act-utilitarianism can entail or in determining the consistency and validity of act-utilitarianism. Nor is it useful in discussing human behavior in most contexts because such behavior is egregiously affected by and therefore heavily determined by lack of information and other limits of reason. Hodgson's ideal act-utilitarian world is a world peopled, if that verb can be so broadened in meaning, by omniscient and omnibenevolent beings.[52] Reasoning from such assumptions may give us insights to help clarify our thinking, but quick conclusions drawn from such assumptions cannot be held valid for our actual problems.[53]

Refutations of moral theories commonly take two forms. The recommendations of a theory are trumped by "our" intuitions or the theory is shown to be internally inconsistent and contradictory. Peculiar examples are put to use in both kinds of refutation. I will leave the discussion of conflicts between moral intuitions and utilitarianism for later (§34). Efforts to show that utilitarianism is internally inconsistent are almost invariably efforts to show that it would not be utilitarian in some respect to act according to utilitarian principles. Disproof by counterexample is an honorable device in the mathematician's canon because the logical standing of the example is usually not in question.

---

52. D. H. Hodgson, *Consequences of Utilitarianism* (Oxford: Oxford University Press, 1967), esp. chap. 2. Also see Dan W. Brock, "Recent Work in Utilitarianism," *American Philosophical Quarterly* 10 (October 1973): 241–276, who, at p. 258, finds this kind of argument persuasive.

53. Again, Pareto gives sensible advice: "Perfecting a theory is completely different from seeking to destroy it by foolish and pedantic subtleties. The first task is sensible and useful, the second is not very reasonable as well as fruitless, and someone who has no time to waste does better not to bother with it" (Pareto, *Manual of Political Economy*, chap. 3, sec. 31, p. 112).

Arguments from examples in ethical theory are also useful, but when one's common sense is violated by the examples, one's suspicions should be aroused. An artificial example should be especially suspect. It may serve a role in clarifying the structure of an argument or in helping us discover a class of problem. But if there is a point of persuasion in using it, we should be able to find real or literary instances to illustrate our point. If we cannot, we should doubly wonder about the force of our claims from the invented example.

In general, the focus on paradoxes and peculiar examples misplaces our interest, which should be on whole systems of thought. A supposed counterexample will seldom be adequate to knock down a major theory. Rather, one must wonder whether the theory, if it is venerable and well worked out, is not ground for doubting something about the counterexample.

Efforts to show the supposed inconsistency of utilitarianism depend very heavily on the principles imputed to utilitarianism and on deductions of consequences of following the principles. If the deductions are, as they often are, from science fiction examples or problems, as in James's and Hodgson's arguments, the first thing to note about their discussion is that it is remarkably narrow-minded and underargued. Anyone who discovers such a powerful argument and then fails to follow up its full range of implications deserves censure for temerity of intellect. We might follow Antony Flew's advice against a putative conclusion of Bertrand Russell: "Yes, it does seem absurd; 'but,' as Groucho Marx would have it, 'don't be misled. It is absurd.' "[54] A world that encompassed James's bargain, Hodgson's beings, or, say, Newcomb's genie would defy virtually all our understandings. In analyzing it we could not reach quick or definitive conclusions; it is a stupefying task to transport ourselves in our minds to so radically different a world and also to work out an ethical system in that world.[55] But if we are interested in moral theory we have no reason to analyze

54. Antony Flew, *An Introduction to Western Philosophy* (Indianapolis: Bobbs-Merrill, 1971), p. 369. The view of Russell's that Flew considers absurd is that we have no immediate knowledge of external objects but only sense data from which we may infer existence on the supposition that something must have caused us to have the sense data (ibid, p. 368).

55. Wittgenstein notes that if "you imagine certain facts otherwise, describe them otherwise, than the way they are, then you can no longer imagine the application of certain concepts, because the rules for their application have no analogue in the new circumstances" (Ludwig Wittgenstein, *Zettel,* transl. G. E. M. Anscombe [Oxford: Basil Blackwell, 1967] §350, p. 64e). See further below, §34. Even in our own world, where our imaginations are not so sorely tried, our problem is that, as James says, "Everywhere the ethical philosopher must wait on facts" (James, "The Moral Philosopher and the Moral Life," p. 208).

such a world. If we are to reason sensibly about moral theory, we must begin with the world that we understand best, the one in which our theories will have practical application.

Again, as with the use of crucial examples, there can be value in considering the import of radically altered circumstances. Recall Hume's discussion of the circumstances of justice: "Reverse, in any considerable circumstance, the condition of men: Produce extreme abundance or extreme necessity: Implant in the human breast perfect moderation and humanity, or perfect rapaciousness and malice: By rendering justice totally *useless,* you thereby totally destroy its essence, and suspend its obligation upon mankind" (E188).[56] Or consider Sissela Bok's constructive effort to test the value of keeping secrets by posing four worlds as nearly different from ours as Hodgson's is. In the first of these we are transparent while one or more others are fully protected against our prying. In the second, others are entirely transparent while we are protected. In the third, all are completely transparent to anyone who wants to know their inmost thoughts. In the fourth, all are fully protected against prying if they wish to be. In few words, Bok notes how pervasively the world under each of these conditions would differ from our own world.[57] One might extend her discussion to note how different our so-called commonsense moral principles would likely be in each of these worlds. When all are transparent, for example, truth telling loses its moral significance. It must therefore be a contingent moral concern. Showing that in some idealized world there would be no value in truth telling says little about our own world or our own moral theory. The one lesson we can solidly infer from such an exercise is that our moral theory cannot be purely abstract but must be based in the contingencies of the kinds of lives it should govern, as Hume forcefully argues.

Before leaving this topic, let us reconsider the moral impulse of James's morality play. His essential point is some variant of the usual issue in distributive justice that it is wrong to let some benefit at the expense of others just because the benefits outweigh the costs. Rawls makes a related claim. He says that "justice denies that the loss of freedom for some is made right by a greater good shared by others. It does not allow that the sacrifices imposed on a few are outweighed by

---

56. David Hume's *An Enquiry Concerning the Principles of Morals,* in Hume, *Enquiries,* 3d ed., ed. L. A. Selby-Bigge and P. H. Nidditch (Oxford: Clarendon Press, 1975). Cited here and hereafter in parentheses with an E followed by section and page numbers.

57. Sissela Bok, *Secrets: On the Ethics of Concealment and Revelation* (New York: Pantheon, 1983), pp. 15–18.

the larger sum of advantages enjoyed by many."[58] As usual, Rawls's point is more complex than the simple one that benefits for some cannot be justified by their being greater than the costs for others. He allows a slighter injustice to be compensated by avoidance of a greater injustice.[59] He merely disallows that an injustice in the form of a violation of right be compensated by essentially "greater" welfare effects.[60] So, for example, it may not violate justice that some lose their freedom when they are drafted into military duty to protect the rights of the rest of us, who may be enslaved if our society is not defended. But it would seemingly be wrong to draft some in order to protect our land, which produces what wealth we have, if those who wish to take our land will ignore us and our rights of freedom if we simply let them have the land and we retreat into the barren hinterlands.

In our understanding of this general range of issues, we may profit from the exploration of examples of the implications of various principles or theories, but only if we keep the examples realistic rather than rhetorically impossible. Realistic examples may help us understand just what it means to assert, as Rawls does, that justice is a first virtue of human activities and that welfare is secondary.[61] They may still not help us resolve the rightness of alternative theories each of which depends on centrally important intuitions (see further, §34).

58. Rawls, *A Theory of Justice*, pp. 3–4.
59. Ibid., p. 4.
60. As will be discussed below, §27, this seems odd, because Rawls's value theory seems to stipulate lexicographic priority to rights over welfare effects, so that the latter cannot be greater.
61. Ibid.

2

The Strategic Structure
of Moral Problems

Apart from cognitive limits of reason, the major obstacle to an individual's achieving good outcomes is the fact that the individual typically is not directly in control of outcomes: they result from the joint actions of many people. The ways in which outcomes are determined by actions of two or more people at once are many and varied. Nevertheless, we may generally characterize them as variants of a small number of types. Sometimes we share purposes, sometimes we merely need to keep from blocking one another, sometimes one of us may do something beneficial for another without any action by the other. We may jointly benefit from erecting a fence between us, as in Robert Frost's "Mending Wall."[1] My well-being on the highway may depend on whether you drive right or left although I may know and care nothing else about your existence. Your life may depend on my actively stopping to help you, who otherwise care nothing about me. Whether we are concerned with our own narrow interests or with the general welfare, we depend unavoidably on the actions of others to accomplish our purposes.

It is impractical to consider many of these issues without using the framework of game theory. Therefore, I will use a small number of representative games to order the discussions that follow. However, there are few points to be made from these games beyond keeping the structures of various interactions clear. One could verbally make sense of such interactions as the Prisoner's Dilemma and of coordination games, but it would be a needlessly arduous task and the result would probably be opaque to most readers. Unfortunately, for its task game

1. Robert Frost, "Mending Wall," in Frost, *Complete Poems of Robert Frost* (New York: Holt, Rinehart and Winston, 1949), pp. 47–48.

theory is badly named: it has little or nothing to do with games, and it is hardly a theory. It is preeminently a descriptive framework for categorizing social interactions. There is theory in the theory of games, but much of it is mathematical theory that often has little applicability to problems that interest social theorists. Game theory is of great value in social theory primarily because it affords conceptual clarification and descriptive simplification and generalization of problems that interest us. Theorists have been able to understand many of these problems without game theory, as, for example, Hume did for many of the problems of concern here. But they have been less successful in communicating their arguments to others than in getting them right in the first place. A strength of game theoretic representations of social interactions is their extraordinary transparency and consequent ease of generalization to structurally similar interactions, although it may require long exposure to begin to see through them.

For reasons that will become increasingly clear, I wish to begin discussion of these problems with the limited value theory that assumes only ordinal ranking of outcomes by each participant in an interaction and no interpersonal comparability of valuations among the participants. Hence, I will use ordinal game theoretic representations in which the outcomes have only ordinal values. One cannot say anything more than that one prefers the first ranked outcome to the second, and so forth. In particular, one cannot say that the first ranked outcome has any particular value, such as a cardinal number of utils or dollars. And there is no sense in saying that the value of your payoff from a particular outcome can be added to that of mine for that outcome.

All the game structures that will be discussed here can be divided into those that involve only conflict, only coordination, and a combination of these two. An ordinal game involves conflict if it is true that anytime a change in outcomes makes some player better off it makes some other player worse off. A two-person ordinal game can involve *pure conflict* in that every change in outcome leaves one player better off and the other worse off or it leaves both at the status quo. A game involves coordination if in it it is true that some change that makes one player better off makes another better off as well. A game is *pure coordination* if in it every change that makes one player better off makes all players better off.

If we could make comparisons among individuals' values to say that the "sum" of our payoffs in one outcome is greater than the "sum" in another payoff, most of the point of considering the strategic structures here would disappear. A utilitarian could then simply sum all of the payoffs in each outcome and select that outcome with the highest sum.

(There would still be some point in keeping straight the incentives that self-interested participants face as these incentives are represented in the strategic structures of their interactions.) *The vast bulk of technical game theory is based on the assumption that such sums make sense and is therefore of little relevance in much of what follows here.* Indeed, the very labels of the strategic categories of games in the large game theoretic literature are different from the "coordination" and "conflict" labels used here. One of the most important divides in games in which payoffs of players can be added to yield a sum is the distinction between *constant sum* and *variable sum* games (sometimes the latter are confusingly called "positive sum"), whose meanings should be apparent. A game is variable sum if the sum of payoffs to all players in every outcome is not a constant. The label "zerosum" is sometimes used, misleadingly, to cover the more general category of constant sum games. If payoffs are in dollars, poker is generally played as a constant sum game. The sum is generally zero in a neighborhood game, but it is negative for the actual players in a game played in a casino that takes a fixed cut from the winnings. A variable sum game is, in the terminology above, at least partly a game of coordination. A constant sum game is, in that terminology, a game of conflict.

Unfortunately, in the usual jargon of game theory for games in which payoffs can meaningfully be added, "conflict" means lack of any possibility of reaching prior agreement on how to play. In this sense, poker is generally played under conditions of conflict. Indeed, if I made a prior agreement with another player on how we would play our cards, you would rightly think I was cheating. The opposite of conflict in this jargon is "cooperation," which means the condition of being able to make prior, binding agreements, as when we sign a contract. I will not use the usual jargon of additive game theory in any of what follows.

One of the worst of all confusions in game theoretic terminology is the tendency to speak of pure conflict games as zerosum. Ordinal games, such as in virtually all the strategic structures discussed in this book, can be pure conflict in the clear sense defined above, but they are obviously not zerosum. They are not because there can be no comparative weighing of payoffs that are strictly ordinal. Suppose a real interaction could be conceived as zerosum in whatever counts as welfare in a utilitarian moral theory. In that game all outcomes would be equally utilitarian. Hence, there would be no utilitarian ground for advising on the choice of strategies. Zerosum games and the more general category of constant sum games are therefore of little or no interest in utilitarian moral theory.

In what follows, I will lay out the strategic structures of categories of interactions that must be properly regulated if we are to achieve good outcomes. As already noted (§3), the game structures will represent the narrowly self-interested values of various outcomes to individual participants. These values can be viewed as the baselines against which more generally utilitarian choices may be made. As discussed earlier (in §4) moral theory has historically been at the small scale of virtually face-to-face interactions, whereas many of the problems that interest us are at the large scale of collectivities and whole societies. It is instructive to divide the strategic categories of moral problems into small-number and large-number interactions to see how we may generalize from the one to the other. The problem of beneficence at the dyadic level is in important respects analogous to distributive justice at the collective level (§9). The problem of promise keeping is partly analogous to that of political order (§10). And the problem of coordinating our actions to meet for lunch is partly analogous to that of grand social conventions for monarchical succession, inheritance, and the transfer of property (§11). Despite strategic relationships between small- and large-number problems, generalization from quotidian small-number contexts to large-number contexts is not always simple. How far we may go in deducing a moral duty to act in various circumstances turns on how much we can know about the relative values of outcomes for all participants. Demands for such knowledge are far more severe for beneficence and distributive justice than for the other problems and are often more severe for large-number than for small-number contexts (§12). A clear grasp of the strategic structures of the problems we face helps to clarify the morality of promising (§13) and the supposed principle of generalization that is often given as the answer to the question, "What if everyone did that?" (§14). Finally, recognition that our actions and choices are of strategies that only indirectly produce outcomes suggests a central difficulty in the concept of agency in social interactions (§15).

Roughly speaking, the difference between dyadic interactions and large-number interactions is the difference between the morality of everyday life and the morality of political institutions. Once we have made clear what are the strategic relationships between various categories, we will turn, in Chapters 3 and 4, to the analysis of political principles in what we may call institutional utilitarianism, first in the structure of legal rights that might be justified without interpersonal comparisons of welfare (Chap. 3) and then in more general institutional provisions that require interpersonal comparisons (Chap. 4). The background strategic structure will be the same as that we survey in the following sections.

§8 The Strategic Categories

Problems of social interaction may be regulated by moral motivations, by self-interest, or by institutional arrangements that couple self-interest with the more general interest. Which of these will work will depend on the incentives that individuals and groups of individuals face. Suppose we start, with the early utilitarians from Hume to Mill, from the assumption that the chief problem in motivating people to act for good outcomes on the whole is that their own interests are often better served by acting against the general interest. Then to discover whether good outcomes will occur spontaneously in particular contexts we must check the fit between individual and collective interests. Since the outcomes of concern will often be determined by the actions of more than one person, we will often have to survey the incentives to many people at once. The most perspicuous way to do that is with game theoretic payoff matrices.

We may roughly approximate all possible interactions with a typology of six game structures ordered according to two dimensions. First there is a dimension of the number of participants in an interaction. Some problems involve small-number—indeed, often dyadic—interactions whereas others involve large-number or society-level interactions. There is also a dimension of strategic or game theoretic structure. As will be explained more fully below, at one extreme our interactions may involve unreciprocated actions that, in game-theoretic terms, imply a pure conflict of (narrow self-) interest. At the other extreme, some interactions involve only coordination without any conflict. Between these extreme categories are interactions that involve a combination of conflict and coordination. Table 2.1 presents these problems in a two-dimensional strategic typology.

The typology of problems in table 2.1 is similar to the range of

Table 2.1. The Strategic Structure of Moral Problems

	Scale of the Interaction	
Strategic Type	Dyadic and Very Small Number	Large Number
Pure conflict	Beneficence	Distributive justice
Mixed-motive	Promise keeping	Justice as order; collective action
Coordination	Coordination promises	Conventions, e.g., for monarchical succession

problems at the center of Hume's moral and political theory. Hume considers exemplars of four general categories of problems: (1) beneficient actions; (2) promise-keeping and its analogues; (3) justice, allegiance, and their relatives; and (4) conventions such as those governing the succession of monarchs and the inheritance of land. The second and third of these are virtues that are "artificial" in the sense that they are socially contrived, often by convention. They are artificial because their virtue is contingent on how society is arranged. The first is one of many "natural" virtues not unlike those familiar from Aristotelian ethics.[2] The fourth category is not itself of direct concern to Hume—indeed, most of his discussion of conventions, except for his discussion of the objects of allegiance (T3.2.10), is carried on in long footnotes. Conventions are of interest to him primarily because they are useful in restricting the vast set of possible institutions for resolving certain problems in his second and third categories.

In the typology of table 2.1 there are two categories that were not in Hume's list. These categories are large-number beneficence and small-number coordination. The former is perhaps best exemplified by what is often called distributive justice, as opposed to the kind of justice—which Sidgwick derisively calls "order"[3]—that concerns Hume. The second can be exemplified by a kind of promising that is used strictly for coordination—as in our promise to meet for lunch tomorrow at noon (with any luck, in Paris)—as opposed to the kind of promising that is used to secure some sort of exchange for mutual benefit. Clearly, omission of the category that includes distributive justice is a major omission from any serious moral or political theory, although it is

2. The distinction between natural and artificial virtues is briefly drawn in David Hume, *A Treatise of Human Understanding,* 2d ed., ed. L. A. Selby-Bigge and P. H. Nidditch (Oxford: Clarendon Press, 1978), book 3, part 3, sec. 1, p. 579. This reference is hereafter cited in parentheses in the text in the standard fashion as (T3.3.1, p. 579).

3. Henry Sidgwick, *The Methods of Ethics,* 7th ed. (London: Macmillan, 1907), p. 440. Anthony Quinton observes that justice "is first and foremost a distributive notion" (in "Utilitarian Ethics," pp. 1–118 in W. D. Hudson, ed., *New Studies in Ethics* [New York: St. Martin's, 1974], 2:76). *Now* it may be foremost a distributive notion, but first it was otherwise, and at least very early it was a notion of order. The thirty-first Principle Doctrine or Sovran Maxim of Epicurus is: "The justice which arises from nature is a pledge of mutual advantage to restrain men from harming one another and save them from being harmed" (Whitney J. Oates, ed., *The Stoic and Epicurean Philosophers* [New York: Modern Library, 1940], p. 37). When Locke claims that the proposition, "*Where there is no Property, there is no Injustice,*" is as demonstrably certain as any proposition in Euclid, he is concerned with justice as order (John Locke, *An Essay Concerning Human Understanding,* ed. Peter H. Nidditch [Oxford: Clarendon Press, 1975]; 4.3.18, italics in original; see also Hume, T3.2.2, p. 501). Moreover, it is generally true that without property there is little to distribute.

plausible that Hume thought its omission a virtue. The omission of the category of small-number coordination interactions, however, is not particularly important for a moral theory.

There is one other conspicuous omission from Hume's account: he does not discuss what one should do in large-number Prisoner's Dilemmas for which there is no regulating institution. Voluntaristic collective action can secure the general benefit in such cases, but it often fails, typically because it will not be in any individual's interest to contribute toward the collective provision.[4] What is one's moral obligation to participate in collective action in such cases? Despite his apparent grasp of the logic of collective action,[5] this is not a question that Hume raises. Various efforts to answer the question can be read into or out of Kant, Mill, and the massive twentieth-century literature on various generalization arguments, beginning with Broad.[6] As I will argue below, Hume's neglect of this issue is related to his neglect of the problem of distributive justice (see §§9 and 10). There is reason to suppose that his neglect was deliberate, that it was not merely an oversight.

Hume's clear grasp of strategic grounds for different resolutions of various problems of social interaction did not become a part of the utilitarian tradition, and it seems generally not to have been understood except in piecemeal cases. Perhaps the reason for this failing is that strategic understanding is particularly difficult. It seems more likely that later writers missed the analysis simply because no analytical treatment of the general problem of strategic interaction was available to them.[7] In fairness to later writers, Hume does not explicitly discuss the strategic structures of his problems; rather he considers specific examples of problems whose resolutions he clearly relates to their strategic structures. His grasp of the latter is shown, not by his labeling the categories according to their strategic structures, but by how resolutely he divides his subject into its categories and by how thoroughly he bases his resolutions of various problems in their strategic structures.

4. Mancur Olson, Jr., *The Logic of Collective Action* (Cambridge, Mass.: Harvard University Press, 1965); Russell Hardin, *Collective Action* (Baltimore: Johns Hopkins University Press for Resources for the Future, 1982).

5. Hume, T3.2.7, p. 538; see further, Hardin, *Collective Action*, pp. 40, 132.

6. C. D. Broad, "On the Function of False Hypotheses in Ethics," *International Journal of Ethics* 26 (April 1916): 377–397.

7. As William Baumol notes of the logic of collective action, "writers, sometimes even those who had considered these ideas elsewhere in their writings, continued to make mistakes and omissions which greater familiarity with the analysis in question might have prevented" (William J. Baumol, *Welfare Economics and the Theory of the State* [Cambridge, Mass.: Harvard University Press, 1952], p. 143).

§9 Pure Conflict Interactions

The usual problem of beneficence has the simple ordinal structure of Game 2.1. In each cell of the game, the first payoff is to Row, the second to Column. Column is in need of help that Row can offer. Column has no relevant choice in the matter while Row can choose either to help or not to help. If helping entails some cost to Row and Row is narrowly self interested, we might suppose that Row's preference is not to help. Row ranks her not helping first and her helping second while, of course, Column ranks these in the reverse order. Hence, their preferences are in direct conflict. Without entering other possible outcomes, such as that in which Column rewards Row after the fact for Row's helping, they have no interest in cooperation.

                          Column

          Not help   1,2

    Row

          Help   2,1

Game 2.1. Beneficence

In general, it is better to say that the interests of Row and Column, rather than their preferences, are in direct conflict, because one may suppose their *interests* have the orderings of Game 2.1 even if Row happens to prefer to act beneficently and to help Column or even if Row and Column are mistaken about their interests. Morality is typically of greater concern when it conflicts with interest. Therefore, while game theorists generally speak of preferences, it is interests that are of concern here. Hence, the payoffs in the game matrices here do not represent preferences except in the narrow sense of *preferences over one's own outcome independently of the outcomes to others* when one correctly understands what is at issue. The outcome one ranks first should be that which serves one's own interest best. Furthermore, it should be clear that the concern here is only with benefits and costs to the donor and the recipient of beneficence, so that the interaction of Game 2.1 should be viewed as independent of its players' interactions with any other persons.

Suppose I am Row and you are Column. Should I help you? It depends. If the overall state of affairs in the outcome in which I do help you is better than that in which I do not help, then the utilitarian judgment is that I should help you. Let us leave discussion of how to determine whether the overall state of affairs is better in one outcome than in the other for later (see §12) and suppose for the moment that the utilitarian judgment is that I should help you. In doing so I suffer a loss while you enjoy a gain, one might say a gratuitous gain. There need be no particular sense in which you deserve the gain or in which I owe you the loss that I suffer other than the utilitarian one.

This is the two-person or dyadic instance of beneficence. It can be generalized to cover the large-number or society-level case. In general, however, n-person games cannot be pure conflict; in such games there is typically room for some subset of the players to cooperate in their own interest, perhaps but not necessarily against the interests of other players. Nevertheless, we can view the problem of n-person beneficence as one of pure conflict if we make what will often be a natural simplification. We must simply suppose that there are two groups, one of which is the potential benefactor group and the other the potential beneficiary group. It may be true that within the benefactor group several of us would rather cooperate with each other in not joining the effort to help the beneficiary group and that therefore our game at the individual level is not strictly a game of pure conflict. But at the group level it is sensible to view it as pure conflict: one group's interest is contrary to the other group's interest. It is also often generally sensible to view problems of distributive justice as essentially group-level problems involving the interests of the well-off and the less well-off. For example, the interests of the masses in the Sahel may be leveled against the interests of affluent Americans. Moreover, in the most important theory of distributive justice of our time and perhaps of any time, John Rawls supposes in his Difference Principle that we compare the interests of the worst-off group to those of everyone else, then of the next worst-off group to those of everyone above them, and so forth. At each comparison, the interests are those of two groups in a strategic situation of pure conflict.

In both the dyadic and the large-number problems here, the utilitarian motive for Row to help Column is simply that the help will make for a better state of affairs on the whole, with the 'whole' defined in each case with respect only to those in the relevant interaction. In both cases, Row is a net loser from helping and Column is a net gainer. In neither case need there be any obligation other than that of utilitarian concern. It may be that the kind of help that is likely to be of concern in dyadic cases is typically different from what is likely to be of concern in distributive justice cases. In the former, one may most often expect to perform some service whose costs are in time and energy. In the second, one may most often expect to transfer resources of, say, food or money, whose costs are indirectly but ultimately still in time and ener-

gy. Structurally, however, distributive justice is simply mass beneficence.

Earlier I noted that a strength of Hume's theory of morality is his
grasp of what are central issues and his clarity in putting them into a
strategic account. Yet he dismisses distributive justice, one of the most
important classes of issues. In part, at least, the dismissal follows from
the fact that he was trying to explain our typical moral responses. He
supposes that benevolence is motivated by sympathy and cannot be
directed toward a distant, ill-defined crowd.[8] Hence, what he calls
"extensive benevolence" is "too remote and too sublime to affect the
generality of mankind."[9] Moreover, in his time a concern for egalitarian distributive justice was apparently not one of the standard moral
responses. It had earlier been a concern in the time of the Levellers. It
came to the fore again in the French Revolution and in the Radical
criticisms of the English industrial revolution. Mill and Sidgwick are
greatly concerned with it. Today one can hardly address the notion of
justice without considering distributive views, which are, of course,
central in the theory of Rawls and in the vast body of contemporary
political theory that he has helped to stimulate.[10]

In part the change that has occurred is that moral theorists increasingly have turned to basing their accounts on what, as Hume says
(T3.3.1, p. 583), "reason requires" rather than on what psychology
commands. There are, however, other grounds for the difference between many contemporary theorists and Hume. Briefly, the two of
perhaps greatest significance are the following. First, the power of
states has radically increased since Hume's time. Hume's England and
Scotland lacked even the capacity to levy and collect taxes on income.
That is not to say merely that they lacked the will to do so but that even
with the will they would have lacked the organizational and administrative capacity. As Hume says, perfect equality is "impracticable."

8. In his account Hume is fundamentally concerned with a theory of motivation—of
the passions—and he speaks of benevolence, the willing of good, rather than of beneficence, the doing of good. His purpose is to explain moral actions and political institutions
by relating them to the passions and to reason. He typically speaks "of the origin of," for
example, justice, property, and government (T3.2.2, p. 484; 3.2.7, p. 534). The psychological basis of benevolence, Hume argues, is sympathy. Hence, his discussion of
benevolence in the *Treatise,* book 3, "Of Morals," is clearly secondary and adjunct to his
discussion of justice and its relatives. The more extensive discussion of it appears in book
2, "Of the Passions," particularly in part 2. It is a natural virtue that comes up in book 3
largely in counterpoint to the artificial virtues to show why the latter more richly involve
reason.

9. See T. A. Roberts, *The Concept of Benevolence* (London: Macmillan, 1973), p. 101.

10. John Rawls, *A Theory of Justice* (Cambridge, Mass.: Harvard University Press,
1971).

The second ground for Hume's position is that he, like such modern theorists as Hayek, was explicitly anti-egalitarian for principled or social theoretic reasons. He supposes that, in contemporary language, equalization would sap incentives and therefore reduce everyone to a worse level. Equality would be "pernicious" (E3.2, p. 194).[11] Rawls tries to meet this second concern with his Difference Principle, allowing inequalities that are generally beneficial.

Whatever may have been the case in Hume's own time with respect to the capacities of the state, contemporary states can probably make substantial redistributions. Moreover, while it might be pernicious to strive for "perfect" equality, as Hume supposes, it may be possible to achieve radical reductions in the extent of inequalities without substantially affecting productive efficiency.

There is one other obstacle to achieving equality: the inability to measure it. This issue will be taken up in §12 below. The institutional problem of distributive justice will be considered more generally in §27. These later discussions, however, depend on a prior grasp of the argument for justice as order in the following section.

§10 Mixed-Motive Interactions

Let us turn now to such issues as promise keeping and justice as order. These involve elements of both coordination and conflict. I might be better off this moment if I could break my promise, but I would be worse off in general if I could not use promising to secure mutually beneficial trades with others. Similarly, although I might wish that I alone had a ring of Gyges so that I might steal with impunity, I would gladly give up the ring if by doing so I could be sure everyone else would give it up. With that mythical ring, one could become invisible and thereby enter another's house with no fear of being found out. In Plato's *Republic* Glaucon supposed that while wearing such a wondrous ring not even the just man "would stay on the path of justice" but would plunder and rape at will.[12]

In essence, these problems are instances of the well-known Prisoner's Dilemma, whose payoff structure is displayed in Game 2.2. In this game the choices or strategies of the two players can be viewed as choices whether to turn over something to each other in a trade that, if it were consummated, would be mutually beneficial. Column can yield x or keep it; Row can yield y or keep it. Column prefers y to x; Row

11. These issues will be discussed further in §27 below.
12. Plato, *The Republic*, book 2, 360b–c.

prefers x to y. There may be no structure of dyadic interaction more prevalent than this.[13] In the payoff matrix, the outcomes are ranked ordinally from first to fourth preferences for each player.

		Column	
		Yield x	Keep x
	Yield y	2,2	4,1
Row			
	Keep y	1,4	3,3

Game 2.2. Prisoner's Dilemma or exchange

To see that the ordinal payoff structure of the Prisoner's Dilemma is precisely that of an ordinary exchange, one can suppose that x is your old car and y is my $1000. If it makes sense for us to trade, it must be the case that I prefer your car to my money while you prefer my money to your car. Obviously, as first preferences each of us would most like to have both the car and the money. As second preferences we would like to make the trade. Our third preference is to fail to trade and to remain at the original status quo. Our fourth choice would be to lose our own holding without gaining that of the other.

Promising enters because we may not be able to consummate both sides of our trade in the same moment. I may need your help in changing a tire today in return for my promised help in moving your piano next weekend. Suppose I make the promise and you help me with the tire. Morality aside, should I then help you with the piano moving? In the massive philosophical literature on promising it is often supposed that I should not if my only concern is my own interest. Hume says on the contrary that "interest is the *first* obligation to the performance of promises" (T3.2.5, p. 523). Hume is right for the kind of promising that concerns him and, he seems to assume, almost all promisers. Let us consider why.

How does interest enter my mind when next weekend it is time to move your piano? Obviously, you are not likely to be just any randomly selected person. Rather, you are likely to be a near neighbor or an otherwise close associate. Hence, even though I might wish, as Anthony Heath supposes,[14] that as far as your helping to change my tire is concerned, bygones are bygones, in fact I have other incentives to

13. Russell Hardin, "Exchange Theory on Strategic Bases," *Social Science Information* 21 (1982): 251–272, esp. pp. 251–253.

14. Anthony Heath, *Rational Choice and Social Exchange* (Cambridge: Cambridge University Press, 1976), pp. 59–60.

be fair to you. The main incentive is that it is likely to be useful to me in the future to have your cooperation or at least your goodwill in other endeavors. Hence, just as your incentive to help was your expectation of reciprocal help from me in the future, so I will look to the future before I lazily refuse to keep my bargain to hoist your piano.[15]

In the context of ongoing relationships such as ours in the case above, promising is essentially a device to allow us to deal with exchanges repeated over time. Ian Macneil calls these "relational exchanges."[16] The incentive structure for such exchanges is that of the iterated rather than that of the single-play Prisoner's Dilemma. That incentive structure is clearly to cooperate.[17] This distinguishes it from beneficence, in which there is no incentive to "cooperate" because the giving is one-sided. There is reputedly a notion in Soviet society, translated by recent Russian emigrés as "senseless kindness," that evidently covers acts of beneficence that are not within relationships of reciprocity.[18] In many contexts one can only hope there will be enough senseless kindless to get us through. In most contexts one may be glad that promise keeping does not depend on senseless kindness.

Hume argues that promise keeping in ongoing relationships is an "artificial" virtue because it runs against our immediate passions, such as my passion for indolence when it is time to move your piano. "Hence," he says, "I learn to do a service to another, without bearing him any real kindness; because I foresee, that he will return my service, *in expectation of another of the same kind, and in order to maintain the same correspondence of good offices with me or others.* And accordingly, after I have serv'd him, and he is in possession of the advantage arising from my action, he is induc'd to perform his part, as foreseeing the consequences of his refusal" (T3.2.5, p. 521; emphasis added). On this account, promise keeping is not generally a moral problem. This conclusion might sound surprising to readers of moral philosophy through most of this century when concern with promise keeping may have dominated any other more clearly moral problem.

Before turning to the large-number generalization of the problem of relational exchange or promise keeping, note that promises take at least two other forms, as will be discussed below (in §13). The other forms are the promissory equivalents of beneficence and of coordination. The

15. Hardin, *Collective Action*, pp. 213–216.
16. Ian Macneil, *The New Social Contract* (New Haven, Conn.: Yale University Press, 1980).
17. Hardin, *Collective Action*, pp. 213–216.
18. As reported by Sylvia Rothchild, author of *A Special Legacy: An Oral History of Soviet Jewish Emigrés in the United States* (New York: Simon and Schuster, 1985), in conversation, August 1984.

latter will play some role in the discussion of the general problem of coordination interactions (§11).

Just as self-interest leads to promise keeping, so too in small-number interactions, such as in small towns or in the small societies studied by anthropologists, it can lead to scrupulous adherence to the rules of justice. "The same self-love, therefore, which renders men so incommodious to each other, taking a new and more convenient direction, produces the rules of justice, and is the *first* motive of their observance" (T3.2.8, p. 543; Hume's emphasis). As Hume seems to recognize, this problem is the larger number analogue of the two-person Prisoner's Dilemma of Game 2.2.

It is generally supposed that cooperation in the Prisoner's Dilemma, even when play is iterated, falls off as the number of participants increases. While my close associates might hold me accountable for my free riding on their cooperative efforts, a very large number of people with whom I do not individually interact typically cannot hold me accountable.[19] Hence, "when men have observed, that tho' the rules of justice be sufficient to maintain any society, yet 'tis impossible for them, of themselves, to observe those rules, in large and polish'd societies; they establish government as a new invention to attain their ends, and preserve the old, or procure new advantages, by a more strict execution of justice" (T3.2.8, p. 543). Hume's "impossible" is perhaps too strong a term: we could, of ourselves, refrain from theft. But no one believes all of us will do so, and we welcome the "more strict execution of justice" in securing the more general cooperation.

For Hume there are two major roles for the institutions of justice: first, they protect property and its possession; second, they secure common interests. In each of these roles the problem that must be resolved is strategically equivalent to the Prisoner's Dilemma. Let us briefly discuss the first of these, which is Hume's greater concern, and then turn to the second, which Hume evidently takes for granted but does not discuss at length. In his emphasis here he is transitional between Hobbes, who is concerned almost exclusively with order, and Smith and the nineteenth-century political economy theorists of the state, who focus on the state's role in providing collective goods.

Hume's view of the conditions of human life is more benign, less paranoid than Hobbes's view often seems to be. Hume does not suppose we are threatened by war of all against all. Rather, our pervasive problem is that our passions in the short run defeat our interests in the

19. But see Hardin, *Collective Action,* pp. 173–187.

long run by leading us into momentary acts of injustice. Hume's account of how our passions defeat us sounds like an account of the juvenile quality of the Soviet-American arms race: "You have the same propension, that I have, in favour of what is contiguous above what is remote. You are, therefore, naturally carried to commit acts of injustice as well as me. Your example both pushes me forward in this way by imitation, and also affords me a new reason for any breach of equity, by shewing me, that I should be the cully of my integrity, if I alone shou'd impose on myself a severe restraint amidst the licentiousness of others" (T3.2.7, p. 535). A modest institutional framework of police protection of property and its possession is sufficient to deter us both from destructive disorder and injustice. All that is needed is a small number of people who, "being satisfied with their present condition, and with their part in society, have an immediate interest in every execution of justice, which is so necessary to the upholding of society" (T3.2.7, p. 537). Those who are satisfied with their present conditon of wealth may suppose their short-term interests are not affected by government action or policy, so that their more destructive and self-seeking passions will not be evoked by the opportunities of government service. Rather, they may be motivated by long-term considerations of the general benefit of the society that justice will bring. Commitment to justice on the part of a few makes justice prevail for the many. Smith thinks self-interest is sufficient to make the economy go; Hume thinks more, but only a bit more, than self-interest is required for political order in a large society.[20]

Turn now to the second role of the state. Its first role is simply to protect us in our spontaneous endeavors to create wealth. Once government that is concerned with protecting our general well-being exists, however, it can actively promote our welfare by creating wealth in contexts in which we could not spontaneously do so. First, through government

> men acquire a security against each others weakness and passion, as well as against their own, and under the shelter of their governors, begin to taste at ease the sweets of society and mutual assistance. Then government extends farther its beneficial influence; and not contented to protect men in those conventions they make for their mutual interest, it often obliges them to make such conventions, and forces them to seek their own advantage, by a concurrence in some common end or purpose. . . .

20. As noted above, in a small society self-interest is generally sufficient to bring about justice.

> Thus bridges are built; harbours open'd; ramparts rais'd; canals form'd;
> fleets equip'd; and armies disciplin'd; every where by the care of govern-
> ment, which, tho' compos'd of men subject to all human infirmities,
> becomes . . . a composition that is, in some measure, exempted from all
> these infirmities. (T3.2.7, pp. 538–539)

How does all this work to defeat the usual incentive not to cooperate in
a very large-number Prisoner's Dilemma? Largely by changing the
incentives to individual citizens. And what motivates the governors?
Hume supposes, again, that they are simply men whose short-run
interests are not at stake so that their actions are determined by the
calmer passions of concern for the longer run. One might rather note
that the governors are not strictly in a large-number Prisoner's Dilemma. If it is in my power to decide whether we all cooperate in or all
defect from some mutually beneficial endeavor, my interest may quite
clearly be identical with the collective interest. For example, a national
leader with the power to raise an army is not like a mere citizen in the
face of foreign attack. If not coerced by government, the citizen faces a
severe problem of the logic of collective action. The leader faces no such
problem but can simply decide whether to defend against or to surrender to the attack.

This way of resolving broad problems of collective action has in it
the conspicuous risk that those with power will abuse their positions
for their own benefit. Hume's sanguine dependence on finding a Pericles to govern would, if successful, avoid this risk. But a historian of
Hume's stature should face the fact that there might be no Pericles.
Hence, resolving our initial problem of order by creating government
permits both the furtherance of other collective purposes and the abuse
of the collective population. Both these prospects may be only parasitic
on the creation of modest institutions for securing justice as order, but
they are practically unavoidable.

Provision of collective goods and abuse of power are not the only
outcomes parasitic upon the institution of justice as order. Such beneficence as is seen in the specific care of the needy or in general efforts at
distributive justice may also be furthered by the prior creation of government to maintain order. Similarly, such niceties as the enforcement
of contracts may follow in the wake of government, so that even dyadic
exchange relations come to depend on the state. This is particularly
useful for securing an exchange whose halves must be fulfilled at different points in time. Such an exchange may fail when the second party's
interest is not served by fulfilling the promise. This can happen if the
cost of fulfilling the promise is high relative to any likely gains the
second party can expect to receive from future dealings with the other

party, a condition that will be met for almost all promissory exchanges between strangers. In order to secure promises to complete exchanges in these cases, we resort to contracts enforceable at law. The enforcement mechanisms are available because the state is already there to protect property and its possession. That such contract enforcement has in fact been parasitic on justice as order is suggested by the relatively late development of contract law.[21]

This is the general category of justice as order that, of course, is the subject of jurisprudence and the law. It brings to mind problems of procedure and institutions rather than of the distribution of resources. Some of the procedures are merely conventions; they could as well be other than what they are but, given what they are, we are bound by them. Philosophers interested in justice commonly are concerned with both justice as order and distributive justice, although they do not always keep their categories clear and they often argue past one another.

After we have considered all that the state is likely to do on our behalf in organizing the provision of collective benefits, there remains a large class of cases that fit into the cell of large-number Prisoner's Dilemma problems in table 2.1. This is the class of collective action problems that do not affect more or less the whole society. These problems would seem to be unresolvable if we all have Hume's moral psychology: we will not act from benevolence except in small-number cases and, by the logic of collective action, we cannot rationally cooperate to resolve such problems.

If it is not narrowly rationally incumbent on one to contribute to a collective provision, is it nevertheless morally incumbent? For a straightforward utilitarian the answer may often seem to be simple: Yes, if one can effect more good with one's contribution than it costs. This is to make one's action a matter of beneficence, motivated of course by what reason requires rather than by what sympathy commands. But the answer is not so simple in general, as I will argue in §12 below. The complicating factor to be discussed there is the grievous difficulty of determining that one's contribution effects more good than it costs.

§11 Pure Coordination Interactions

Many choice situations we face are problems of coordination. There is no single best action for me independently of your choice of action.

---

21. On Roman developments, see Barry Nicholas, *An Introduction to Roman Law* (Oxford: Clarendon Press, 1962), pp. 159–167.

This is not true of an isolated play of Prisoner's Dilemma, in which I have a dominant strategy choice, which is not to cooperate no matter what you do. In a simple coordination game how you choose will affect how I should choose. For example, in the coordination game whose ordinal payoffs are displayed in Game 2.3, I will prefer to choose my strategy I if you choose your strategy I; otherwise I will prefer to choose my strategy II.

Column

	I	II
I	1,1	2,2
II	3,3	1,1

Row

Game 2.3. Coordination

Because coordination in an interaction of the form of Game 2.3 may simply be motivated by self-interest, there is little that is distinctively moral about it. Hence, coordination problems are at best on the fringes of ethics. That is evidently Hume's view: he relegates much of his discussion of coordination issues to footnotes. However, as noted above, Hume is concerned exclusively with coordination on the large-number or society-level rather than in dyadic or relatively small-number contexts. Before turning to the more important large-number issues, let us discuss the dyadic problem.

An obvious, common example of dyadic coordination is a coordination promise of the kind in which you and I promise to meet for lunch. We make the promise because we think our interests are fully congruent. If we raise the possibility of meeting but then discover, as all too often happens, that we cannot find a time in the near future, so that the effort to coordinate fails, it does not follow that there is a failure of morality. The same is true, of course, for an exchange promise. If we decide in advance that the proposed exchange is not mutually beneficial, it does not follow that our failing to promise is a failure of morality. Moral considerations may enter only after the promise is made.

A clear difference in the obligatoriness of a Prisoner's Dilemma or exchange promise and a coordination promise can be seen in the difference in the implications of breaking them. If we have mutually promised to meet for lunch and I call you to break the promise, because on afterthought I do not really want to do it, perhaps because I am too busy, you may not feel abused unless in the interim you have made special arrangements for the meeting or you have passed up another opportunity. If I have promised to help you move your piano in return for your assistance in changing my tire and I call to break the promise after my tire is changed because on afterthought I do not really want to do it, you are almost sure to feel cheated.

In lawyer's terms, your interest in the coordination promise is a *reliance* interest: that is, you have no interest until you have come to rely on the expectation of fulfillment in undertaking action in the interim. For example, you may have turned down some splendid opportunity that is then lost to you if I do not fulfill. Your interest in the exchange promise is a *restitution* interest: in a sense, you want to get back at least what you paid out as in any exchange.

The difference here is strategic in the following sense. In making a promise to help you move your piano I know it will not be in my interest next Saturday morning actually to fulfill the promise except in, say, Hume's sense of my enlarged interest in future exchange with you or others. But I would not make a coordination promise unless I thought it would be in my interest at the moment when I should fulfill the promise to do so. Moral considerations might enter for such a promise only when the parties make it in a state of what turns out to be inaccurate knowledge of their future interests. If reliance on the promise alters the behavior of one of the parties, fulfilling the promise becomes increasingly obligatory for the other (or others). Unless that happens, however, the promise carries no moral weight.[22]

When a large group or society faces a coordination problem, it may not simply be able to use a coordination promise. But, as Hume argues, it may readily resolve its problem by convention. If the problem recurs often enough, any successful coordination by much of the relevant population may signal how to coordinate again at the next recurrence of the problem. The strategy onto which the group happens may become a convention in the sense that it is the obvious choice of virtually everyone whenever the standard problem occurs.[23] Any one of several other strategy choices might have been as good but once the convention is established no other strategy makes sense.

How does the particular strategy that becomes the convention get selected? It does not much matter. Hume says, "Sometimes the interests of society may require a rule of justice in a particular case; but may not determine any particular rule, among several, which are all

22. See further, P. S. Atiyah, *The Rise and Fall of Freedom of Contract* (Oxford: Clarendon Press, 1979), pp. 1–6.

23. David K. Lewis, *Convention* (Cambridge, Mass.: Harvard University Press, 1969); for a brief account, see Hardin, *Collective Action*, pp. 155–161.

equally beneficial. In that case, the slightest analogies are laid hold of, in order to prevent that indifference and ambiguity, which would be the source of perpetual dissension. . . . Many of the reasonings of lawyers are of this analogical nature, and depend on very slight connexions of the imagination" (E3.2, pp. 195–196).[24] As in this passage, Hume is generally interested in those conventions that define or regulate his institutions of justice. It is by convention that rules for the inheritance of property and for the succession of monarchs are established. It is by convention that certain devices and not others mark the transference of property. The rules and devices differ from one community to another for reasons of historical accident in the uses of the imagination in finding what Thomas Schelling calls prominent points for coordination.[25]

In an instructive error, Jonathan Harrison thinks one would expect Hume "to hold the view that what caused men to feel that they ought to obey one rule, in preference to any other, was always their *belief* that this rule was more useful than any other, and that they were justified in thinking that this rule ought to be obeyed, if this rule was *in fact* more useful than any other."[26] There are two responses one may make to Harrison's complaint. The first is one he himself makes in another context:[27] there might be no rule which is "*in fact* more useful than any other." The equivalence of what results from following any one of many rules is what defines a coordination problem. If coordination problems are commonplace, it is silly to insist against the facts that there be a single best rule for resolving one of them, and one would not expect Hume to do so. This response applies most obviously to the occasion of first coordination.

The second response to Harrison is that once a convention has been established, the rule of that convention may indeed be more useful than any other rule. In principle we should be indifferent between a rule of all driving on the left and a rule of all driving on the right. But once we have established the convention, say, of all driving on the right as in the United States, it may very well be true, therefore, that this rule is better than any other (although in another context we may suppose that such a rule is not best, as in the case of Sweden discussed below). Not only may an extant convention be effectively best when there are others that

24. See also the long footnotes, T3.2.3, pp. 504–513; and the account of allegiance, T3.2.10, pp. 553–567.

25. Thomas C. Schelling, *The Strategy of Conflict* (Cambridge, Mass.: Harvard University Press, 1960), pp. 54–58.

26. Jonathan Harrison, *Hume's Theory of Justice* (Oxford: Clarendon Press, 1981), p. 214.

27. Ibid., p. 226.

are in principle as good, it may even be effectively best when there are others that are in principle demonstrably better. The standard American typewriter keyboard, fondly called "qwerty" after the arrangement of keys in its first alphabetic row, is a hindrance to far faster typing times. Indeed, it was designed by Christopher Sholes, who invented the typewriter in 1867, to slow down typists who, using the hunt and peck technique, were so fast on an alphabetically arranged keyboard that they jammed his crude machine. More than half a century later in 1930, after touch-typing and better machines made typing much faster, August Dvorak proposed a new arrangement of the keyboard. (Many other keyboards have been patented and even produced, but all fell to qwerty.) On the "dvorak" keyboard 70 percent of the strokes (in typical English) are made on the so-called home row where the fingers rest, as against a mere 32 percent on the qwerty keyboard. Again more than half a century later, we still clumsily use the qwerty keyboard despite dvorak's being about twice as fast and less prone to error.[28] Presumably, we still cling to it because the costs of switching would be massive to the present generation of typists and typewriter owners. Perhaps the ease of rearranging the keyboard on modern microcomputers will finally lead to a changed convention.[29]

Before leaving the discussion of coordination problems, note how their resolution may be parasitic upon the existence of institutions of justice. In 1967 Sweden switched its driving convention from driving on the left to driving on the right. This was a change that could not have been made spontaneously by the sum of individual actions freely chosen. As a joke current at the time had it, the government was to make the change gradually, with buses driving on the right the first week, trucks going over to the right the second week, taxis the third week, and private cars last. Spontaneous change would have been as good as this policy. In fact, of course, the change was made all at once, at 5:00 A.M. on Sunday, September 3. Most vehicles were banned from the road for several hours around that time, and those that were on the road had to come to a full stop on the left side of the road by 4:50 A.M.,

28. Steven Leveen, "Tangled Typing," *Science 81* (May 1981): 84–86. Also see Paul A. David, "Clio and the Economics of QWERTY," *American Economic Review Papers and Proceedings* 75 (May 1985): 332–37.

29. In fairness to Harrison, Hume is not completely clear on the strategic significance of conventions for resolving iterated coordination problems (but see T3.2.10, pp. 553–567). He is rather more typically concerned with the origin in the imagination of particular rules than with how their strategic stability increases through their iterated application. Not surprisingly then, Hume's strategic grasp is weaker here than in his accounts of promise keeping and of the utility of institutions of justice.

then shift to the right side of the road and park until 5:00 A.M., when the signal was given to "drive right."[30]

Ironically, the original convention of driving on the left was more nearly a spontaneous growth. It was presumably already custom when an eighteenth-century royal decree required it for Swedish mail coaches.[31] England did not enact a law mandating the rule until 1835. Before that it was merely a custom, as sung in the ditty:

> The law of the road is a paradox quite,
> As you're driving your carriage along.
> If you go to the left you are sure to go right,
> If you go to the right you go wrong![32]

It was a custom that required little or no enforcement other than that implied in the last line of the ditty. The law of 1835 was presumably intended more to tidy things up and perhaps to bring local deviants into line than to determine overall behavior. Re-coordination from left to right could not now take place spontaneously without mayhem. Nevertheless, it is easy to suppose that switching to driving on the right in the rising tide of tourism was, by 1967, better for Sweden than continuing to drive on the left—even at a cost of roughly $120 million and, no doubt, considerable momentary inconvenience. In particular, on long streches of the open road, Swedes in Sweden must be killed less often by foreign drivers forgetfully reverting to their home custom and Swedes driving abroad must be killed less often by their own reversion to custom.[33] Indeed, since Swedish cars were built with the driving wheel on the left, just as most cars everywhere are built, Swedes must be less often killed while passing on the open road in Sweden now than they would have been under the old convention.

Because what happened almost spontaneously before could not spontaneously be undone, the state intervened to force re-coordination. It was evidently a utilitarian decision. More generally we may expect modern states to decide on rules to resolve many new coordination problems so that the role of spontaneously generated conventions may seem less important than it once was. It would be misguided, however, to see state intervention in these coordination problems as

30. Paul J. C. Friedlander, "H-Day Is Coming in Sweden," *New York Times,* August 20, 1967, sec. 10, pp. 1, 31: *Time Magazine,* September 15, 1967, pp. 39–40.

31. Ibid.

32. *New York Times,* September 9, 1967, p. 30.

33. At the time of "H-Day," for Höger, which means "right" in Swedish, there were 97,000 kilometers of highway, of which only 250 were divided superhighways (Friedlander, "H-Day Is Coming," p. 31). It must have taken vigilance for most foreigners to avoid drifting into the wrong lane on most Swedish roads.

somehow comparable to state regulation of Prisoner's Dilemma problems, such as protection of property.

§12 Value Theory Issues

Because beneficent actions involve a pure conflict of interest while Prisoner's Dilemma and coordination interactions involve the achievement of mutually beneficial outcomes, the former require a far more stringent value theory to justify them. Beneficence generally makes utilitarian moral sense only on the assumption that the relevant interpersonal comparison of utility is possible. To say that I *ought* to behave beneficently toward you is to imply that there is something I can do that will benefit you more than it costs me. Otherwise, although I may behave beneficently toward you, it is not the case that I ought to.

At some risk of belaboring this point, I should make sure it is clear. An act involving greater loss to the donor than gain to the donee may be an act of benevolence. But to assert a utilitarian *moral duty* to act beneficently implies the opposite relationship. Similarly, one may be obligated, because of a prior commitment or official duty, to do something for another that costs oneself more than it benefits the other. But this is not an act or a duty of beneficence. I am only concerned here with acts of beneficence *tout court,* which are acts independent of any other source of obligation.

Let us carry the central point further. One can say that my action to benefit you is benevolent without making an interpersonal comparison of utility. Indeed, the outcomes in Game 2.1 above are ranked only ordinally for each player without any implication as to whether the differences between their respective first and second choices are comparable in any way. But it is not sensible to assert that I *ought* to act with beneficence toward you unless one can make at least a crude judgment that you would benefit more than I would lose from my action.

Finally, note that one should be able to make a comparison that is stronger than merely ordinal. One should be able to say that you benefit *substantially* more from my benevolence than I lose from it because if comparisons are not cardinally precise they cannot be ordinally precise either. Hence, one cannot make compelling ordinal claims about borderline cases. A comparison that is based exclusively on ordinal information can make sense in the preference scheme of a single individual but not in an aggregation of preferences across individuals unless the interpersonal comparison per se is very strong—that is, I must seem to have an ordering of preferences quite similar to yours.

In sum, what is needed for moral claims to act with beneficence is weakly cardinal, interpersonally comparable utility information. Such information is often not available. However, I think it wrong to suppose that such information is never available on the claim that, as many economists assume, interpersonal comparisons are wholly meaningless. The rejection of even rough interpersonal comparisons would lead to some odd choices. For example, suppose I face you in a once-only interaction with the monetary payoff structure of Game 2.4.

You

	Cooperate	Defect
Cooperate	1¢,$100	−2¢,$100,000
Defect	2¢,0¢	0¢,$99

(I, to the left, spanning both rows)

Game 2.4. Prisoner's Dilemma with strong interpersonal comparison

Strategically, Game 2.4 is a simple Prisoner's Dilemma. Morally, it is much more: it poses for me a choice between a wonderfully benign but cheap action and a savagely unbenign action. Is it plausible that I would choose not to cooperate? Suppose you are a stranger to me and I have no expectation of further dealings with you, so that I have no incentive from self-interest to benefit you. But it is reasonable—isn't it?—to suppose you are a decent person of ordinary means.

It is with hesitation that I argue from an apparently bizarre example of the sort used by recent philosophers to trick readers into confusion. However, here there is nothing to confound any of one's beliefs, as I think the suppositions of Newcomb's problem, James's bargain (§7), and many other contrived choice problems do. Indeed, in the days of live television I once saw a version of Game 2.4 actually played out. As I recall the show, a "contestant" had to place a collect call to a randomly chosen long-distance telephone number. If the answering party was willing to accept the charges, the contestant won a hefty prize. The contestant, whose name was evidently unknown to the called party, was permitted to give no explanation other than that the call was very, very important and that there was no mistake in dialing. If one had been watching the show and had been at the randomly dialed number, how should one have acted?[34] No matter how we might have acted, most of us would be willing to acknowledge that accepting the call would have hurt us less than it would have helped the contestant.

---

34. The contestant, although she pleaded desperately, failed to convince her answerer to accept the small charge. She got no prize.

Before going on to large-number beneficence problems, note how strikingly small-number Prisoner's Dilemma and coordination problems differ from the beneficence problem. Resolution of Prisoner's Dilemma and coordination problems need not require interpersonal comparisons of even the weakest kind because all are ordinally better off in one outcome than in another.

If we can make sufficiently strong interpersonal comparisons in Game 2.4, we might suppose that the utilitarian outcome in such a case is clearly in the upper right cell. But if there can be no agreement on such comparisons in a Prisoner's Dilemma, we can still be sure that the upper left outcome is superior to the lower right. If the lower right is the status quo, we therefore know how we can improve our collective lot. We can make similar claims for a Prisoner's Dilemma involving any number of people and for any coordination game. Hence, in such contexts we can know how to make utilitarian improvements even in the face of one of the weakest of value theories: that in which there are no valid interpersonal comparisons and there is only ordinal information for individual preferences or interests.

Since in general we surely can make at least crude interpersonal comparisons, one might suppose we can ignore the constraints of the very weak value theory that denies such comparability. But many of the moral choice problems that we face will be cases in which crude comparisons will be inadequate for ranking outcomes. The larger range of possible outcomes over which we could make credible comparisons will not be at issue. Often we will be concerned only with a range of outcomes over which we cannot make meaningful comparisons. In these cases, we can make only ordinal, noncomparative utilitarian judgments over our range of actions. In Prisoner's Dilemma and coordination contexts, this constraint will not cripple our moral judgment. *But it substantially restricts the field in which we can claim that someone is obligated to act beneficently.*

Again, if we can make crude interpersonal comparisons, we can have a utilitarian duty to act with beneficence toward another in dyadic cases. (When we cannot do so, we do not have such a duty.) But what of the large-number problem? When can we know we have, either individually or as a group or class, a duty of beneficence to a large group or class? The answer is that the judgment typically, though not always, will be far more complex than in the dyadic case.

If we had an interpersonally comparable, precisely cardinal value theory, we might in principle suppose there to be a very discriminating answer to the question whether it was utilitarian for us to act with beneficence toward some group. That is to say, it would generally be either right or wrong to act and only rarely a matter of moral indifference. If comparisons are cruder, the indifferent cases must bulk larger. As we aggregate across a larger number of vague valuations, the penumbra of vagueness in the sum becomes relatively larger.

Suppose the m members of group A may act beneficently toward the n members of group B. Suppose further that m is not larger than n and that there are m members of B each of whose benefit from A's beneficence is found, in one-on-one comparisons, to be greater than the cost to the respective member of A. In this case we may be able easily to say that A is obligated to act beneficently toward B. (Whether A is obligated to act may, of course, turn in part on A's other relationships and obligations at the time.) But if the one-by-one comparison does not work out or if m is larger than n, the case will be trickier, and we may not be able to conclude that A has a duty of beneficence to B if we can make nothing stronger than ordinal comparisons between members of the two groups.

Perhaps the most perplexing conclusion for the account of group-level beneficence concerns the obligation of an individual member of a potentially beneficent group A whose other members do not contribute to the beneficent action toward group B. Suppose the conditions above would clearly be met so that we can say that A has a duty of beneficence to B. As an individual in A, am I obligated to act even if others in the group do not? Plausibly not. If I do act, my beneficence may result in far smaller per capita benefits to B. Now it may no longer be true that there is a member of B whose benefit from my action exceeds my cost. Hence, whether I am individually obligated may depend on whether enough others shoulder their part of our group obligation.

This result may seem less perplexing in the light of its coherence with an analogous result in the problem of voluntaristic collective action. Such problems are, again, those cases of large-number Prisoner's Dilemma problems that are not regulated by institutions of justice. It is utilitarian on strictly ordinal, interpersonally noncomparable valuations for all to cooperate rather than defect in a Prisoner's Dilemma. Hence, we do not require a particularly demanding value theory to reach a utilitarian conclusion. But suppose we face a collective action in which few contribute. Since it is a Prisoner's Dilemma that we face, my contribution to its resolution would cost me more than it would benefit me but not as much as I would benefit overall if everyone contributed.

But suppose there are so few contributors that my benefit from all actual contributions will be less than my own contribution. Now my contribution would be an act of beneficence to others in the group. To decide whether I ought to contribute, I now need interpersonally comparable measures of costs and benefits. If these have no merit and I only make assessments of my own costs and benefits, the only plausible meaning of the utilitarian injunction to produce the greatest good sounds like a modest version of a principle of fairness. If I get more from the collective provision than my contribution costs and my contribution makes a difference, then I ought to contribute; otherwise not. Hence, in a world without interpersonal comparisons, the dictates of fairness and of utilitarianism may not be in conflict despite commonplace claims to the contrary.

It is not fairness per se that is determinative, however, as can be seen from the discussion of group beneficence immediately preceding. It would be odd to say that whether I have a duty to contribute to the relief of misery in the Sahel turns on a concern with the fairness of my action in the light of others' contributions. We do talk as though my contribution were a matter of doing my fair share. But, insofar as one can make precise claims about the content of such usages of ordinary language, here the claim is perhaps best seen as referring to how much each and every similarly situated person ought to contribute in general, not to whether I ought to contribute such a "fair share" depending on how many others have done so. The concern in ordinary language is presumably with my acting fairly toward the people of the Sahel. In the above analysis of collective action the equivalence of the prescriptions from fairness and from utilitarianism has to do with their reference to my own group, not some outside beneficiary group.

There is another respect in which the distinction between collective action and group beneficence may blur. In many collective action problems there is no simple, indivisible action x that each of us in our group must undertake for us to provide ourselves with some collective benefit. Rather, there is some kind of resource varying amounts of which each of us may invest in providing our group benefit. I might be capable of bearing the full cost of our provision even though it would not be in my interest to do so. More generally, there might be an enormous set of cost-sharing arrangements that would be pareto superior to not providing ourselves our benefit.[35] If our value theory is inadequate for precise comparisons of utility, it cannot rank the set of cost-sharing arrangements to tell us which is best. Often in such contexts we are wont to assert that certain arrangements are fairer than others. If our instincts are to count as correct, however, we must be able to make comparisons that are in some degree precise. Otherwise, the notion of fairness is apt to be meaningless or arbitrary. Hence, as in the discussion of collective

35. See further, Hardin, *Collective Action,* pp. 90–100.

action above, claims for such fairness are consonant with utilitarian claims.

It is a realization that fairness often cannot be measured in terms of utility or welfare that leads many to measure it rather in terms of bald resources, such as money and time.[36] Such measurement cannot be finally compelling. It may get its apparent appeal from thinking about cases in which we may readily assume that relatively precise comparisons are possible, as we commonly do when we are dealing with our own peers. If our values are quite similar and our resources, as measured in baldly objective terms, are relatively equal, we can suppose we know the answer to relatively precise comparative questions. For example, I may suppose it clear that a $20 or $20,000 loss to you is worse than a $10 or $10,000 loss to me. Hence, measures in resources and in welfare terms coincide. When they do not coincide, however, concerning oneself strictly with measures of bald resources cannot be appealing.

To see this issue clearly, consider the following dyadic beneficence problem. If I render great service to you at very small cost, the action may seem unproblematic. But if I render a service to you that seems to benefit you only somewhat more than you would value its cost in resources if you had done it for yourself, it seems to matter whether we are similarly situated. If I am far worse off than you in the status quo, it seems perverse that I should be obligated to make you even better off at real cost to me. At first this may sound like an argument from fairness. But it is not merely that; here our capacity for making precise comparison is very much in question. If we are not similarly situated, comparisons of marginal utility to us cannot be precise. We may both be morally nearly certain that I am far worse off than you. But we may be able to make no serious claims about whether my small act of beneficence to you benefits you more than it costs me. It is only because we can contrive linguistically to speak of such problems that the issue even arises. We cannot typically conceive resolutions of such issues in actual as opposed to abstract contexts.

To fall back on resources when welfare measures are in princple imprecise is to let our reason be subject to meaningless linguistic contrivance. Objective measures of resources may be superb proxies for

---

36. For a thorough account of this issue, see Brian Barry, *Theories of Social Justice* (Berkeley: University of California Press, forthcoming), especially the section, "Want-Satisfaction versus Resources." Also see Ronald Dworkin, "What Is Equality? Part I: Equality of Welfare" and "Part II: Equality of Resources," *Philosophy and Public Affairs* 10 (Summer 1981): 185–246, and (Fall 1981): 283–345.

subjective measures of welfare when there is reason to suppose the two coincide. But when the two do not coincide, concern with resources should not displace the more fundamental concern with welfare.

This is not to say that marginal comparisons are only possible over equals but that if inequalities are great the margins that can be compared must be very broad margins. For example, a desert nomad living on the edge of subsistence cannot generally have any obligation of beneficence to a wealthy sheik. But we might easily suppose the nomad should yield a day's supply of food and water if necessary to save a starving sheik who has crashed in his private jet in the desert. For such radically differently situated people one cannot make symmetric claims of obligation. For the nomad to be obligated to the sheik requires a gross effect on the latter of a modest cost to the former; for the sheik to be obligated to the nomad need require only a modest effect. As Martial elegantly noted to one of his wealthy benefactors,

> So, Quintanius, when a man who's poor
> Sends nothing to a rich friend, it's an act
> Of generosity—in point of tact.[37]

To be as generous as Martial, Quintanius would have to give far more than he got. Martial graciously proposed to spare him that loss.

Issues of justice arise in small-number contexts of beneficence and in large-number contexts of distributive justice and justice as order. To give a utilitarian resolution of apparent problems of beneficence and distributive justice we must make interpersonal comparisons of welfare. For problems of justice as order we may go very far even without such comparisons. For other social interactions, such as exchange relationships and coordination problems, we can generally expect self-interest to give a sufficient motivation to resolve problems in ways that are utilitarian.

§13 Promising

One of the most common tactics for showing the inconsistency of utilitarianism either with its own principles or with "our" moral intuitions is to argue that a utilitarian cannot be bound to keep promises in various circumstances. Many such proofs are faulty in their strategic misconception of the nature of relevant promises. Much of the exten-

37. Martial, *Epigrams,* book 6, no. 18, in James Michie, trans., *The Epigrams of Martial* (London: Hart-Davis, MacGibbon, 1973), p. 87.

sive discussion of promising and promise keeping by moral philosophers has been distorted by a failure to recognize the different kinds of
interactions within which promising takes place.[38] Moral lessons
drawn from one context may not generalize to others.

As we have already seen above, the problem of promising and
promise keeping arises in distinctively different contexts. First, there
are exchange promises that facilitate exchanges made over time. Second, there are coordination promises that facilitate our getting together
or otherwise accomplishing some joint venture. Promising also occurs
in contexts of pure conflict. For example, I may simply promise to do
something for you without any explicit or implicit expectation of a
return action from you either before or after my action.[39] In the law
such promises are called gratuitous. Gratuitous promises are the promissory equivalent of acts of beneficence: there is no quid pro quo, no
evident benefit to the promisor. The motive to keep such a promise
may be some combination of the motive to act with beneficence and the
motive, once the promise has been made, to fulfill an obligation to
which one has freely consented.

Despite the prominence of gratuitous promises in philosophical discussion, they are surely of little practical import in the sense that one
does not often actually make such promises. Largely, no doubt, because of their oddity, they do have some place in the case law.[40]
Coordinating promises may have an even more prominent place in
philosophical discussion. Oddly, while they may be of great practical
import, they are of little moral significance for the simple reason that
conformance to them can almost always be understood as the straightforward implication of self-interest. In this respect they are like most
exchange promises in actual life.

In one important respect, the tendency to blur all categories of
promising into a single generic category is consistent with our actual
practice of promise keeping. To break any kind of promise is to cast
doubt on one's reliability for promising in general. Hence, to make
even a gratuitous promise changes the incentives one faces for action

38. Although she does not put her analysis in strategic terms, Vera Pretz seems to
grasp the strategic differences in "Promises and Threats" (*Mind* 86 [October 1977]:578–
581). J. L. Mackie gives a solid account of exchange or Prisoner's Dilemma promises and
coordination promises in "The Disutility of Act-Utilitarianism" (*Philosophical Quarterly*
23 [October 1973]: 289–300), esp. pp. 293–297.

39. In richly ongoing relationships, such as that of a parent and a child, we may
commonly suppose there is some degree of implicit expectation for return. Or we may
not.

40. See esp. John P. Dawson, *Gifts and Promises: Continental and American Law Compared* (New Haven, Conn.: Yale University Press, 1980).

thereafter. If I break a gratuitous promise, perhaps excusing myself by pointing out that it was utterly gratuitous and that you therefore were owed nothing from me, I actually lose something. Making such a promise is a form of self-manipulation, an instance of what we might call a Ulyssean strategy of constraining oneself, of metaphorically tying oneself to the mast. [41] To the extent this is true, however, it means that even the kind of promises, gratuitous promises, that would seem to require a purely moral motivation from a duty or obligation entered into solely by the act of promising itself may often be motivated by the usual concern with reputation, a concern that can be partly or even exclusively based in self-interest.

More important, it may be that all other promising is parasitic on the more fundamental form of promising to complete mutually beneficial exchanges. We might agree with P. S. Atiyah: "In much philosophical writing, it seems to be assumed that the paradigmatic case is of a promise which is wholly gratuitous and is given for charitable or benevolent purposes. It seems to me far more likely that the source of both legal and moral obligations concerning the binding force of promises is derived from the more common case where the promisor obtains, or expects to obtain, some advantage from his promise, and that cases of charitable and benevolent promises are the result of extrapolating from the common case."[42] More generally, Atiyah argues, as Hume does, "that *most* promises are performed because it is in the interests of the promisor to perform."[43]

Suppose, however, that you have done some service for me and that the time has come for me to reciprocate by fulfilling my promise to do a service for you. And suppose for a moment that I am not motivated by self-interest but only by utilitarian concern and that my self-interest here is not affected except by my sacrificing whatever it takes to perform the promised service to you—I will not lose anything from failed future opportunities. In a standard move, D. H. Hodgson argues that, if I am an act-utilitarian, I should now do what is best on the whole independently of what I have promised. If what is best is to perform the promised service, I perform it; if not, not. But that just means that the promise has no role. Hence, promising is irrelevant.[44] One who has a

41. Jon Elster spells out the case for self-manipulation in the title essay of *Ulysses and the Sirens* (Cambridge: Cambridge University Press, 1979), pp. 36–111.
42. P. S. Atiyah, *Promises, Morals and Law* (Oxford: Clarendon Press, 1981), pp. 145–146.
43. Ibid., p. 145.
44. D. H. Hodgson, *Consequences of Utilitarianism* (Oxford: Clarendon Press, 1967), pp. 38–42.

strong intuition that promising is morally relevant must therefore dismiss utilitarianism as immoral.[45]

This move is too quick. What motivates us to exchange, say, my x for your y is that I value your y more than my x and you value my x more than your y. In Hodgson's tale, I now have your y and must decide de novo on utilitarian principles whether to give you my x as promised when the time comes. That decision turns on whether you or I value my x more, not on whether we have engaged in our promising game. Note that this conclusion requires interpersonal comparison, perhaps very precise comparison, whereas our initial motivation to exchange x and y requires no such comparison. Suppose we cannot make such a comparison in this case. What then should I, as a utilitarian, do if you have already delivered your y to me and the time has come for me to deliver my x to you? Unless I complete the exchange, I cannot know that there has been a utilitarian improvement. Hence, I have no utilitarian defense against fulfilling my side of the bargain.

This conclusion is stronger than it may seem at first glance. If we are each well informed of our interests, I will typically not be able truthfully to say that transferring your y to me was alone enough to increase the overall welfare. I can only know that consummating our exchange, with the help of my promise, increases overall welfare. There may be cases in which we would agree that half the exchange would alone increase overall welfare. For example, if our sheik above had landed in the desert and offered a small payment in advance to the impoverished nomad to turn over his next-born goat, we might easily suppose that the transfer of the sheik's money was by itself welfare enhancing even without the nomad's reciprocal action. But in the overwhelming range of contexts in which exchange promises are made and in the typical cases discussed by philosophers, the only credible indicator of welfare improvement will be agreed upon and consummated exchange. Indeed, *it is strictly because my valuations of things are not the same as yours that we could even want to enter into an exchange.* You may often know a great deal about the differences between your and my valuations but you will typically be unable truthfully to assert that my surrendering particular assets to you or doing particular services for you without your reciprocation would increase overall welfare.

45. Hodgson audaciously concludes, "Because the making of promises and the communication of information would be pointless in our act-utilitarian society, so that these practices would not be engaged in, there could be no human relationships as we know them" (ibid., p. 45). The whole argument is forcefully rejected by Jan Narveson on grounds not quite those to follow here ("Promising, Expecting, and Utility," *Canadian Journal of Philosophy* 1 [December 1971]: 207–233, esp. pp. 220–228).

Hodgson says that "the fact that persons promise and communicate with each other *presupposes* either ignorance or irrationality in, or some actions done on non-act-utilitarian criteria by, at least some of these persons."[46] This might often be true of communication, because there would often be no point in my communicating to you something of which you were not previously ignorant. It is less clearly true of promising, unless we include within the vale of presupposed ignorance our ignorance of exactly what will happen in the future. But it is clearly true of coordinating promises that their purpose is to overcome a certain degree of ignorance. If you are going to show up for lunch with me tomorrow, I wish to show up also. If you are not going to show up, I also wish not to show up. Either of these is a relatively good outcome, although, if neither of us is otherwise unable to do so, it might be that the best outcome would be that we both show up. We arrange to do so by promising. We thereby communicate some information of which we might have been ignorant: that neither of us is otherwise unable to do so and that both of us now plans to do so.

Hodgson concludes, in an extravagant move, that "advocacy of act-utilitarianism . . . involves either advocacy of no communication of information between such persons, or advocacy of the ignorance or irrationality which would be necessary to allow communication in an act-utilitarian society."[47] On these matters a sensible act-utilitarian merely advocates living well in the kind of society we live in. It is not even clear what intellectually it could mean to advocate ignorance or nonignorance in Hodgson's sense. We simply and fundamentally have no choice about the matter. We are ignorant and we will remain ignorant of much that would make our lives better. Certain kinds of ignorance are constitutive of our nature and hence of our understanding of moral and other human relations. If we knew so much about each other and about relevant causal relations that promising became otiose, then it would simply be otiose. And there would be no moral implication per se in the elimination of the moral or other value of promising, because that value *comes from* the contribution promising makes to our actual conditions, not from any a priori rightness above such value.

Promising makes sense primarily because of uncertainties. It is cous-

<hr>

46. Hodgson, *Consequences of Utilitarianism*, p. 46.

47. Ibid. G. J. Warnock agrees with this absurd argument: ". . . if the general felicific beneficence were the only criterion, then promising and talking alike would become wholly idle pursuits. . . . And thus, towards the betterment of the human predicament, the simple recipe of general beneficence must be, while admirably intentioned, very minimally efficacious" (*The Object of Morality* [London: Methuen, 1971], pp. 33–34). Dan Brock also finds it troubling to utilitarianism in "Recent Work in Utilitarianism" (*American Philosophical Quarterly* 10 [October 1973]: 241–276).

in to honesty and truth telling, which are of value precisely because others do not already know the truth about certain matters. If they did, lies would have no force. My truth telling has utilitarian value because it allows you to act intelligently toward your own purposes, which you generally can be expected to know better than I know them. Similarly, in our world of great uncertainty and ignorance, promises have the function of strategically binding us to bring about better results than might otherwise occur with uncoordinated action. Indeed, insofar as one of the uncertainties we must deal with is the akratic doubt we may have in our own future behavior, making a promise can be a strategic maneuver a bit like burning one's bridges. It increases the costs of not going ahead with the (promised) action, as noted above in the discussion of gratuitous promises.[48]

In the extremity of so-called desert island or deathbed promises, however, there may be no strategically devised costs of violating one's promise. There seems to be a general if sometimes inarticulate understanding of the self-interested motivation for keeping promises in ongoing relationships. But suppose that an ongoing relationship is about to end or has ended, for example through the death of one of the parties. Before dying, I ask you to promise that you will do something for me that you, when the time comes, will consider utterly counter to the greater good. For example, Adam Smith requested of his friends attending him in his dying days that they burn most of his unfinished manuscripts. It might have inflicted considerable pain on Smith to refuse to promise what he wanted. It might have inflicted real loss of pleasure on others to carry out such a promise. If promise keeping and lying are a priori inviolable moral principles, the friends faced the choice of lying and breaking a promise or of causing harm, either to Smith or to others. We cannot judge the utilitarian merits of the case without a great deal more information on the quality of the manuscripts and perhaps on Smith's reasons for thinking them inferior. But we may suppose that friends who promised a living Smith to burn the manuscripts might well have reneged on their promises after Smith was dead.

Smith, evidently understanding all of this, played to win by insisting that the manuscripts be burned as he watched, thereby forcing one of

48. Alan Donagan, who is not a utilitarian and who is not concerned with the self-interested implications of his strategic analysis, states the strategic value of promising well: "The institution of promising enables a moral agent to make himself responsible for his failure in the future to do what it will be in his power to do. It thereby extends from the past and present to the future the range of his acts of will, and hence of his voluntary actions, about which a man can give assurances to others" (Donagan, The Theory of Morality [Chicago: University of Chicago Press, 1977], p. 92).

his friends to choose between two harms rather than between harms and certain pristine moral principles.[49] But he did not finally win the whole issue, because chief among his manuscripts to be burned were lectures, of which diligent students had made thorough notes. If they were virtually complete versions of what he read in his lectures, the original lectures in Smith's hand must have served his memory and the cause of social theory better than the students' notes.[50]

§14 Generalization

It is characteristic of moral theory that its dictates are considered universal in some sense. What it is right or wrong for me to do in particular circumstances it is right or wrong for any other similarly situated agent to do. Religious ethics, as in the Old Testament, often do not seem to conform to such a principle of universalization but philosophical and commonsense ethics generally do. There is another supposed principle that seems at casual glance to be derivative from the principle of universalization. It is the principle of "generalization" that is given as an answer to the question, What if everybody did that? The principle of generalization seems to be a bit of commonsense Kantianism in that it might plausibly follow from the Categorical Imperative to adopt only those moral principles that one could will to be universal laws.

Alas, the principle of generalization is not generally valid without further conditions packed into it. If everybody did "that" in many contexts, the result would be a bad state of affairs. Reputedly, King George VI, in bestowing upon Bertrand Russell the Order of Merit in June 1950, said to him, "They tell me you have led a very adventurous life. But it would not do if everyone tried to lead such a life, would it?" To which Russell sensibly retorted, "Postmen go about knocking on

49. Dugald Stewart, "Account of the Life and Writings of Adam Smith, LL.D.," pp. 269–351 in Adam Smith, *Essays on Philosophical Subjects,* vol. 3 of *The Glasgow Edition of the Works and Correspondence of Adam Smith* (Oxford: Oxford University Press, 1980; Indianapolis: Liberty Press, 1982), pp. 327–328n. Stewart rationalizes Smith's decision as coming from higher motives, to prevent inadequately worked out and possibly erroneous views from being given undue authority as coming from the hand of Smith. Stewart simultaneously calls the burning of the manuscripts an "irreparable injury to letters" (ibid., p. 327).

50. The student notes of the burned lectures are in Adam Smith, *Lectures on Rhetoric and Belles Lettres* and *Lectures on Jurisprudence,* vols. 4 and 5 of *The Glasgow Edition of the Works and Correspondence of Adam Smith* (Oxford: Oxford University Press, 1983 and 1978). There are grounds for supposing that the losses were far greater than merely more polished and more complete versions of the original lecture notes (Knud Haakonssen, private conversation, October 1987).

doors, even though it would not do if everyone went about knocking on doors." His Majesty, more philosophical than one might have thought, is supposed to have changed the subject.[51]

Perhaps the most commonplace, if trivial, problem to which the principle of generalization is applied in contemporary philosophical literature is taking a shortcut across a lovely lawn or garden. If everybody did that, as many do in many locations such as my own university campus with its visually pleasing but not always convenient placement of sidewalks, the result would be unaesthetic paths etched in the grass, trampled flowers, and broken hedges. Since if everybody did that it would be bad, the quick inference is some version of the principle that no one should do that. M. G. Singer and others have elevated variants of this principle to the status of firm moral rules, usually with utilitarian groundings. Singer dubs his variant the "generalization argument," or GA.[52] As is true of promising and of many other moral principles, the force and applicability of such a generalization principle depends on the strategic structure of the problems to which it is applied. For example, Singer's principle and many criticisms of it are partially misguided because they fail to deal with the variety of contexts to which the principle might apply.

Singer's GA is: If the consequences of no one's doing x would be undesirable, while the consequences of everyone's doing x would be desirable, then everyone ought to do x.[53] An alternative, which is stronger in that it applies far more generally, is Lyons's comparative version that, if valid, lends itself readily to appropriation by utilitarians: If the consequences of everyone's doing a certain sort of thing would be worse than those of some alternative, then it would be wrong for anyone to do such a thing.[54] Because the notion 'would be desirable' is ill-defined except in a comparative sense, which must be implicit in the use of the phrase, one must assume that the point of the GA is best captured in a comparative version. One might, therefore, readily accept Lyons's restatement of the argument except that he has made another change: his principle clearly applies to each individual whereas Singer's applies to "everyone." If Singer means "each individual,"

51. Alan Wood, *Bertrand Russell: The Passionate Skeptic* (New York: Simon and Schuster, 1958), p. 209.

52. Marcus George Singer, *Generalization in Ethics* (New York: Alfred A. Knopf, 1961). Charles Silver sets out general conditions for the utilitarian requirement of participation in collective action in "Utilitarian Participation," *Social Science Information* 23 (1984): 701–729.

53. Singer, *Generalization in Ethics*, pp. 72–73.

54. David Lyons, *Forms and Limits of Utilitarianism* (Oxford: Clarendon Press, 1965), p. 25.

then Lyons has greatly altered the principle. If Singer means "each and every individual," then Lyons has greatly altered it.

For the moment, let us suppose Singer is concerned with ethical principles for individual action and that Lyons has his meaning right. Among its other applications, Lyons's strong version of the GA should apply to coordination situations *in which a defective convention has been established*. But the principle of individual action derived from the GA for those situations would commonly be wrong. As an example, consider the Swedish driving convention discussed above (§11). Suppose it was true before September 1967 that it would have been better if everyone in Sweden had driven on the right than if everyone had driven on the left. It follows from the strong GA that it would have been wrong for anyone to drive on the left. Hence, had I been driving in Sweden then, I should have driven on the right. This is an absurd—murderous and suicidal—conclusion. Surely, if it yields such a conclusion, the strong GA is not generally valid for situations that meet its conditions.

Perhaps Singer's GA should not be taken as a principle for individual choice. Neil Dorman supposes that indeed it should not in his modified GA (MGA): If the consequences of not having a rule against y would be undesirable, then there ought to be a rule against y.[55] Clearly this principle is less applicable to individual choice than to lawmakers' choices. While the strong GA recommends an absurd conclusion in the Swedish driving case, the MGA speaks not to Swedish drivers but only to someone whose action would actually bring about a simultaneous switch by every driver in Sweden, as Swedish government action did. Cyrus might be instructed by Dorman's MGA; his subjects could not be. Hence, the GA as applied to "each and every individual" is a less interesting moral principle than the strong GA that applies to "each individual." That a government ought to do what promotes greater welfare in preference to what promotes lesser welfare is not an innovative conclusion.

It is hard to read Singer and most proponents of such generalization principles without supposing that they mean to have their principles apply to individual actions just as Kant's imperatives do. Can we readily clean up the strong GA, which is directed at individual action rather than government or collective action, to yield a valid principle? One way to do so would be to follow a suggestion of Edna Ullmann-Margalit to restrict its application to Prisoner's Dilemma situations.[56]

55. Neil A. Dorman, "The Refutation of the Generalization Argument," *Ethics* 74 (January 1964): 150–154, esp. p. 154.

56. Edna Ullmann-Margalit, *The Emergence of Norms* (Oxford: Clarendon Press, 1977), pp. 53–58.

Then we are not faced with absurd recommendations for action in the face of poor coordinations. Unfortunately, we are faced with other problems analogous to difficulties in promising.

Suppose we are in a Prisoner's Dilemma situation and some of us are cooperating while others are not. What should I do? Under the GA I should cooperate. But suppose that in cooperating I wind up worse off than I would have if not only I but also all the other cooperators had not cooperated. Have I helped make the general state of affairs better? Quite plausibly not. If relatively precise interpersonal comparisons of utility or welfare are not possible, I cannot deduce that my cooperation while many do not cooperate adds enough to the welfare of others to outweigh the loss in welfare to me. Hence, only if it is true that enough others are cooperating for all of them and for me to be net beneficiaries from our cooperation can I say that it is better for us to cooperate than for us not to. While every Prisoner's Dilemma by definition meets the conditions of the GA, it does not follow that in every Prisoner's Dilemma any single individual ought to cooperate if others are not cooperating. Therefore, even for many Prisoner's Dilemma situations, while the GA may give valid recommendations to a lawgiver, it will not in general give valid recommendations to particular individuals. Again, the GA is not a perspicuous principle for individual action.[57]

§15 Agency in Social Interactions

Much of moral theory and even many whole moral theories are about actions rather than about outcomes.[58] Action-based moral theories are concerned with what an individual does, with the natures of actions and individuals, with the relationship of actions to character rather than to consequences more generally. Such theories generally issue in rules for action, as in the Ten Commandments. The focus of such rules is on what *I* do rather than on what happens. Traditionally the concern with what *I* do covered kinds of choices that governed a relatively limited range of the problems we wish to address in moral and, perhaps especially, political theory. When what happens depends on strategic interactions, what *I* do is inherently less important than what we do; indeed, what I should do may depend on what you have done or will do. When we see our problems as those of the very different categories

---

57. For further discussion, see Russell Hardin, "The Emergence of Norms," *Ethics* 90 (July 1980): 575–587, esp. pp. 584–586.

58. Samuel Scheffler, *The Rejection of Consequentialism: A Philosophical Investigation of the Considerations Underlying Rival Moral Conceptions* (Oxford: Clarendon Press, 1982).

of table 2.1, we necessarily see them as problems of getting the outcomes right, so that actions are of concern only as means.

Suppose we focus on outcomes rather than actions. What does this
do to our theories of action and agency? It complicates them severely
because it forces them to be theories of strategic action or of choices of
strategies. While one might immediately conclude from an action that
directly implies a particular outcome whether it is right or wrong, that
is, whether it is a relevant means to its end, one cannot so readily
conclude from a choice of strategy whether it is right or wrong. Why?
Because a choice of strategy does not imply a particular outcome—in
general it only restricts the range of achievable outcomes. For example,
when, as Row player, I choose the lower strategy in the Prisoner's
Dilemma of Game 2.2, I do not determine a final outcome. Rather, I
only eliminate the outcomes (2,2) and (4,1) from the range of achievable outcomes. I have—by definition, as represented in my preference
ordering—a preference over the outcomes here but I clearly cannot
simply choose the one I want most. Indeed, if I try to obtain the one I
like best (1,4), I can generally suppose you will want to block my choice
and force us jointly to the poor outcome (3,3).

Philosophical discussions of action and agency do not generally deal
with the nature of strategic interaction and its impact on the whole
notion of agency except by treating specific cases, generally in ad hoc
ways. A driving insight of consequentialist ethics is that results of
actions are not immediately deducible from kinds of actions. In social
contexts, action is often inherently *interaction*. Indeed, it is only in the
pure conflict situations of table 2.1 that we can ignore the mutuality or
interactive aspects of the problems and focus strictly on an individual's
or group's actions toward another. In the mixed-motive and coordination situations of that table, a significant part of the determination of the
rightness of a choice of strategy may depend on what others choose.
(This may also be true for individual choices in large-number instances
of beneficence; see §§27 and 31.) It would therefore be odd if a strictly
action-based theory could yield morally compelling results for these
interactions. If one wishes generally to defend rules for action over
consideration of consequences, the argument must be derived from a
concern with consequences that is tempered by a recognition of human
limits and weaknesses, as in G. E. Moore's resolution that a utilitarian
should follow commonsense moral rules.

The nature of strategic action implies that Kant's Categorical Imperative, if it is generally supposed to apply to kinds of acts, cannot be
compelling as *the* or even *a* moral principle, just as the generalization

argument cannot be generally compelling (§14). If we are to hedge about the definition of an act enough to bring into it the conditions that make for various kinds of outcomes rather than others, we reduce the notion of an 'act' to silliness. But if we stipulate any general claims that certain kinds of acts are always right or wrong independently of such conditions, we can only produce injunctions that are perverse, as in the injunction that I should have driven on the right in Sweden before 1967.

Appendix to Chapter 2: THE COMPLETENESS AND RELEVANCE OF THE TYPOLOGY OF MORAL PROBLEMS

Because there are seventy-eight logically distinct 2 × 2 ordinal games,[59] one may wonder how complete is the typology of social interactions in table 2.1. It is in fact quite complete in the following sense. Every game or interaction involves either pure conflict, pure coordination, or some mixture of the two. Three of the seventy-eight 2 × 2 games are pure conflict and three are pure coordination; all others are like Prisoner's Dilemma in that they involve a mixture of conflict and coordination. Of the latter, however, many (eighteen) are de facto coordination games in that both players agree on what outcome is most preferred, so that the conflict is over which outcome is second or third best as in Game 2.5. But it does not matter that they disagree about second, third, or fourth best if they are going to select the most preferred outcome in any case. Hence, we have three games that are pure conflict, three that are pure coordination, and a much larger number that are effectively coordination even though not pure coordination. The remaining fifty-four games are effectively mixed-motive.

This account includes only games in which both players have strict preferences over their outcomes, that is, they do not rank two outcomes equally best. If we allow for such indifference, the number of distinct 2 × 2 games radically increases. Many of these games will pose genuine coordination problems in the sense that the players will now not automatically see which strategy is best but will need to know what strategy the other is choosing before knowing which is best for themselves. Some of these games will also be essentially degenerate in

59. There are seventy-eight strategically nonequivalent ordinal 2 × 2 games in which each player ranks the four outcomes from first to fourth choice without ties. Two games are equivalent if merely changing the labels of one or both players' strategies or of the two players in one of the games produces the payoff matrix of the other game (Anatol Rapoport, Melvin J. Guyer, and David G. Gordon, *The 2 × 2 Game* [Ann Arbor: University of Michigan Press, 1976], p. 17).

strategies for one or both players because the player or players will be indifferent between their two strategy choices. Hence, they will include games that are equivalent to such simple games as that in which one player has only one choice and the other has two choices, as represented in Game 2.1. With these additions to fill out the set of all 2 × 2 ordinal games, however, we still have only games that are effectively pure conflict, pure coordination, and mixed-motive.

If an interaction involves pure conflict, interpersonal comparisons will be required for determining moral obligations. If it involves pure coordination, there are not generally likely to be serious moral issues at stake. If it involves a substantial mixture of conflict and coordination, we can generally restrict out of the range of *moral* choice those outcomes from which coordination would be sufficient to yield better ordinal results. For example, in the Prisoner's Dilemma of Game 2.2, the lower right cell can be ruled out of consideration as a moral outcome. To the extent interpersonal cardinal comparisons are possible, we may be able to go further and prescribe a best utilitarian outcome. In the Prisoner's Dilemma of Game 2.4, in which there is impressive interpersonally comparable utility or welfare information, we may further conclude that I should cooperate while you defect. In this respect, Prisoner's Dilemma is typical of most mixed-motive games.

To see how other strategic structures fit this analysis, consider another game, of unequal coordination, as shown in Game 2.6. Suppose you are Column and I am Row. Clearly we both prefer to be either in

Column

		I	II
	I	1,1	3,2
Row			
	II	2,3	4,4

Game 2.5. Virtually pure coordination

Column

		I	II
	I	3,3	2,1
Row			
	II	1,2	4,4

Game 2.6. Unequal coordination

the lower left or upper right cells rather than in the upper left or lower right cells. Hence, we face a problem of coordination. But I prefer to be in the lower left cell and you prefer the upper right. Hence, we also face a problem of conflict. This could represent an interaction in which we all benefit from the general efficiency of hierarchical organization. But each benefits most from being at the top of the hierarchy. On the strictly noncomparable analysis, we can morally resolve only the coordination problem to recommend that we coordinate on either the lower left or upper right cell, for example, by creating a hierarchy. To go further and morally resolve our problem of conflict over which of us should be on top as well we require interpersonal comparisons.

For the large-number classes of moral problems in the right-hand column of table 2.1, we cannot stipulate what all the possible nonequivalent games are: their number grows at an alarming rate as the number of players grows. Still we may conclude that they are all either pure conflict, in the restricted sense in which we discussed large-number beneficence (§9), or pure coordination, or a mixture of conflict and coordination. We cannot assimilate all interactions that are mixed-motive to the Prisoner's Dilemma, but in interactions of interest we can generally speak of central tendencies as we have done here for two-person games. When an interaction has important elements of both coordination and conflict, we must still conclude that we can deal only with the coordination choices if we have only noncomparable welfare information on the participants. To reach moral conclusions about the conflictual choices we will require some degree of comparability.

Hence, our typology of moral and political problems is complete. We should merely note that the middle category of mixed-motive games cannot be represented fully by the remarkable game of Prisoner's Dilemma. Nevertheless it is useful to focus on the Prisoner's Dilemma in the discussions of this chapter (especially §10) because that strategic structure is particularly prevalent in human interactions in various guises, most notably in what are forthrightly seen as exchange relationships, and because it poses an extreme mix of conflict and coordination.

There is one respect, however, in which the game theoretic representation of these problems is not a realistic representation of interactions in real life. We commonly think of a game analytically as though it were somehow isolated from all other interactions, from all else in life. This is conspicuously unrealistic. For example, consider the very notion of "pure conflict." Normally, to say that an interaction is pure conflict is to say that the interaction *all else held constant* is pure conflict *and* that threats governing the interaction cannot be based in all else rather than in the interaction at issue. Of course, in actual life one generally can base threats in "all else": "I'll blow us both up if you don't give me your watch." To make such a threat credible, it may be necessary to arrange causally for it to be fulfilled if its conditions are met, as the superpowers seem to have done with their nuclear retaliatory forces. If carrying out such a threat is possible in an interaction, then the interaction is not fully characterizable as pure conflict, because both parties may prefer to coordinate on avoidance of the threatened outcome over letting it come about. Consequently, there can be virtually no real interaction that is genuinely pure conflict. More generally, viewing any interaction as though it were isolated from all else is in principle wrong, although it may be reasonable to do so as an approximation in many instances. It is more reasonable to do so for interactions between individuals or other parties who are not utterly oblivious of the interests of those with whom they interact, so that they will not generally use radical threats of mutual harm to get their own way.

3

Institutional Utilitarianism I:
Without Interpersonal Comparisons

Interactions that are pure coordination do not generally pose moral problems. At worst they pose technical problems in how to succeed in doing what everyone wants to do. Interactions that are mixed-motive are at least partially moral problems because they have an element of conflict of interest, and hence of conflict of welfare. When no interpersonal comparisons are plausible or when such comparisons as are plausible cannot resolve such problems, the problems can generally be satisfactorily resolved to a large extent by at least addressing their coordination element. This involves coordinating on the best of the outcomes on whose overall ranking there is agreement. I wish in this chapter to discuss the extent to which such resolution, without making use of interpersonal comparisons of welfare, is likely to be plausible in important contexts. To make the boundaries clear at times, this will involve pushing problems beyond the point at which such resolution is possible and suggesting when interpersonal comparisons must play a role if we are to commend a welfare-enhancing resolution.

Because there is a partial conflict of interest in mixed-motive interactions, they commonly require some kind of external motivation to help strictly self-interested parties to them reach a stable coordination. Because there can easily be lack of full understanding of the degree of agreement among all parties about the mutually advantageous outcome that can be achieved, even utilitarians may require external intrusion to organize the coordination.

In general, the form that external intrusion will take in small-scale interactions, such as in dyads, is the range of incentives that come from the ongoing nature of the relationships between the parties to a particular interaction this moment. Hence, the parties can sensibly be seen as

playing a much larger game in which the element of conflict is displaced
by the element of coordination. In the abstract, I might have no interest
this moment in fulfilling my promise to you. But in the actual longer-
run relationship I have with you, I have a strong interest in doing so
because I value the continuation of the relationship.

For large-number interactions, the form the external intrusion is
likely to take is an institutional or a conventional regulation of the kind
of interaction in which we are involved. It is such institutional or
conventional regulations that I wish chiefly to discuss here. Typically in
many modern societies they take the form of rights and other protections. These can often be designed to secure mutual advantage for all
even though there can be no interpersonal weighings of advantages.
They are the best feasible solution of many problems of social interaction when interpersonal comparisons are not possible, which in the
view of some may be always. This may be part of the reason that many
anti-utilitarians assert that rights are prior and utility of supposedly
little concern: their objection is largely to the addition of utility across
persons. Even if one rejects addition across persons, however, it does
not follow that rights are prior. Indeed, on any account one must
wonder what is the point of rights if they do not work to enhance
human welfare. Of course, if this is their point, then they are not
prior—rather, they are merely a means to the enhancement of welfare.

Even if one believed strongly in the possibility in principle of adding
utility or welfare across persons, one might have need of such institutional devices as rights protections to regulate relationships in the face
of severe limits to information about individual welfares across a large
society. If there were no such problems of information, there would
plausibly be no point in rights protections as a device for enhancing
welfare, which could be done by direct intervention or allocation.
Again, as noted earlier, what makes the categories of mixed-motive
and pure conflict interactions complex for a utilitarian account is that
the interpersonal, additive utility or welfare theory and the other
knowledge that would be necessary for a direct, general resolution of
these kinds of interactions instance by instance are often not available
even in principle. What we must do, therefore, is create institutions to
regulate the interactions in ways that typically enhance welfare.

In what follows, I wish to argue that morally defensible rights are
sensibly grounded in a concern for consequences and that the character
of particular rights therefore depends on more general strategic considerations of the nature of the society and of incentives for action within
it. Although some rights might seem to be valuable in almost any
society we may know, few if any rights can be given an a priori ground-

ing independently of a fairly articulate account of the society or societies in which they are to be defended. The first issue for discussion here is the strategic structures of the justifications for various rights (§§16–20). Once these are established, we then need to understand the structure of a utilitarian institution for defending the rights and, hence, the justification of restrictions on the behavior of those who hold roles in the institution (§21). The justification of individual behavior in institutions is radically different from the traditional rule-utilitarian focus on practices and rule following, with which it is often confused (§22). Finally, I will discuss the apparent implication of Amartya Sen's "liberal paradox" that a utilitarian theory of rights is inherently contradictory (§23) and then briefly discuss the supposition that we can construct a political theory for dealing with such problems as those that motivate this chapter through contractarian devices (§24). As we progress through various categories of problems—especially as we reach issues of group rights—it will appear increasingly implausible that we can resolve them merely from welfare considerations without interpersonal comparisons.

§16 The Strategy of Rights

It is sometimes supposed that utilitarianism cannot support or yield a system of rights with moral force. In part this may seem to follow from arguments of early utilitarians that "natural rights" are inherently meaningless. Given Bentham's, Austin's, and Mill's clear commitment to law and its use in protecting individuals, one cannot sensibly suppose that they thought positive, legal rights would be ineffective *means* to securing welfare. In a more articulate criticism, however, Lyons rejects the association of rights with utilitarianism.[1] His conclusion turns, as does his earlier argument for the extensional equivalence of act- and rule-utilitarianisms,[2] on pristine requirements for knowledge and understanding. Just because we cannot have adequate knowledge to judge the utility of certain actions from the position of a central adjudicator or administrator, however, we effectively decentralize judgments and decisions to the level of those who have better knowledge, and we commonly enforce their judgments with legal backing. In particular, we enforce such individual and dyadic rights as the rights of property

---

1. David Lyons, "Utility and Rights," pp. 107–138 in J. Roland Pennock and John W. Chapman, eds., *Nomos* 24: *Ethics, Economics, and the Law* (New York: New York University Press, 1982).

2. David Lyons, *Forms and Limits of Utilitarianism* (Oxford: Clarendon Press, 1965). See the earlier discussion of Lyons's argument in §5.

and of exchange. If there were no knowledge constraints and no difficulty in making interpersonal comparisons of welfare, then utilitarians
might plausibly conclude with Lyons that rights make no sense—if
anyone can meaningfully have confidence in deducing anything from
such strong assumptions beyond all experience.

The chief reason society cannot simply judge the rightness of particular outcomes by their welfare effects is that, even at egregious costs,
institutions for such particular, one-by-one judgments would be unre-
liable. For example, in the Matthew and Luke problem of R. B.
Braithwaite and Brian Barry, Matthew likes to play jazz trumpet while
on the other side of a thin wall Luke likes to play classical piano.
Hearing the jazz trumpet disturbs Luke's piano playing enough that he
gives up his pleasure. Clearly, then, the full utility of Matthew's action
of playing his jazz trumpet depends on whether there is a Luke who
lives beyond a thin wall.[3] Playing a trumpet is not simply an action *tout
court,* it is an action with contingent consequences. As a result, the
rightness of Matthew's action depends on its effects on Luke. To judge
directly from utility in practice in general would require an account in
each case of all such effects. The institutions for gathering such information would be costly. A far less expensive set of institutions may get
us closer to the "ideally best" outcome: a set that simply establishes
rules for conduct in typical cases and that leaves some freedom to the
relevant parties to work out their own better solutions or to recur to
political institutions to prevent others from violating the rules. We need
an institutional structure of rights or protections because not everyone
is utilitarian or otherwise moral and because there are severe limits to
our knowledge of others, whose interests are therefore likely to be best
fulfilled in many ways if they have substantial control over the
fulfillment.

This is how traditional rights should be understood. They are institutional devices for reducing the burden of gathering information
and calculating consequences. They differ from rules in the lexicon of
most twentieth-century rule-utilitarians in their being backed by institutional force but they are similar to the rules of thumb of some rule-
utilitarians in their actual function. Unlike rules of thumb that an individual would follow to reduce information and calculation costs,
however, such institutional rules as legally defined rights cannot easily
be overridden when calculation shows that in a particular case a better

3. R. B. Braithwaite, *Theory of Games as a Tool for the Moral Philosopher* (Cambridge:
At the University Press, 1955); Brian Barry, "Don't Shoot the Trumpeter—He's Doing
His Best," *Theory and Decision* 11 (1979): 153–180, and *Theories of Justice* (Berkeley:
University of California Press, forthcoming).

outcome would follow from violating the rules. This follows for relatively complex reasons of the strategic structure for the establishment and enforcement of the rules. Again, the reason for not violating relevant institutional rules in practice in particular cases is related to the reasons for having them in the first place: the costs of setting up the devices for deciding on when to violate the rules are too great to be justified by the gains from violation. When this conclusion seems not to follow in a particular case, then we may institutionally, as we do individually, resolve that case against the rules.

Conceiving of rules for individual behavior as rules of thumb to be violated when calculation recommends it gives rule-utilitarianism very little force. It is nothing more than simple decision theory applied to moral choosing. Hence, it can be judged to be fully consistent with straightforward act-utilitarianism. Much of twentieth-century ethical debate has clearly been motivated by a sense that there is more to rule following than this.

In part, one might suppose that the reason for seeing more to rule following is that the individualist focus of much of deontological ethics, the focus on the rightness of individual actions, has pervaded even the ethical thinking of utilitarians. If there is any force to the kinds of insights that many have had about rule-utilitarianism, however, it cannot be that deontological concerns should pervade utilitarian thinking. Rather, it is that many of the rules that we would commonly accede to in our daily lives are conspicuously utilitarian in their consequences and that we cannot imagine living without such rules. This class of rules is generally the class of institutionally determined and—generally but not always—institutionally enforced rules. Much of the mid-twentieth-century effort to read earlier utilitarians, such as Mill, as really rule-utilitarians largely misses the point of the earlier concern, which was with institutional arrangements that would help to secure good consequences and not with individual rule following.[4] To avoid such confusion we should speak not of rule-utilitarianism but of *institutional utilitarianism*. Perhaps the largest concern of institutional utilitarianism in a modern society is with rights legally defined.

Even if one granted all of the above, one might still be bothered by a nagging suspicion that somehow concern with rights and concern with outcomes or utility are quite different concerns. Part of the reason for

4. J. O. Urmson, "The Interpretation of the Moral Philosophy of J. S. Mill," *Philosophical Quarterly* 3 (1953): 33–39. Many discussions of this issue in the interpretation of Mill can be found in *Canadian Journal of Philosophy,* supp. vol. 5, *New Essays on John Stuart Mill and Utilitarianism,* eds. Wesley E. Cooper, Kai Nielsen, and Steven C. Patten (Guelph, Ontario: Canadian Association for Publishing in Philosophy, 1979).

this suspicion is perhaps that rights are generally related to the strategic structure of various interactions and not directly to outcomes in the following sense. Rights are not generally about particular outcomes but about particular classes of action. Hence, they might seem to be pre-eminently deontological in character. The difference between typical rights theories and utilitarianism on this point is, however, less significant than it might seem. The utilitarian judgment of an action is in fact a judgment of the outcome the action helps to bring about. But few actions that interest moral theorists bring about outcomes on their own. Generally, as argued in Chapter 2, outcomes of moral concern result from the interactive effects of the actions of more than one person. But we cannot generally legislate that certain kinds of outcomes should result and not others and also make clear who is responsible for what results. Instead of decreeing that outcomes of type x are to happen, we legislate that actions of type q are legal, or required, or illegal insofar as they typically would not hinder, would bring about, or would prevent outcomes of type x. In many cases, however, it would be prima facie ludicrous to suppose that we actually care about whether actions of type q are undertaken *tout court*. For a trivial but important example, we do not a priori care whether people drive on the right or the left. Rather, we only care whether they drive in such a way as to cause harm. Requiring everyone to drive on the right or, alternatively, requiring everyone to drive on the left is justified merely because it brings about a good outcome in general. We constrain individuals' choices of strategy in order to produce a better outcome than would have resulted from unconstrained choices.

Against much of this argument one may still wish to assert that rights are fundamental, that they are not derivative from other considerations, such as consequences or respect for persons among leading moral theories. I do not wish to take on such a view here other than to note some advantages of a derivative account of rights, in particular an account derivative from considerations of welfare. If rights are viewed as metaphysical, abstract, or directly intuited rather than contingently derived, they must be defined very simply without many subclasses, distinctions, or exceptions. Legal rights, as opposed to moral or human rights, do not suffer from this disability in principle. They can be modified to meet new situations or conditions, and they can be highly articulated with manifold subclasses, distinctions, and exceptions. If a situation in which the application of a particular right leads to undesirable outcomes, perhaps because suboptimal, then the right can be redefined or slightly altered to fit the relevant situation. Hence, in an institutional system of rights the persistent occurrence of bad outcomes should be rare, or at least only short-lived until the relevant modifications can be made.

Similarly, on the derivative, utilitarian account of rights presented here, rights may change through time as the conditions of social interaction change, and they may differ across societies in understandable ways to adapt to strategic considerations. What set of rights should be defended will depend on what set will produce desirable results under the circumstances. For example, the right of contract should change as economic conditions change. Perhaps at one time—under the conditions of the nascent industrial economy and early market of, say, eighteenth-century England—the right of contract should have been nearly untrammeled in order to encourage productive activities. Today perhaps the right of contract should be restricted in certain systematic ways to prevent imbalances of economic power from grievously affecting certain kinds of transactions and to prevent certain kinds of external effects, such as air and water pollution and neighborhood destruction. Anyone who tries to defend an unvarnished right of contract for any two parties to do whatever they want to do under any circumstances will be met with vacant stares from most moral and political theorists today.

The derivative utilitarian view of rights is largely an account of what institutional protections we should have. Hence, it is a normative account of what legal rights we should have. To some extent it may also seem to give an explanation of the system of legal rights and institutional protections we have—*if* we further assume that desirability somehow produces relevant causal forces. To some extent such an assumption may be compelling. If we have constructed institutions that work against individuals' interests, we may expect them under certain circumstances to try to change those institutions. Hence, if some of our legal rights are not utilitarian, we may expect some pressure to change them toward more utilitarian rights. No one could sensibly suppose that such pressure would be overwhelming or that there might not be powerful countervailing pressures toward less utilitarian rights. Therefore we cannot sensibly suppose that a normative and largely conceptual account, such as that presented here, necessarily yields easy explanations of actual rights.

In general, the point of traditional legal rights is to secure the aggregation of individual benefits. We may, however, distinguish three ways in which this is accomplished: we may secure benefits to individuals that are independent of other individuals' benefits, we may secure benefits that are mutual but that are generally available only to dyads or very small numbers independently of benefits to the larger society, and we may secure benefits to larger groups or even the whole society. As will become clearer below, the first of these cases involves protection of some against intrusions by others, and the latter two involve protection of some against their own strategic incapacities to benefit themselves. To some extent all can seemingly suggest problems of paternalism (which I will discuss later, in §§28–30).

Many of the protections that interest us may plausibly be seen as falling into more than one of the classes above. For example, the freedom of contract is dyadic at base but may have large implications for the whole society, even large enough to justify enforcing it independently of our concern with pairwise exchanges. Similarly, the right of ownership of property may have far more important implications for the larger society than for individual property owners considered separately. Both these rights, as do many others, may have external effects that go far beyond particular relationships. Hence, we may wish to secure them for their particular effects, their more general collective effects, or both.

There is a sense in which one could say that securing any of these benefits is a benefit to the larger society, especially if the way in which the benefits are secured in particular cases is through the workings of an ongoing institution. To secure a right that benefits me is, in this sense, to secure it for everyone or nearly everyone. However, for the present discussion I wish to speak of securing benefits in particular cases in order to show that the way in which this is done may depend on the strategic structures of the cases. That the same strategic structure recurs commonly is good reason for creating an institutional protection and, one may say, widespread recurrence makes the protection a collective benefit.

A rights protection may explicitly apply individual by individual, dyad by dyad, or only collectively, and it is useful to keep clear which kind of case is at issue. Exemplars of the three classes of rights are (1) rights of privacy, (2) rights of voluntary exchange or contract, and (3) rights of freedom of speech or freedom from servitude or rights to redistribution of welfare. At first, it may not be obvious why these should be put in their respective categories, but I hope to make clear that their strategic structures justify the categorizations. In the following four sections I will discuss these three categories by focusing on central examples of each. From the general grounding of liberalism in individual protections (§17) I will go on to discuss what is perhaps the best understood of the more complex cases, the protection of the dyadic right of voluntary exchange (§18). This right, like certain individual protections, is generally considered to be fundamental to liberalism by utilitarian as well as by deontological rights theorists. Of course, utilitarians consider the right to be derivative from concern with welfare consequences whereas many rights theorists posit it from a priori reason or directly from intuition. Finally, I will discuss the strategically most complex of all the classes of rights, the collective rights, some of which are positively directed at creating a beneficial form of government (§19), some of which, the so-called inalienable rights, are negatively directed at preventing certain failures of collective action (§§19 and 23), and some of which, often called welfare or group rights, are positively directed at benefiting particular groups (§20). In general, the strategic structures of these protections provide the underlying logic of liberalism.

§17 Individual Protections

One ground on which virtually all individual protections can be based is the supposition that individuals are generally the best judges of their own interests. Hence, guaranteeing them control over their lives to determine their own consumptions will generally make them better off. The same grounding can be given for dyadic rights as well. The principle is essentially paretian and utilitarian: protecting an action that makes someone better off while making no one worse off produces a better state of affairs on the whole. Moreover, protecting certain classes of action can make virtually everyone better off. Ensuring certain rights supposedly has just this effect. For example, as all the great English political philosophers assert, ensuring the right to ownership of property guarantees that certain actions I take to better my condition will indeed better it. Without the security of expectations inherent in such a right I would be far less likely to exert myself to create the property and to make myself better off.

Although the protection of property is the central concern of early liberal theory, one can defend virtually any individual protection on the same argument. (Arguably, Locke includes more under property than we are wont to do. In particular, life and liberty may be covered by property.) From the freedom of religious practice that exercised Locke to the right of privacy that has exercised jurists and legal theorists in our century, these protections generally have in their favor that they let people make the best of things for themselves without capricious and destructive intervention by others, particularly by others who have the power of the state with them. These protections represent the simplest of the logics of liberalism. Indeed, their violation for the purpose of imposing values that others hold is the defining instance of paternalism and of the odious implications that that term has. Too easy generalization from the logic of this class of protections produces claims for rights that are inherently contradictory and criticisms of state policy as paternalistic when it is in fact far more complex and difficult to evaluate than that label suggests. The complexity of the issue of paternalism should become clearer as we address protections that are inherently concerned with more complex strategic problems involving more than one individual.

§18 Dyadic Protections

The class of dyadic protections is fundamentally concerned with exchange and agreement to exchange. Its chief exemplar is the freedom of contract, which largely grows out of the concern to have fuller control over property.[5] Hence, it is an extension of the private aspect of certain individual protections. The larger role of contract has probably become rather the enabling of greater control over future plans of diverse kinds with control over property per se as a relatively small part of the whole body of contract. Let us briefly consider the strategic structure of exchange and then turn to the regulation of future fulfillments of exchanges by contract.

Simple dyadic exchange has the strategic structure of the Prisoner's Dilemma, as represented in Game 3.1. In this game, you as the Column

	Column's Choices	
	Yield Car	Keep Car
Yield $1000	2,2	4,1
Row's Choices		
Keep $1000	1,4	3,3

Game 3.1. Exchange (Prisoner's Dilemma with ordinal payoffs)

player own a car and I as the Row player have $1000. I would rather have your car than my money and you would rather have my money than your car. Hence, we can move from the status quo, in which you have the car and I have the money, to a unanimously preferred state of affairs, in which I have the car and you have the money. In the game matrix, the payoffs are ordinal with, again, my most preferred outcome ranked first, or 1, and my least preferred ranked fourth, or 4, and

5. P. S. Atiyah, *The Rise and Fall of Freedom of Contract* (Oxford: Clarendon Press, 1979), pp. 85–90.

similarly for your preferences over the outcomes. Either of us would most like to have both the money and the car. But an exchange is better for both of us than the status quo.

The payoffs in Game 3.1 can be used to illustrate two different classes of rights. In securing the right of exchange we must also secure one's right to keep what one "owns." I can meaningfully have the right to exchange my money for your car only if you have no right to take my money for nothing in return. Hence, we first protect my right of ownership and then we further protect my right to exchange what I own with someone who wants to make a, presumptively, beneficial exchange with me. If we assume that players in such a game as Game 3.1 will not voluntarily move from one outcome to another that is inferior to it in their preference schedule, then the protection of the right of ownership is guaranteed by blocking the (1,4) and (4,1) outcomes from happening as the result of a move from one of the other outcomes. (One of these, say the (4,1) outcome, might occur as the status quo. But then it would be wrong to represent our "interaction" as including the possibility of my choosing my lower strategy. The protection of your right to own both the money and the car implies that I cannot unilaterally act to put you in the less advantageous position of any of the other payoffs.) Further protection of the right of voluntary exchange then requires that we be permitted to move from the (3,3) outcome to the (2,2) outcome that we both prefer to it.

There are basically three ways such exchanges are regulated. One is for us to face each other in a given moment and make an instantaneous exchange under the threat of violence if either should try to take from the other and run; the second is to have a rich ongoing relationship that guarantees that we will each want to treat the other fairly in order not to jeopardize the future of our relationship; and the third is to have an external power enforce our voluntary agreement on whether to exchange. Macneil calls exchanges regulated in the latter two ways relational exchanges because they involve ongoing relationships, in the second case between the parties themselves, and in the third case between each of the parties and the state.[6] In a complex society, the state typically enforces voluntary agreements through the law of contracts. Indeed, for a very large number of exchanges, it also enforces the reliability of each of us in discrete exchanges of the second type by outlawing and punishing theft so that, as Macneil argues, virtually all

6. Ian Macneil, *The New Social Contract* (New Haven, Conn.: Yale University Press, 1980); see also Russell Hardin, "Exchange Theory on Strategic Bases," *Social Science Information* 21 (1982): 251–272.

exchange is relational and the economists' favored category of discrete exchange is virtually empty.

We want the state to intervene to protect our voluntary exchanges when we exchange with people who are strangers to us, when our exchanges involve unusually large values so that even close associates might not be trustworthy, and especially when either or both of these conditions are coupled with the need to consummate our exchange over time with one of us fulfilling now and the other later. Because all are arguably made better off and no one is harmed by such exchanges, it is a Pareto improvement to have an efficient regulator of exchange, as the state can be. Indeed, if we are restricted to considering only utilities to individuals without comparisons across individuals, this paretian concern is virtually all that remains of utilitarianism. We can say that an institutional protection of exchange and of contract is utilitarian if everyone seems likely to be better-off with it than without it. In contemporary economics, the grandchild of utilitarianism, one speaks of Pareto efficient changes in the state of affairs rather than of the maximization of social utility. In its weakest version—unanimity—the Pareto principle is perhaps the most generally accepted principle of social choice. But for Sen's well-known views, one might suppose it was unanimously accepted.[7]

Since the possible range of states of affairs without state protection of exchange and contract may be quite large, it may not easily be shown that such protection is utilitarian, but this is an issue that goes beyond the present concern, and I will leave it for later. If we were concerned only with a particular exchange of the moment, we might easily conclude that it would be utilitarian compared to not making the exchange. Surprisingly much of social and political theory has been argued as though this were the only concern: justifying piecemeal actions against the background of everything else held constant. That this is a fundamentally flawed way to frame political theory is the argument of much of Chapter 4, in which the effects of institutionalizing particular resolutions of classes of problems are at issue.

Suppose now that we have a relatively efficient state empowered to intervene to prevent theft, so that virtually discrete exchange is possible, and to enforce contracts, so that fairly complex exchanges, such as those that must take place over time, are possible. Our original insight and model concerned dyadic exchanges. But there are at least three

---

7. Sen supposes that the weak Pareto principle violates liberalism, which he thinks counts against it as a general principle of social choice. See further below, §23, "Rights versus Unanimity."

classes of contracts that the state might enforce. First, ordinary contracts for mutual benefit through exchange between two or more parties in cases in which all of the benefits of the contracted action derive from "internal" sources, that is, from and to the contracting parties. Second, contracts for mutual benefit between two or more parties when one of the parties is a member of a larger class of people who share a common interest in not being able to enter such contracts. For example, the class of all workers may share an interest in not being able individually to contract to work during a strike. Third, contracts such as those among members of a group to enable them to support their interest in a conflict with another party, in which case the benefits of contracting derive from "external" sources, that is, from the conflicting party. The second and third of these classes are the subjects of the following two sections on collective protections. It is enforcement of only the first of the classes that seems Pareto efficient in plausible cases. Enforcement of the second and third classes of contract will make some people better off at the expense of other people.

Perhaps, one might suppose, the way to keep to paretian results is to restrict contracts to dyads and to leave others to their own spontaneous devices by not enforcing group contracts. Alas, to do so may automatically give advantage to certain interests over others. In particular, if there are greater difficulties in collective action for the larger group, restrictions on the enforcement of group contracts will typically give advantage to the interests of small numbers against those of large numbers in many contexts. For example, for a large group case, recall the early history of labor unions in the United States. The Supreme Court held that collective efforts by workers to negotiate for higher wages were illegal, that workers must individually enter dyadic contracts with their employers. In principle, of course, workers could all have coordinated on negotiating individually for the same wage level they might have got collectively. But, for reasons of the logic of collective action, one would not expect them to have great success in doing so in factories with large numbers of employees or even more generally in any factory that could draw its workers from a relatively large pool. Restriction of contracts to dyads only, therefore, virtually guaranteed greater bargaining power to employers over potential employees than they would have had against employees legally capable of bargaining collectively.

For a small group case, consider the Chicago–East Coast railway cartel in the latter half of the nineteenth century. Overlapping dyadic contracts between the very small number of railway companies could easily have been arranged to accomplish anything a group contract could have accomplished. If the state had enforced the dyadic contracts, the result would have been monopolistic pricing in an effectively stable cartel. That the state chose to try to block the cartel did not turn on the fact that its organization was of more than two parties. The frequency of failures of the cartel, given that the state would not enforce its agreements, may well be explained by the fact that there were several parties to it with strong incentives to take advantage of those cooperating. But basing the cartel on dyadic as opposed to group agreements would not have made it a more liberal achievement. One might suppose, therefore, that the rulings against workers trying to bargain collectively likewise did not turn on the stated concern with the protection of freedom of—implicitly dyadic—contract.

Interestingly, the two kinds of case, involving small- and large-number collectives, differ enough strategically that they may finally differ legally. To stop cartelization of some small-number industries might require positively outlawing agreements and informal coordination because the relevant firms might each be able to reckon that its gains from cheating on an agreement would be outweighed by its probable losses from the failure of the agreement caused by its own cheating. To stop unionization, however, may require little more than refusing to enforce contractual agreements among workers. The general sense very early on that workers needed the union shop to protect their interests was probably well-grounded. Samuel Gompers argued this in 1905, when he said that "persons who are desirous of becoming beneficiaries of an agreement should become parties to that agreement, and . . . they should bear the equal responsibility which such an agreement involves."[8]

Is it liberal for the state to intervene as a partisan in a conflict of interests? Since partisanship one way or the other either by enforcing or refusing to enforce contracts is unavoidable, a liberal must either answer this hard question or define it away. One might answer that no one loses from the enforcement of certain classes of contracts and that therefore they should be enforced; but for classes of contracts that bring benefits to some parties at the cost of others, the state should not act as enforcer. Where then should it stand with respect to contracts that benefit some at the cost of others but that do not require state enforcement? Should the state intervene to block these? Answers to these questions do not follow straightforwardly from considerations of rights sensibly defined. In the case of the railway cartel, one can sensibly argue that much of the monopolistic pricing of rail transport—for

---

8. Samuel Gompers, "Discussion At Rochester, N.Y., on the Open Shop—'The Union Shop Is Right'—It Naturally Follows Organization," *American Federationist* 4 (April 1905): 221–223, quote on p. 221.

example, to small towns served by only one line—did not directly harm anyone in a way that simply not offering the rail transport would not have harmed them. Hence, running lines into small towns and charging monopolistic prices was clearly a benefit to the small towns. But it would be hard to argue on grounds of liberal rights that the railways were required to serve anyone, so that it is hard to see how any rights were violated by the monopolistic pricing of a railway that chose to serve an isolated community. There may have been violations of justice and utility, but not of rights.

If the state has the power to enforce or not to enforce contracts, if therefore unavoidably has the power to decide for one party against the other in certain conflicts of interest. The liberal's disinterested state cannot be disinterested. More generally, liberal support for the freedom of contract cannot be unlimited. It is not easy to present arguments that are exclusively rights based for why contracts to monopolize prices would be wrong so long as the state does not intervene to prevent competitive entry into the market. A utilitarian account that turned on ordinal comparisons between the benefits to the contractors and the costs to the parties against whom they have contracted could, however, yield relevant qualifications on the freedom of contract. Hence, a derivative theory of utilitarian rights stands up better to the problems we face than does a theory that is nonderivatively, fundamentally rights based. In large part this is because strategic considerations are of overwhelming importance not merely between any two parties to a transaction that is protected by right but also between them and many others who may be unable to influence the transaction.

§19 Collective Protections

In traditional views there are at least two basic classes of collective protections, as indicated by the locutions "freedom of" or "right to," and "freedom from":

1. those that help to bring about particular collective benefits more or less to the whole society, as in the right to vote, freedom of assembly, freedom of speech, freedom of press, and other such guarantees as those in the Bill of Rights of the United States Constitution;
2. those that protect particular classes against themselves and against adversary classes, as in various so-called inalienable rights, such as the freedom from servitude.

These two classes of protections address somewhat different strategic problems and should generally be kept separate in discussion. Rights or freedoms of the first class are generally permissive for the individual: they simply guarantee that the individual may do certain things if the individual wishes to. Those of the second class are generally binding on the individual: they require that the individual not do certain things. In this sense, rights of the second class are sometimes considered duties.[9] But the label "duty" fits them no more perspicuously than the label "rights" because these protections are not so clearly directed at particular individuals as at classes or groups.[10]

Let us consider these two classes of protections in turn. Those of the first class typically function to establish the form of governance of the society. In typical liberal societies, they tend to make politics and collective decision making more open, less fettered by particular powerful interests. In the vocabulary that many liberals like to use, they help to guarantee that politics takes place in a marketplace of ideas with open debate, careful scrutiny of government action, and strong protection of individual rights of participation. Although formulated as individual protections, they secure the genuinely collective benefits of democratic government. They do so not because they mandate that people act in certain ways but because they give people the freedom to act from their own incentives and on their own initiative.

These protections can be successful in their intendment only if people take advantage of the freedoms they provide to control and direct their government. Moderately egoistic people and reasonably utilitarian people can both be expected, from our experience, to take such advantage of these freedoms in many societies. For this contingent

9. Peter Gärdenfors, "Rights, Games and Social Choice," *Nous* 15 (1981): 341–356.

10. Despite a commonplace claim to the contrary, therefore, there is a meaningful distinction between "negative" and "positive" liberty or freedom. Gerald MacCallum argues that "what many persons distinguishing between positive and negative freedom apparently fail to see or see clearly enough" is that all freedom is a triadic relationship of the form freedom of A from hindrances q to do z. Hence, all freedom is freedom from *and* freedom to, so that in using one or the other of these locutions one "can, at most, be said to be attending to, or emphasizing the importance of only one part of what is always present in any case of freedom" (Gerald C. MacCallum, Jr., "Negative and Positive Freedom," *Philosophical Review* 76 [July 1967]: 312–334, p. 318.) Depending on what is the strategic form of the protection, however, it may be extraordinarily difficult to specify the content either of q or of z, in this formula, without making a ridiculously exhaustive list. When the range of hindrances (q) is easily specified while the range of permitted actions (z) is not, we can quite sensibly speak of negative freedom or freedom from; when it is the range of actions that is the more easily specified we naturally speak of positive freedom or freedom to. MacCallum's deeper point, that freedom is not more importantly seen as either negative or positive but that it is simultaneously both, is compelling. The sheer difficulty of stating the content of the range of hindrances or actions for some freedoms in their full triadic form may be responsible for our sometime supposing that freedom inherently is a function of only the one or the other of these.

reason, the rights can be strongly defended by utilitarians in such societies—and perhaps also by most egoists, as libertarians assert (although an egoist with great resources might be expected to want to subvert them rather than to defend them). They can also be strongly defended by many contractarians of both actual-consent and rationalist varieties, although one might suppose that such contractarians are very nearly utilitarian.

One can make a sophisticated claim that the protection of private property falls in this class of collective protections rather than in the class of individual protections discussed above. The value of the right of ownership of property lies not only in the enjoyment of what one has without fear of its being taken away but also, and perhaps even more so, in the strategic or structural impact of such a right. The protection of private property gives extraordinary incentive to anyone capable of doing so to enhance the well-being of all or many of us by creating new wealth. This is, of course, the eighteenth-century Whig view of Smith and Hayek. Much of the early concern with freedom of contract is similarly in fact a concern with allowing anyone who can satisfy demands of others by producing and selling particular goods to do so without restriction.[11] One might, as libertarians such as Robert Nozick commonly do, simply assert such rights out of direct intuition as strictly justified at the level of the individual independently of their effects on the larger society. But if the economic and social theories of Hume, Smith, Mill, and other political economists are sufficiently compelling, they can be solidly grounded in their general utility.[12] On this point, contrary to his own apparent belief, Hayek is utilitarian.[13]

Turn now to the second class of collective protections. A typical

11. However, "to a considerable degree, freedom of contract began by being freedom to deal with property by contract" (Atiyah, *The Rise and Fall of Freedom of Contract*, p. 85).

12. Even Blackstone sees this: "Had not therefore a separate property in lands, as well as moveables, been vested in some individuals, the world must have continued a forest, and men have been mere animals of prey" (William Blackstone, *Commentaries on the Laws of England* [Chicago: University of Chicago Press, 1979; facsimile of 1st ed. of 1766], 2:7).

13. Hayek supposes that the utilitarian program necessarily falters on the problem of limits to our knowledge to predict outcomes well enough for us to be act-utilitarians or to construct the rules to be rule-utilitarians. His complaint against utilitarians is not that the moral content of their theory is wrong but that the way they speak of applying it is wrong because they do not take account of human ignorance and social complexity, constraints that a rational chooser must recognize. Hence, his criticism of utilitarians is just his criticism of social theorists more generally (F. A. Hayek, *Law, Legislation and Liberty*, vol. 2, *The Mirage of Social Justice* [Chicago: University of Chicago Press, 1976], pp. 17–23.) Norman Barry accepts Hayek's view of himself as not utilitarian (Norman P. Barry, *Hayek's Social and Economic Philosophy* [Atlantic Highlands, N.J.: Humanities Press, 1979], pp. 129–131).

view of so-called inalienable rights is that they are, and even must be, grounded in concern for individual autonomy. To quote an unlikely source, Knight says that freedom "is a 'value,' a thing the individual ought to want, even ought to have if he may not choose it, a part of the modern ideal of the dignity of the person. Thus the laws of liberal states do not allow men to sell themselves (or their children) into 'involuntary servitude,' even if they so choose."[14] In fact, however, the strategic case for the inalienability of certain rights is compelling and has long been recognized. These rights protect the interests of relevant *classes* of individuals by changing, in their favor, the terms on which they face other classes.

Consider Mill's example of the problem of reducing the workday from ten to nine hours: "Assuming then that it really would be the interest of each to work only nine hours if he could be assured that all others would do the same, there might be no means of their attaining this object but by converting their supposed mutual agreement into an engagement under penalty, by consenting to have it enforced by law."[15] Because factory workers as a class face a difficult collective action problem, in which the logic is for all to favor the nine-hour day as a general rule but to work ten hours in their particular cases, they will wind up working ten hours for a day's pay if they are not prevented from doing so. Hence, what they need is not the simple right to a nine-hour day but the inalienable right to a nine-hour day. Indeed, the force of the logic of collective action may make the simple right of little value. We might simply extend the freedom of contract to allow the members of such a class to contract among themselves to hold together in seeking their interest against another party. But that freedom would not help a very large group. Hence, Mill's workers would require that their right be effectively inalienable. The problem of voluntary servitude is plausibly analogous as may be the problem of marriage in perpetuity.

In all of these cases, the members of a relevant class are potentially pitted against each other to their collective harm, and the only way to secure them against that collective harm is to deny them singly the right

14. Frank Knight, "The Role of Principles in Economics and Politics," pp. 251–281 in Knight, *On the History and Method of Economics* (Chicago: University of Chicago Press, 1956), p. 259. Knight is here openly in favor of autonomy even for those who do not value it.

15. John Stuart Mill, *Principles of Political Economy*, ed. J. M. Robson (Toronto: University of Toronto Press, 1965), book 5, chap. 11, sec. 12, p. 958. Also see Mill, *On Liberty*, pp. 209–310 in Mill, *Essays on Politics and Society*, ed. J. M. Robson (Toronto: University of Toronto Press, 1977), vol. 18 of *Collected Works of John Stuart Mill*, chap. 4, par. 20, p. 289.

to free-ride on the abstinence of other members of the class. If one holds, as many, including Mill, do, that a right is for the benefit of the right holder, one might find it odd that when it is ever invoked it is actually invoked to stop someone from acting in a particular way. Mill supposes "that the person who has the right, is the person who is meant to be benefited by the imposition of the duty" that is correlative to the right.[16] Therefore, libertarians can argue with some force that so-called inalienable rights are not rights but the denial of rights because they impose a duty—such as the duty not to sell oneself into servitude—on the supposed right holder. The notion of an inalienable right is somehow contradictory if it is seen in this way as an individual right. It makes sense only at the group level because whatever benefit comes to an individual under the right comes indirectly through its effects on the relevant larger class. It is unfortunate that it has been given the name "right" or that it is associated with the notion of "duty"—again, "protection" would be a better term.

Many of the first class of collective protections can be strengthened if they are made in some sense inalienable. For example, one can choose not to exercise the right to vote, but there are good reasons to block one from alienating it in the stronger sense of selling it. Making alienation in this sense virtually impossible secures the right in two ways. On the one hand, it makes the right to vote meaningful by preventing the destruction of the voting process through the buying of votes. On the other, it is a strategic device to protect holders of the right against coercions to which those rights would otherwise make them subject. In the case of voting, the requisite inalienability can be secured relatively easily by arranging the actual process of voting so that it is strategically almost impossible for one to prove that one has kept any bargain to sell one's vote. But we may go further and make it a crime to sell one's vote.

While the strategic justification for making such protections as freedom from involuntary servitude inalienable has not forced itself upon the understanding of many critics and defenders of the protection, one suspects that the parallel justification for outlawing the selling of votes would easily be accepted. Presumably no one would think it paternalistic to block the selling of votes—perhaps because this would clearly be a case of protecting a good that is conceived to be important generally to anyone and not only to members of a particular class. But one could imagine in most societies a large block of people who would willingly sell their votes. Hence, protecting the right to vote by making

16. John Stuart Mill, "Austin on Jurisprudence," pp. 165–205 in Mill, *Essays on Equality, Law, and Education,* ed. John M. Robson, vol. 21 of *Collected Works of John Stuart Mill* (Toronto: University of Toronto Press, 1984), p. 179.

it inalienable is not qualitatively different from protecting the freedom from involuntary servitude by making it inalienable. Both protections serve the interests of classes.

It is often claimed that people can never be made worse off by being given more possibilities from which to choose. That this claim is specious should be clear in such collective action contexts as those above. Requiring that people *not* take the individual choice that, if taken by all or even many, destroys the possibility of mutually beneficial collective gains helps to secure those gains collectively and hence individually. If I am not required to contribute to a collective benefit, I may prefer along with everyone else not to contribute. But against the outcome of such individualistic actions by all, I might prefer that all, including myself, be required to contribute to the provision of our mutual benefit. The examples I have given are powerful because each involves genuine and important interests of the class that faces a collective action problem. For example, suppose, as Mill assumes, that one of Mill's workers who simply chose to work nine hours while all others worked ten would get nine-tenths the daily wage of all workers if none could work more than nine hours. It follows that all would be significantly better off if they could not work more than nine hours.

One can cite other examples of cases in which more choice—hence more liberty—is worse than less, as Gerald Dworkin does when he canvasses such problems as the duel and coed dorms.[17] Alexander Hamilton may have had little choice but to duel Aaron Burr if he wished to keep a political career. Hence, a scoundrel could impose horrendous burdens on someone who would not choose to bear such burdens. Hamilton had worked to block Burr's accidental election to the presidency over Thomas Jefferson when the Electoral College failed to decide between them in 1800 and he continued the severe conflict with Burr until their duel in 1804.[18] Had dueling been illegal and

17. Gerald Dworkin, "Is More Choice Better Than Less?" pp. 47–62 in Peter A. French, Theodore E. Uehling, Jr., and Howard K. Wettstein, eds., *Social and Political Philosophy*, vol. 7 of *Midwest Studies in Philosophy* (Minneapolis: University of Minnesota Press, 1982).

18. Under the original constitutional provisions, members of the electoral college cast two votes for president. If the person who received the most votes got votes from more than half the electors, he was elected president. The person who received the second highest vote count, if it represented a majority of the electors, was elected vice president. Jefferson's cleverly organized party did not fit the original provisions because its representatives on the electoral college voted for the ticket of Jefferson and Burr, giving each the same number of votes, so that the election had to be decided in the House of Representatives where the opposition Federalist party led by Alexander Hamilton was in the majority. Against more destructive sentiments in his party, Hamilton preferred his enemy Jefferson to the scoundrel Burr. It was a fatal preference. There are many accounts of the conflict and duel, including those of Robert Irving Warshow, *Alexander Hamilton:*

socially scorned, Hamilton would likely have been safe against Burr's efforts to revenge him for his actions and reputed slanders and Hamilton might have lived much longer. The strategically similar complications of life under the social pressures of coed dorms may be left to the reader's imagination. In these, as in the other cases above, the only way to secure an individual benefit without undue cost may be to secure the collective benefit by denying certain courses of action.

In a minor aside, Rawls says that a person does not "suffer from a greater liberty." But H. L. A. Hart rightly counters that "it does not follow that a liberty which can only be obtained by an individual at the price of its general distribution through society is one that a rational person would still want."[19] For example, I might want to have available to me the recourse to perpetual servitude in the event of severe economic duress. But if the only way to have it available to me is to have it available to everyone, the result might soon be a relatively widespread instance of slavery with substantially poorer prospects overall for hired employment. Hence, Rawls's Difference Principle might require that there be no slavery, as suggested by the following argument.

Suppose there are crudely three conditions into which the worst-off members of our society might fall: destitution without opportunity to work for support but with general freedom otherwise, slavery, and wage labor with general freedom. One can imagine that virtually everyone might prefer these in reverse order. Hence, without an inalienable right to freedom, the destitute might readily consent to slavery. If they were barred from consenting to slavery, however, you who need their labor would choose to hire them while leaving them generally in freedom. We could now apply the Difference Principle to two ways of organizing our society: one that imposes an inalienable right to freedom, and one that does not. In both societies, the worst-off class would be destitute. But in the society with the inalienable right to freedom the next worst-off class would be wage laborers, while in the society with the right even to alienate one's freedom the next worst-off class would be slaves. By Rawls's criterion, the first organization of our society, with the inalienable right, is more just.

Many examples of the creation of de facto inalienable rights in the

First American Business Man (New York: Greenberg, 1931), pp. 207–220; Allan McLane Hamilton, The Intimate Life of Alexander Hamilton (New York: Charles Scribner's Sons, 1910), pp. 357–431; and Nathan Schachner, Alexander Hamilton (New York: A. S. Barnes, 1946), pp. 419–433.

19. Rawls, A Theory of Justice (Cambridge, Mass.: Harvard University Press, 1971), p. 143; H. L. A. Hart, "Rawls on Liberty and Its Priority," University of Chicago Law Review 40 (1973): 534–555, p. 551.

actual laws of the nineteenth century in the United States and England involved breaking the supposed sanctity of the freedom of contract since they involved laws that protected classes against actions by their own individual members in contracting, for example, for longer days. Much of the legislation that protected specific classes of people by giving them legally inalienable rights is generally called paternalistic. That may often have been its stated motivation, but it can easily be understood as in fact an effort to redress strategic imbalances. The political rhetoric of the time had liberals such as T. H. Green defending the defenseless in order that they might eventually become autonomous, developed persons and conservatives defending the inviolable freedom of contract.[20] But note what a restrictive quality contract had, perhaps especially in early nineteenth-century American law. Contracts were dyadic, between individuals, not between a large class and an individual or another large class. To outlaw collective negotiations was inherently to disadvantage that class whose collective action problem was the more severe.

We may not be able to know what were the views of the workers, women, tenant farmers, and children protected by various pieces of supposedly paternalistic legislation over the decades, but it is plausible that, had they been able to express a collective will by voting rather than by individually entering their separate contracts, many of the groups would overwhelmingly have chosen to restrict themselves as the legislation eventually did. If so, then governments eventually took the side of one party against the other after having long defended the other. In these cases, government action did not better the lot of the members of the relevant class against the members' own judgment, as paternalistic actions generally are supposed to do, but rather in support of their judgment of their interests. How one should morally judge such a government change of heart turns on how one would evaluate the distributive justice of the two arrangements. To judge it as a violation of rights would be uninformative, because either way, before and after the change of heart, a presumptive right is violated.

§20 Group Rights

The rights discussed in the foregoing section are collective in the particular sense that they protect members of a class, somehow defined.

20. See T. H. Green, "Liberal Legislation and Freedom of Contract," in Green, *Political Theory*, ed. by John R. Rodman (New York: Appleton-Century-Crofts, 1964), pp. 43–74.

They are similar in that they generally protect the class as a whole against individual members of the class. There is another sense in which we often speak of the rights of groups or collectives: we suppose that a group has a right against some other group or party. For example, we may say of a relevant group that it has a right to be represented in political decision making, or of a population that it has the right of self-determination. Some rights theorists might immediately object to such a locution that rights are inherently individual, not collective. This would be an odd claim, however, since it is clear that the exercise of many rights by individuals requires actions or forbearances by collectives.[21] Such actions or forbearances are duties correlative to the rights. Hence, there is something inherently collective about the nature of many rights that are couched in supposedly individual terms. Of course, on a welfarist conception, there is no prima facie reason for excluding group rights from our concern.

The strategic structure of a collective right to secure welfare or interests is a straightforward generalization of the strategic structure of a dyadic right to voluntary exchange or contract.[22] The strategic structure of dyadic exchange is simply that of the Prisoner's Dilemma, as represented in Game 3.1 above. Given this general structure of the right of exchange, we can immediately generalize to the problem of collective action in which a group of people are in a many-person Prisoner's Dilemma. The welfarist justification of the dyadic right of exchange ought similarly to generalize to the many-person case. In principle it does. But the practical judgment of when a collective right of exchange should be exercised is a particularly difficult problem in a way that does not inherently afflict the judgment of the dyadic right of exchange. Voluntarism is often a virtually sufficient indicator of whether a specific dyadic interaction should be protected in order to enhance the welfare of the relevant parties. Voluntarism is generally not an adequate indicator for whether a collective exchange is welfare enhancing. Voluntarism in dyadic contexts typically indicates or, in contemporary economic jargon, reveals preferences and, hence presumptively, welfare. In large-number collective action contexts it does not.

Consider why revealed preferences may typically make sense in the context of dyadic rights, such as the right to freedom of exchange or contract, but often not in the context of group rights. Because the asymmetrical outcomes in which one of the parties to a dyadic ex-

21. For example, see Alan Gewirth, "Can Utilitarianism Justify Any Moral Rights?" pp. 143–162 in Gewirth, *Human Rights: Essays on Justification and Applications* (Chicago: University of Chicago Press, 1982), p. 143.
22. See further, Russell Hardin, "Exchange Theory on Strategic Bases."

change receives both parties' holdings are ruled out in market contexts, we can get a forced comparison between the (2,2) and (3,3) outcomes in a dyadic exchange Prisoner's Dilemma. Hence, we can obtain a direct, if sometimes rough, revealed preference over those outcomes. In large-number or collective action cases, we might get such a revealed preference in a vote between the all–cooperate and all–defect outcomes, as in a referendum. But typical actions in voluntaristic, large-number contexts without voting do not generally reveal actual preferences in full because no individual ever has a choice between all–cooperate and all–defect in such contexts. Since it may require collective action even to get an issue on the agenda—for example, by bringing it to a referendum—we may have at best very crude "revealed" preferences over many possible issues affecting groups. Moreover, once a collective right has been legally established, there may still be a collective action problem in getting it enforced.

Any strong principle of group rights, therefore, threatens to fall into the trap of revealed preference theory if the purpose of a collective right is to enable a group to achieve such outcomes as the defense of the group's interests. When choices are over collective provisions and not over individual consumptions, revealed preferences typically cannot be complete. Hence, we often cannot know what liberties people genuinely want to have protected. To say that a group has a right to have its interests represented is odd if it cannot even be known what the group's interests are. In collective choice contexts the credibility of revealed preference theory is severely undercut. One cannot simply choose an outcome when outcomes are determined in large part by the choices or actions of others; one can only choose a strategy. Preference theory, however, is generally about the ranking of outcomes or states of affairs. There are too many factors entering into a typical choice of strategy in a social choice context for us to deduce much about others' preferences as revealed by their strategy choices.

One immediate implication of the greater difficulty in determining welfare effects of large-number than of dyadic exchanges is that, practically speaking, we should expect to have easier justification of dyadic than of group rights. The easier revelation problem for dyadic exchanges means that we can typically be far surer of piecemeal claims in defense of the benefits of exercising dyadic than of exercising group rights. Hence, not only can we choose to decentralize the choices for dyadic exchanges, because dyads will not have perverse problems in the logic of collective action, but we can also centrally determine that dyadic rights are worth protecting. For large-number collectives, the problems of centralized knowledge to justify a rights claim are no less severe than the problems of such knowledge to justify, directly, a welfare claim. Insofar as limits of reason justify enhancing welfare indirectly through the creation and enforcement of rights, the strategy of protecting individuals and dyads through a system of individual and dyadic rights makes far better sense than the like strategy of protecting groups through a system of group rights.

Note that the problem of limits of reason is of quite different forms in the dyadic and collective cases. In the dyadic case, there is little problem with limits of reason at the level of the dyad itself; but it would be hopeless for the central government to decide which dyadic exchanges should take place in the interests of the parties. Hence, the sensible policy at the central level is to protect individuals in those dyadic exchanges they choose to enter, not to decide when they should or should not exchange. In the collective or group case there may be severe limits of reason at the group level, and there are perverse incentive effects. Here, the government may be able to judge reasonably well what exchanges should be made in the interests of the members of the collective, but there may not be a simple rights formulation that would enable the collective to act in its members' interests. One might generally conclude that the strategy of creating rights to protect collective interests as we create them to protect individual and dyadic interests is therefore not likely to be useful.

This general conclusion against group rights is not categorical because it is possible to imagine circumstances in which knowledge would be good enough to recommend the enforcement of a collective right in a case in which one would expect individual incentives to be adequate to motivate relevant action under the right. For example, one might conclude that the failure of a governmental agency or other general decision-making body to address the interests of some part of the population would justify giving that part of the population representation, by right, in the body. One could typically expect relevant individuals to come forward in the exercise of such a right. A policy of affirmative action on behalf of racial minorities or women in contemporary societies can arguably be justified in just this way: group welfare is enhanced by giving the group a right. In such a case one might even sometimes suppose that what is at issue is much less a matter of a conflict of interest—between the protected group and others in the larger society—than of the simple neglect of the interests of the protected group. Hence, giving the group representation by right might be a very nearly Pareto move.

§21 The Institutionalization of Rights

Once we have justified the creation of institutional safeguards for
individual rights we face the problem of individuals who have institutional and not merely act-utilitarian norms to follow. In "The Adventure of the Abbey Grange," Sherlock Holmes explains this problem to
Watson when he speaks of why he does not share his clues with Inspector Stanley Hopkins:

> You must look at it this way: what I know is unofficial, what he knows is
> official. I have the right to private judgment, but he has none. He must
> disclose all, or he is a traitor to his service. In a doubtful case I would not
> put him in so painful a position, and so I reserve my information until my
> own mind is clear upon the matter.[23]

Those who know Holmes may be wont to ask why then he withholds
from Watson and from us, who do not share Hopkins's disability. But
we can nevertheless grant that there is a valid moral point in his withholding from Hopkins (as there is a literary point in his withholding
from us and, hence, from Watson). Hopkins is rightly not free to act
simply on his own momentary judgment of what is best on the whole;
rather, he must act according to the norms or rules of his role as a police
official. We would not trust a police force whose officers chose to act
for justice on their own interpretations. Hence we want stringent controls on police practice.

There are several utilitarian reasons for wanting such controls,
which give officials incentives to act in relevant ways (the incentives are
therefore strategic—they focus on actions or strategy choices and not
on kinds of outcomes). For one, we may distrust many police officers
and others in the criminal and civil justice system. For another, we may
suppose from our own behavior that people in such roles are apt to
suffer from a professional deformation that might incline them to over-
zealousness. More generally we simply want the officers of that system
to carry out their charge as we have defined it and not some other way.
In a meaningful sense we do not want such role holders to act in their
roles as though they were fully autonomous. We create a system to
make judgments of guilt or innocence, and it cannot sensibly be left up
to the individuals within the system to make or second-guess those
judgments on their own. By a related argument, we prefer a civilized
system of civil and criminal law to the primitive system in which

23. Arthur Conan Doyle, "The Adventure of the Abbey Grange," in *The Annotated
Sherlock Holmes,* ed. William S. Baring-Gould (New York: Clarkson N. Potter, 1967),
2:491–507, quoted on p. 504.

revenge regulates social interactions. In the institutionalized legal system the enforcers and punishers are hirelings who are more likely to conform to rules and less likely to be swept away by passions than are ordinary citizens in the heat of conflict.[24]

A commonplace criticism of utilitarianism has been that it cannot in fact justify merely the punishment of the proven guilty but must go further and demand the fraudulent punishment of anyone when such action produces better results on the whole. For instance, E. F. Carritt argues, it might be supposed that hanging an innocent after a well-publicized trial would deter actual murderers from killing many other innocents. Surely, then, as utilitarians we would want the one innocent hanged.[25] This argument has been given its most cogent rebuttal by Rawls in "Two Concepts of Rules." Rawls writes that

> the failure of Carritt's argument lies in the fact that he makes no distinction between the justification of the general system of rules which constitutes penal institutions and the justification of particular applications of these rules to particular cases by the various officials whose job it is to administer them. This becomes perfectly clear when one asks who the "we" are of whom Carritt speaks. Who is this who has a sort of absolute authority on particular occasions to decide that an innocent man shall be "punished" if everyone can be convinced that he is guilty? Is this person the legislator, or the judge, or the body of private citizens, or what? It is utterly crucial to know who is to decide such matters, and by what authority, for all of this must be written into the rules of the institution. Until one knows these things one doesn't know what the institution is whose justification is being challenged; and as the utilitarian principle applies to the institution one doesn't know whether it is justifiable on utilitarian grounds or not.[26]

Rawls goes on to underscore his argument by supposing that we had an institution for fraudulently punishing innocents—an institution of "telishment"—when such actions would produce better outcomes on the whole. The complaint that utilitarians must want such actions withers in the face of his apt ridicule—although it may still return to print for generations to come.[27]

24. I owe this observation to Richard A. Posner.

25. E. F. Carritt, *Ethical and Political Thinking* (Oxford: Clarendon Press, 1947), p. 65.

26. John Rawls, "Two Concepts of Rules," *Philosophical Review* 64 (1955): 3–32, at pp. 10–11. Rawls's institutional understanding of utilitarianism is shared by Sidgwick (Henry Sidgwick, *The Methods of Ethics,* 7th ed. [London: Macmillan, 1907], p. 458).

27. Two decades after Rawls disposed of this objection, Leslie A. Mulholland still objects that utilitarianism faces a paradox in the supposed conflict between act-utilitarian and properly rule-governed prescriptions in various contexts (Mulholland, "Rights,

It is consistent of Rawls to present an argument defending the creation of institutions on a particular moral ground and defending
practices within the institutions on the ground of their coherence with
the structure of the institutions. His theory of justice requires a similar
move: it is not about particular actions but about the structure of society. His principles apply to legislative actions, not to court actions, to
the establishment of general principles rather than to the application of
them. As Alan Schwartz notes, common law courts cannot apply the
Difference Principle and a complaint that judges do not apply it would
be beside the point,[28] just as Carritt's complaint was beside the point.

If utilitarianism recommends an institution for punishment of properly convicted persons, then that is the kind of institution a utilitarian
would want. We must create institutions to achieve utilitarian ends
because individual actions unconstrained and unguided by institutional
structures will not achieve them as well. There is perhaps no more
grievous limit to individual human reason than this. It is precisely the
point of such an institution as that for criminal justice to override
individual reason for the social good.

Suppose more generally that one believes, as liberals generally do,
that the way to secure the best results for individuals in their own lives is
to protect them in their freedom of action from infringements by others
and by the state. It follows that the relevant freedoms should probably
be protected by law. But this means that, if a certain right may in a
particular application override the general utility, the utilitarian who
defends the institutionalization of the relevant right must plausibly also
defend its apparently perverse applications. If enforcing the right of
private ownership of property is generally better than not doing so,
then it should be enforced. If there are specifiable classes of infringe-
ment of property that would be utilitarian, however, these may also be
institutionalized and enforced. But it is often implausible that we can
design institutions, comparable to Rawls's institution of telishment,
that could be used to make exceptions from our generally institutionalized rules. There is likely to be no person or institution we would
be willing to empower to decide to take A's property to benefit B
simply because that would make the world better. We can, however,
easily imagine laws and institutions to tax all property to benefit all
those in B's class. The capricious sorts of individual interventions that

---

Utilitarianism, and the Conflation of Persons," *Journal of Philosophy* 83 [June 1986]: 323–
340, esp. pp. 336–340).

28. Alan Schwartz, "Products Liability and Judicial Wealth Redistributions," *Indiana
Law Journal* 51 (Spring 1976): 558–589, esp. p. 570.

many moral theorists pose as counterexamples to utilitarian prescriptions can have no institutional home.

Note that Rawls's argument is almost exclusively at the institutional level (although he goes on to apply it to "practices"—see §22 below). One might still ask, What of individuals? Suppose Holmes were Inspector Sherlock Holmes. Should he, acting as a utilitarian in an official role, ever violate the rules of his office? It is at least conceivable that he should. For instance, he might come upon a case in which his private knowledge and judgment of some aspects of an apparently criminal action recommended against punishment. Yet he might well know that his knowledge would have little weight in a trial court and that his reporting the case would likely result in severe punishment. There might be no reason to expect any external bad effects of his failing to report the case other than the slight risk that he himself would be caught derelict in his duty and would be punished with, perhaps, some exceedingly slight effect on the general institution of criminal justice. As a utilitarian, Holmes might conclude both that he should be derelict and that if he is caught he should be punished as a "traitor to his service." His view, as Hume, Bentham, Austin, and presumably Rawls would hold, would not be incoherent.

Incidentally, one suspects that Carritt and other critics of institutional utilitarianism would agree with Holmes's judgment here. To that extent it seems likely that they have no real objection to individual action on utilitarian grounds contrary to one's official role. Rather, their objection is probably to the kinds of actions they portray, which are actions harming one innocent in order to prevent harm to others. Their real complaint, that is to say, is the usual complaint that utilitarianism violates our concern for fairness. This is generally an issue in distributive justice and as such it is addressed elsewhere (in §9 and §27). These are not easy issues, but I trust that any utilitarian would think it right to override fairness in sufficiently gruesome circumstances. One suspects that Carritt would have to agree.

Another complaint against the unjust action in such cases is more pertinent here: that it violates the rights of someone. But this complaint must assume some grounding for the affected rights. If rights are derivative from general utility, there can be no objection to overriding them in favor of general utility if there is no institutional complication such as that discussed above. That is to say, there may be no institutional way to override institutionalized rights. For example, we may constitutionally prohibit legislative actions, such as bills of attainder, against particular individuals because we are better off on the whole without such legislative powers. We may then suffer when we cannot intervene legislatively in a particular case, say, to take away the property of someone. But an individual actor may act for the better outcome by violating someone's rights. She may then justifiably suffer institutional sanction, with Inspector Holmes, but she may nevertheless think it morally justifiable to violate the right. Hume, who recognizes that the institutions of justice are artificial—which is to say in large part contingent and conventional—says that those who use the word *right* "before they have explain'd the origin of justice, or even make use of it in that explication, are guilty of a very gross fallacy, and can never reason upon any solid foundation."[29] An individual may support the creation of institutions for the protection of rights, be unable to imagine an associated institution for overriding rights to produce outcomes better on the whole, think it right to act individually to override them for that reason, and also think it right that those who do violate rights even to produce outcomes better on the whole should still be punished for the violation in any case in which there can be no sensibly designed institutional way to exempt them. (This account is familiar from a standard view of civil disobedience, according to which one should disobey a law one thinks bad only if one were then prepared to suffer legal punishment for the disobedience.)

The point of the institutionalization of various protections is not to spare us as individuals of the need to make judgments of right and wrong but to secure certain outcomes that would otherwise not be secured. Institutional arrangements must inherently have a certain uniformity. That is a characteristic of their great value, but it can also be the source of their rigidity in cases in which particular knowledge available to some individuals and not to others recommends against rigid adherence to their norms. Sometimes relevant knowledge is not usably available to an institution because the institutional safeguards on collecting knowledge prevent its using the knowledge. This is typically a problem in American criminal law for the prosecution, which is strategically prevented from collecting information in certain ways by being prevented from using any information collected in those ways. As a result, there must be many police officers and prosecutors who are morally certain of the guilt of many legally unconvictable miscreants. In such a case of regularly recurring failure of the system to bring people to justice, it would be wrong to commend to individual police officers that they should see that "justice" is done. In such a case, we design the

29. David Hume, *A Treatise of Human Nature,* 2d ed., ed. L. A. Selby-Bigge and P. H. Nidditch (Oxford: Clarendon Press, 1978), book 3, part 2, sec. 2, p. 491.

institution to build in a greater likelihood of one kind of failure in order to prevent too great a likelihood of another kind of failure.

If it is supposed that it is utilitarian to fail, specifically for reasons of blocked information, to convict some suspects, then it would be wrong for individuals in the criminal justice system to act against that norm— in large part because such action in standard, recurrent cases would destroy the system. The system that would easily survive the occasional dereliction by an Inspector Holmes on behalf of an accused would soon succumb to the recurrent excess of duty by its several officials acting against unconvictable miscreants. In some abstract sense one might wish to say that the latter actions would be just, but the sense is one that cannot be brought down to ground in a plausible institutional structure. In a meaningful sense, then, the actions would not be just.

§22 Practices and Rules

Rawls supposes that an analog of the analysis of institutions in the preceding section (§21) carries over to social practices. In particular, he argues of the obligation to keep a promise that it is incurred under the practice of promising, which is utilitarian and therefore justified, but that the obligation to keep a particular promise is that one has incurred it, not that it would be best on the whole if one did keep it. Hence, one cannot break a promise merely on the ground that it would be best on the whole to do so.[30]

Against this account, note that promise keeping is largely at issue in dyadic or small-number relationships, and in ongoing small-number relationships at that. In such contexts, the motive that enforces the keeping of promises can be entirely strategic consideration of *self*-interest and not even utilitarian, much less other moral, considerations (§10). Such contexts are *at worst* like an iterated Prisoner's Dilemma between two players: either player can perhaps (though often not) do better on the present play by reneging on the other, but cooperation is far more valuable in the longer run. Hence, it is not entirely idle to suppose that the practice of promise keeping has arisen out of strategic interactions between self-interested individuals. If we sense a strong moral force behind promising, it may well be a norm that has simply emerged, perhaps by a loose-thinking derivation of 'ought' from 'is' or by some psychological motor not well understood.[31] In any case, it

30. Rawls, "Two Concepts," p. 27.
31. Edna Ullmann-Margalit, *The Emergence of Norms* (Oxford: Clarendon Press, 1977); Russell Hardin, "The Emergence of Norms," *Ethics* 90 (July 1980): 575–587.

seems plausible that the practice of promise keeping predates its rise to moral status and that it could govern behavior among otherwise relatively amoral egoists. (Anyone who doubts this last point should ponder the effectiveness of casual, word-of-mouth contracts between agents of business firms.)[32]

This account supports Rawls's view that the practice of keeping promises is worth having and is utilitarian. But this does not establish the analogy of this practice with the institutions of justice. Actions under institutions such as that for punishment are in important respects obviously not analogous to actions under the practice of promising. For one thing, under the latter, all relevant parties can reasonably be thought to expect to have their interests served by making use of the practice in a particular instance in which they might invoke it. For another, in the practice of promising, the role holders are their own judges while in the institutions of justice each role holder can be brought to judgment by an independent and impartial other. For yet another, there are conspicuously very many institutions to which the analysis of §21 would apply, but there seem to be relatively few practices to which the analogous account of practices would apply. (In our society the chief practices are perhaps promising, truth telling, and marital fidelity.)

Not all the differences between practices and institutions may be crucial for our understanding of their exceptionless bindingness, although they are suggestive. The first two mentioned above seemingly are crucial, as I hope to make clear. If they are, then one might suppose that if Rawls's account should apply to a particular practice there ought to be formal institutional enforcement of the participation in the practice—unless, for practical reasons, such enforcement would be unworkable or would cost more than the benefits it would produce.

Rawls says that the point of having a practice of promising would be lost if it allowed the excuse that it was best on the whole to break a particular promise.[33] Before taking up the force of this claim for promising, let us consider its content for the institution of punishment. It might not be strictly true that the point of having an institution of punishment would be lost if the individual officials in the organized system of punishment could invoke "best on the whole" arguments for violating its rules. But it would likely be a shabby institution at best.

32. Stewart Macauley, "Non-contractual Relations in Business," *American Sociological Review* 28 (1963): 55–66; Hugh Beale and Tony Dugdale, "Contracts between Businessmen: Planning and the Use of Contractual Remedies," *British Journal of Law and Society* 2 (Summer 1975): 45–60.
33. Rawls, "Two Concepts," p. 17.

While it is not true that it would be impossible to defend one's violation of one's role in the institution on act-utilitarian grounds in a way that would be acceptable to relevant others in their roles in the institution,[34] the system could not entertain manifold, daily exceptions and still function well. Exceptions would have to be just that: exceptions.

Now consider the practice of promising and the recourse to the exceptional claim that it would be better to break one's promise than to keep it. As discussed earlier (§13), one must be able to make a very strong claim if it is to be credible. Failing to keep one's promise, if it is a moral issue at all, is likely to imply costs to someone in order to achieve supposedly greater benefits to oneself or to another. But, because inter-personal comparisons of the relevant kind cannot be made with precision, it does not follow, as Ross and other critics of utilitarianism commonly suppose, that a utilitarian could sensibly argue for breaking a particular promise in order to achieve better results on the whole "no matter how slight the advantage won by breaking the promise."[35] A utilitarian justification of breaking a promise will require a convincing argument that it is better on the whole to break it.[36]

The practice or rule conception of promising is fundamentally different from the institutional conception of justice as order, as in the institution of punishment, in that the latter is a practical requirement of the success of the relevant institutions while the former seems to be more nearly a definitional and perhaps a moral concern. The problem of promise keeping is not so clearly a practical matter as the problem of obeying the norms of one's role in an institution of justice as order. To see just how different the two are, ask a question analogous to that Rawls asks of Carritt: Who is it who is supposed to decide that it was all right for me to break my promise to you? A legislator, a judge, the body of private citizens, a committee of moral philosophers, or what? As this question applied to the institutional role holder in Carritt's complaint against utilitarianism, the answer implicitly forced upon Carritt was that there was no one to fill this super-role of overseer of role violations.

In the utilitarian practice of promising, however, there is a clear, positive answer to our question: you and I who were party to the promise may exonerate me for breaking it. There is generally no third

34. See, for example, Mortimer R. Kadish and Sanford H. Kadish, *Discretion to Disobey: A Study of Lawful Departures from Legal Rules* (Stanford, Calif.: Stanford University Press, 1973), esp. chap. 2, "Justified Rule Departures by Officials," pp. 37–94.

35. Rawls, "Two Concepts," p. 14.

36. For extended discussion of this point by one who is not sympathetic to utilitarianism, see Joel Feinberg, "Duty and Obligation in the Non-Ideal World," *Journal of Philosophy* 70 (May 10, 1973): 263–275, esp. p. 274.

party with a role in our practice to whom we must turn to justify my breaking my promise, no impartial judge to convene, as we would insist on having for judging an institutional role violation. It is just between you and me: if, under reasonable assumptions including the assumption that you are a reasonable person, I cannot plausibly convince you that I should have broken my promise, then I should not have. If I cannot plausibly convince you, then it cannot plausibly be argued that your loss was outweighed by my or someone else's benefit.

Among the reasonable assumptions that should guide my weighing of whether to break a promise is an assumption that you are not, say, an unbending moralist who thinks adherence to "moral rules" is the chief consideration, that actual consequences cannot weigh heavily against such adherence. If you are such a person, then I, as a sensible utilitarian, should not lightly enter into promises with you. I will have to be very confident of the worthiness of my eventual fulfillment when the time comes. Otherwise, making a promise to you is to set up the likelihood of bringing about more harm than good, either through fulfillment of a promise whose premise has unexpectedly turned sour or through infliction of pain on you. In an ironic twist against the commonplace claim that for utilitarians promising is of no value, it is likely that strongly rule-bound moralists will find uncertainty to be a greater deterrent to working out mutually beneficial arrangements than utilitarians would.

In one limited sense, at least, Rawls's practice account of promising is correct: it will be difficult for me credibly to promise to do something people do not commonly do or promise to do. If no one ever kept promises, it would be pointless of me even to try to coordinate future actions with someone by making a promise.

§23 Rights versus Unanimity

Traditional rights theorists should perhaps be seen as the original strategic or game theorists. Descriptively, to have certain rights is to be free to take particular kinds of action in the context of actions by others. Such rights are therefore ideally suited to game theoretic representation. To say that I have the right to a certain kind of action is to say that my set of available strategies must include that of taking the action. To say that I have an inalienable right such as the right to freedom from slavery is to say that I cannot have available any strategy that includes the possibility of my entering into slavery. When we set up an institution to support particular rights, we basically arrange for outlawing any effort to change the relevant characterization of individual strategy sets. Conflicts of rights occur when the constraints on my strategies constrain your strategies in a way that violates your rights. For example, your freedom of contract is restricted not to include freedom to contract with me for my perpetual servitude to you.

Sen has argued that liberalism is logically even more muddled than our discussion of conflicts between rights suggests. According to his theorem of the "liberal paradox" or the "impossibility of a paretian liberal," the existence of even one right each for two persons is potentially in conflict with the simple principle of unanimity or the so-called weak Pareto principle, according to which, if everyone prefers x to y, then x should be preferred by society to y.[37] Assuming an adequate understanding of what x and y imply for everyone, any utilitarian seemingly must accept the weak Pareto principle. Hence, if Sen's theorem is correct, any theory of rights must potentially conflict with utilitarianism. As he says, "The fact that unqualified use of the Pareto principle potentially threatens all rights gives the conflict an extraordinarily wide scope."[38]

It happens that Sen's motivating example for his theorem is, in game theoretic representation, a Prisoner's Dilemma because it is a simple problem of exchange. A slightly mean, lewd fancier of such (somewhat old-fashionedly) pornographic literature as *Lady Chatterley's Lover* would sooner have her prudish neighbor read the novel than read it herself. Prude, the self-appointed protector of society's morals, would sooner read it than have Lewd read it. Lewd has the right to read it and Prude has the right not read it. But, by unanimous preference they choose to have Prude read it in return for Lewd's not reading it. Hence, Sen concludes, both rights are violated.

Sen's conclusion is transparently wrong for this example. Sen seems to have confused rights with obligatory actions. Liberals do not insist that one must exercise one's rights except in cases of inalienable rights. Indeed, it is obvious that among the most important of all rights in the liberal canon are the right of exchange and its correlative right of contract, rights whose exercise is required for the result of Lewd's and Prude's bargain to work. When I exchange something I own for something you own, I do what I have a right not to do. It is not sensibly said that I therefore violate my right of ownership. As A. D. Lindsay says, the exchange "relation *is* a peculiar one. In it, A gives B what B wants, in return for B giving A what A wants. . . . A is not responsible for B's wants, nor B for A's; and therefore—in this curious relation not A but

37. Amartya Sen, "The Impossibility of a Paretian Liberal," *Journal of Political Economy* 78 (1970): 152–157.

38. Amartya Sen, "Liberty, Unanimity and Rights," *Economica* 43 (1976): 217–245, p. 238.

B decides what A should do: and not B but A decides what B should do.”[39] This statement misrepresents the way many must feel about what kind of work they choose to do: the choice is not entirely on behalf of others. But the relation is indeed peculiar in many cases in the way that Lindsay implies. Sen would have it be not only peculiar but wrong.

For a relevantly chosen example, however, there might be some force to Sen's theorem. Suppose Lewd and Prude struck a bargain to exchange their *inalienable* rights or even merely to override Lewd's inalienable right.[40] This would be a unanimous choice (at least of the two parties most immediately concerned) and yet it would violate a right. On the account of inalienable rights given above (§19), it should be clear why such a violation is blocked even though it might be preferred by the most immediately affected parties. Indeed, on that analysis it is clear that the strategic structure of a utilitarian inalienable right cannot be represented with only two people: it requires consideration of the stake of the larger class of which at least one of the two is a member. If the right is inalienable on other grounds, such as that Sen simply intuits it, there is no paradox in a conflict between *that* right and the Pareto principle. Of course, liberalism is fundamentally a rejection of such notions of right, as is its close relative, utilitarianism. Therefore, we should not jump to conclusions so quickly merely from a consideration of unanimous preferences in the matter of Lewd and Prude to say that liberalism is in logical difficulty. Again, we should realize, with Rawls (§21), that there are two kinds of justification at issue here and that the kind on which Sen is relying is ruled out in advance. Having a right at all is like an institution in that it is justified in general. Actions under the right are then judged not simply by preferences but also by conformity with the right.

Consider for a moment the form of Sen's example and ignore the content of it. He shows that unanimity conflicts with two rights in a society of two people. Now put questions like those Rawls put to Carritt (§21) to Sen. Who is concerned with the supposed rights violations in Sen's two-person society? Why would anyone in that society have conceived of a need for inalienable rights? And if they ever did establish rights of whatever kind for their society, why would they then object to having an override clause in any case in which they both

39. A. D. Lindsay, *The Modern Democratic State* (New York and London: Oxford University Press, 1947), pp. 103–104.

40. Sen alludes to this possibility when he notes that “Mill's strictures about people not having the freedom to sell their freedom [are] possibly relevant here” (Amartya Sen, “Liberty As Control: An Appraisal,” pp. 207–221 in Peter A. French, Theodore E. Uehling, Jr., Howard K. Wettstein, eds., *Social and Political Philosophy*, vol. 7 of *Midwest Studies in Philosophy* [Minneapolis: University of Minnesota Press, 1982], p. 213).

wanted it? Against whom are they protecting themselves with inalienable rights that block them from acting when they unanimously agree on
some action?

If theirs were not a two-person society, we could give sensible answers to these questions. If Lewd's and Prude's rights in a larger society
are and ought to be inalienable, that is because of the effects of their
violation on others. In our larger society, with our need for protections
against certain individually rational but often collectively destructive
actions, we need such rights. Once we have them, we may be no more
able to design the institution for making specific exceptions for ourselves than we can design a sensible institution for telishment. That
present agreements may not seem attractive in the future is so far from
being a paradox that it is among the most important of all reasons for
law and by far the most important reason for the law of contracts.
When the constraints of our general agreement are further exacerbated
by the logic of collective action we get Sen's odd paradox, so called. It
seems paradoxical only because he imposes rights to deal with the kinds
of constraints that real societies face—strategic interactions and severe
limits of reason and information that require that we create institutional
devices to handle them—on a peculiar society or partial society of two
people in which such constraints cannot meaningfully be resolved by
institutional arrangements, in which rights have no reasonable basis.

In the inalienable rights instance of Sen's liberal paradox, it is easily
seen that the relevant right is in conflict with the preferences of the two
actors. But the point of such rights in a contingent theory, as in the
utilitarian theory of rights, is to afford us protections against certain
kinds of actions that we could not individually guarantee for ourselves.
This is necessary in many cases precisely because relevant preferences in
particular moments will lead to a result that, on the whole, we consider
worse than if the actions of all parties were restricted in such a way as
partly to violate their momentary preferences. It is therefore no surprise
that Sen finds his supposedly paradoxical conflict between preferences
and—inalienable—rights. Indeed, his paradox boils down to a special
case of the more general logic of collective action. All prefer cooperation (the maintenance of a certain right, for example) by all to nonco-
operation, but each prefers not to cooperate because there are benefits
to be had from going against the general agreement. That is why we
choose to enforce the general agreement against our own momentary
preferences in specific cases. There is surely no paradox in the action of
constraining our own actions in advance in order strategically to make
ours a better world, considered from our own interests, in which to
live.

Perhaps part of the reason for the confusions of Sen's liberal paradox is that it is expressed in the formulations of Arrowian social choice theory. Hence, it is not about strategy choices but only about actual outcomes.[41] In the Arrowian literature, one simply ranks states of affairs and concludes from rankings of all parties what should be the social or collective ranking of the states of affairs. If this were our business in actual life, we would have no need of rights because we would simply produce a social choice and that would be the end of it (or, in light of all the impossibility results, we might reach impasse and that, alas, would be the end of it). But in actual life we do have need of institutions for getting things done and for ensuring certain rights because we bumble along from day to day and generation to generation trying to make the best of things for ourselves. Since your efforts to make things best for you may tend to make them worse for me, and vice versa, when a little coordination or cooperation might have been better for both, we may both agree to establish certain protections in advance that, in particular moments later on, we might one or the other or both prefer to violate. That is part of the logic of the rights of liberalism.

Sen argues in later defenses of the paradox simply that it would be wrong of us to act from our joint preferences in the face of certain rights restrictions. He seems clearly not to be concerned, in this objection, with the external effects of our joint action but only with the effects on us, the two-person mini-society. He evidently has the view that he can intuit directly that certain restrictions are right. He would therefore presumably reject the contingent theory of rights of the present account. And, eo ipso, he would reject utilitarianism and welfarism of any kind, as indeed he does.[42] In this rejection he is consistent with his views on the liberal paradox. One cannot be entirely sure of the grounds for his commitment to the liberal paradox, however, because he also brings in contingent considerations that seem to be at least partly welfarist. For example, he supposes that the bargain between Lewd and Prude that Prude will read the book cannot be enforced because the police would have to be excessively intrusive to enforce it.[43] Imagine how intrusive they would have to be to ensure that Lewd will *not* read the book. This kind of objection turns very heavily on the difficulties of

41. Russell Hardin, "Rational Choice Theories," pp. 67–91 in Terence Ball, ed., *Idioms of Inquiry: Critique and Renewal in Political Science* (Albany, N.Y.: SUNY Press, 1987).

42. Amartya Sen, "Personal Utilities and Public Judgments: Or What's Wrong with Welfare Economics?" *Economic Journal* 89 (September 1979): 537–558.

43. Amartya Sen, "Liberty as Control: An Appraisal," p. 213.

making certain institutional arrangements workable and is fully consistent with utilitarian views. Hence, there are some contracts that the state should not enforce because it would be too costly to be utilitarian to enforce them. This is a relatively ad hoc argument that will apply to the Lewd-Prude case and to others that pose similar difficulties in enforcement. This is not a happy rescue for the liberal paradox, because it is essentially contingent on specific facts of specific cases and is not analytically captured in the bare essentials of the set theoretic representation of rights and preferences. But the intuitionist defense of certain rights against the unanimous preferences of an entire society is not particularly happy either.

§24 Contractarianism

While this is hardly the place for a full-scale account of contractarianism in moral and political theory, a brief discussion may highlight the limits of a system of protections based exclusively on welfare without interpersonal comparisons. As is true of exchange promising (§10 and §12), the chief value of contracting is the informational content that the initial agreement implies. If you and I contract to exchange my x for your y, in essence we thereby reveal that we will both be made better off by the exchange. We want our power to contract effectively to be protected because we can then spontaneously achieve better outcomes for ourselves by acting on our specific knowledge of our own interests, knowledge that commonly will not be shared by any official body.

The claim that individuals know what is best for themselves can be exaggerated and, at its worst, muted into the claim that what people want is eo ipso right for them. Some versions of contractarianism and the most extreme defenses of voluntarism, especially in exchange, exalt supposedly free choice into the measure of the right. The very notion of free choice per se is fraught with extraordinary complexity and dubious coherence, as suggested by the discussion above of rights that protect collective as opposed to dyadic or individual welfare—and by nineteenth-century concerns with false consciousness and, more generally, the difficult problem of the endogeneity of preferences or values (see §36). Nevertheless, in many contexts we can suppose that free choice is a meaningful exercise and that it will be welfare enhancing. In particular, when our values are not readily comparable across persons, contracting lets us promote our own welfare in ways no one else might be able to do for us.

An appeal of contractarianism in moral and political theory is that it seems to capture this value of actual contracting. It does so by dealing in the expected or ex ante values to relevant parties of arranging things one way rather than another. This often seems superior to regulating interactions ex post because it avoids consideration of the conflictual aspects of a class of interactions whose coordination aspects are more important.

Often, however, contractarianism is defended as though agreement per se were somehow right making, as though it is the act of contracting that renders the outcome we contract to bring about morally right. If we contract because we are moral—for example, because we are utilitarian—the act of contracting is otiose as a justification of our actions under it, which are already fully justified by our morality. If we are utilitarian, then, contracting adds nothing to the goodness of outcomes except insofar as it perhaps changes expectations and therefore affects actions and likely welfares. In this sense and to this degree only, agreement is somewhat right making. But, of course, this is *actual* agreement that is right making because it is only actual agreements that affect expectations.

Hypothetical contracts, such as those that must underlie contractarian moral and political theory, are not right making independently of the goodness of the outcomes they stipulate. That is to say, contractarian arguments add nothing to our evaluation of the goodness of a political or legal order. At most, they can be a proxy for or test of what we think will enhance our welfare. How far can they serve even this function when they are hypothetical? Only as far as we restrict our concern to situations of purely mutual advantage, as in pure coordination games, for which actual or hypothetical contracting is of only technical value anyway, and to situations of partially mutual advantage, as in mixed-motive interactions. When we consider situations that predominantly involve conflicting interests, hypothetical contracting adds nothing to our account beyond its gaining assent to whatever moral criterion we apply to resolve these situations. Agreement does not prove that our criterion is right, merely that it is acceptable to all parties to the agreement.

Suppose we agree to the criterion of enhancing welfare to the extent possible. Now we simply face the difficulties of this book: the difficulties of limits of our reason in determining what advances welfare. Again, the contracting is otiose to any justification we give. And it adds nothing in helping us to resolve our difficult issues, which become most difficult when we run against conflicts of interests in our assessment of the welfare effects of institutions, actions, and policies, as discussed in Chapter 4.

4

Institutional Utilitarianism II:
With Interpersonal Comparisons

Clearly, as argued in Chapter 3, we may justify specific institutional arrangements to secure utilitarian outcomes. The principal reasons for creating such intermediating institutions are to overcome problems of information and other limits of reason and weaknesses of motivation at the individual level. For example, we may especially wish to design institutions that will produce utilitarian outcomes from individually self-interested motivations. Among the foremost of our institutions might be those to secure the outcomes that would follow from a positive assignment of rights (§21).

Such institutions will already raise difficult problems of value theory, as suggested in the discussion of group rights (§20). They will also make other kinds of institutional actions possible because, once we have institutions for the enforcement of rights, we can use them to accomplish broader purposes. In this sense, then, many concerns other than that of the simplest kinds of rights can be parasitic upon the devices for enforcing those rights. It follows that, if we think we have a stronger value theory than one in which no comparisons can be made, then we can use our initial institutions for resolving problems that involve not merely the coordination of interests but also the conflict of interests. Interactions that predominantly involve conflict, so that coordination for mutual advantage can play little or no role, pose the most difficult of moral problems. In a utilitarian theory, these can be regulated only if there is some degree of interpersonal comparison of welfare differences. We must be able to say that a loss to one party or group in an interaction is outweighed by the gain to the other if we are to justify a claim for a utilitarian duty of beneficence or of distributive justice.

Distributive justice and beneficence differ in their actual ranges in that the former can practically be achieved only by institutional arrangements whereas the latter is typically demanded where institutional arrangements are infeasible. Much of the difference is to be accounted to limits of reason that differ for individual and institutional actors. Limits of reason that commend state action in some contexts and against it in others play their role in the institutionalization of rights, in the prohibition of certain forms of paternalism, and in aggregate beneficence, that is, distributive justice. The very different knowledge constraints that individuals face in particular circumstances commend action or inaction that may be contrary to what the state should do. It is generally not for the state to undertake daily kindnesses, and it is generally not for individuals to undertake major corrective action against a pattern of maldistribution.[1]

Discussion in Chapter 3 began with problems for which initially no interpersonal comparisons were necessary. Hence, the focus was on the range of problems that fit in the category of mixed-motive interactions, for which we could prescribe at least partial resolutions without making interpersonal comparisons. In the discussions that follow we will generally require a stronger value theory, one in which interpersonal comparisons can be made at least ordinally and sometimes perhaps even additively. As we view problems of rights more generally, by considering them as they interact or conflict with each other (§25) and by considering them as a full collection of issues rather than piecemeal (§26), we are forced increasingly to recognize the limits of the claims that can be made from such a restricted value theory.

Once we have a justifiable set of institutions for enforcing rights (as in §21), we may see how, with an interpersonally comparative value theory, the institutions can be used to effect distributive justice (§27). This analysis then can be applied analogously to such standard problems as ostensibly paternalistic interventions by the state (§28 and §29), collective responsibility for state actions (§31), and welfare policies that are directed at piecemeal rather than wholesale redistributions (§32). The range of the prescriptions we can make on all of these problems is severely dependent on the strength of our value theory.

1. There are at least two reasons it is not for individuals to correct a pattern of maldistribution. First, they are generally not able to do so. Second, they would not likely do it systematically well even if they had the resources. On the latter, see John Stuart Mill, *Principles of Political Economy*, 7th ed., ed. J. M. Robson (Toronto: University of Toronto Press, 1965), book 5, chap. 11, sec. 13, p. 960. But suppose the state fails to correct maldistributions. There may then be duties of beneficence (see further, §§9, 12, 27, 31).

§25 Conflicts between Rights

Obviously, if there are several rights to be protected, their exercise may come into conflict. There are two general classes of conflicts of rights that are sufficiently common to cause serious problems for a theory of rights. The first, and more widely understood, is the class in which the protected actions of one party coincidentally bring harm to another party, typically because of external effects of the actions. The second is that in which the protected dyadic right of contract conflicts with collective rights that would deny members of relevant collectivities the right to enter certain dyadic contracts. The first of these problems has historically been the focus of much of Anglo-Saxon common law. The second has more generally been handled by legislation or by default of either legislative or judicial intervention.

Both these classes of conflicts between rights are fundamentally problematic for a rights theory that begins with rights and that therefore has no prior principle from which to resolve the conflict. A utilitarian theory of rights would resolve either kind of conflict in principle by settling on that distribution of rights that produces better results overall. In practice, however, it might be nearly impossible to decide how best to allocate rights in particular classes of conflict. Some rights theorists might resolve conflicts that result from harmful externalities in favor of the harmed party on the presumption that harms and benefits are not morally symmetric. Ronald Coase, who counts them as strictly symmetric in his general concern with efficiency of production, argues that overall efficiency is not affected by the allocation of rights.[2] His argument is remarkably simple. He supposes that, if, on the one hand, I have a right to prevent you from undertaking a certain activity, you will bargain with me to allow you to undertake it nevertheless—*if* it is worth more money to you to do it than to me to prevent you from doing it. On the other hand, if you have the right to do it, I will bargain with you to get you to refrain—if preventing you from doing it is worth more money to me than doing it is to you. Hence, irrespective of where the right lies, the activity will either be undertaken or not according as it is more valuable to undertake it or to prevent it.

The only effect choosing the one or the other rights allocation will have is to determine which of the parties in the conflict has the initial advantage in bargaining for the gains from undertaking or not under-

---

2. R. H. Coase, "The Problem of Social Cost," *Journal of Law and Economics* 3 (1960): 1–44.

taking the relevant activity. Hence, the rights assignment is exclusively a matter of distributive, not productive, concern. Insofar as Coase's argument is correct, a utilitarian who thinks that money is an adequate measure of utility often has no ground on which to allocate simple rights in conflict. This follows from the fact that, although it may be distributed differently, the combined fund of money in the hands of the parties to a particular rights assignment will be the same under any assignment. Of course, a utilitarian who thinks money isn't everything faces a tougher analytical problem of deciding which allocation of rights produces the better outcome.

Coase's analysis, which has considerable force for the allocation between two individuals, often fails for the allocation of a right between an individual and a collective. His conditions of perfect information and no bargaining costs are far more unrealistic for a group than for an individual, and his analysis fails to consider problems of collective action that undercut the hope that the parties in a collective can simply bargain their way to an efficient outcome. For example, the residents of Chicago and Northern Indiana cannot realistically expect to bargain directly with relevant firms to stop polluting the air.

The more interesting of the two classes of problems in the conflict between rights is conflicts between dyadic and collective rights. Such conflicts can arise either as simple problems of external effects of dyadic exercises of rights or as inherent conflicts between certain collective protections and the exercise of dyadic rights. Little additional complexity follows from the consideration of the conflicts that arise from simple externalities, which have been discussed at great length by many moral, political, and legal philosophers, while the conflicts between dyadic and collective rights have been less well discussed. I will briefly consider the former before turning to the latter.

The general problem of external effects of the exercise of rights may be exemplified by the following. A pattern of exchanges may produce incentives to coercion apart from that inherent in the relative power of the parties to the exchanges. For example, one might argue that free traffic in, say, drugs or prostitution will spawn violence and that, because the state cannot protect innocents against the consequent harms in any other way, it must do so by prohibiting or controlling the relevant exchanges. Such an argument turns, of course, on complex facts and often cannot *easily* be supported. Many of the apparently paternalistic regulations of modern states may be motivated at least in part by such concerns, and they are therefore not in principle illiberal—although they may be in fact. To decide whether to regulate, one would need an ordering principle to say which right takes precedence or a value judgment about which rights violation produces the greater harm.

Turn now to conflicts between dyadic rights, especially of contract, and collective rights. Much of the politics of the nineteenth century in England and the United States over regulation of contract arose from such conflicts. Ironically, when Sir Henry Maine put the case for the shift from status to contract it was already being succeeded by a further development. As an earlier Arnold Toynbee put the corrective argument, "The real course of development has been first from status to contract, then from contract to a new kind of status determined by the law,—or, in other words, from unregulated to regulated contract."[3] The latter shift is the result of interventions by the state, partly to protect certain parties to contractual relations against others and partly to protect some of us from contractual (and noncontractual) actions by others. If we protect the rights of renters against landlords or of workers against employers, we generally do so by restricting what can be dyadically contracted. For example, workers may be secured the right collectively to negotiate a wage level with a given employer by blocking the "right" of others to contract with that employer to work for a lower wage. Rental and other contracts have implied clauses that cannot be signed away by mutual agreement, and many clauses in actual contracts are unenforceable.

Just because the interests protected by collective rights are inherently subject to problems of the logic of collective action, we cannot generally expect to have relevant classes express their own interests with the force and clarity with which an abused individual or corporation might be expected to express its interests. Hence, if the rights of collectives are to be secured, they will commonly have to be secured by state action on behalf of the affected classes without the kind of general, in-principle agreement that we might expect to support the simpler dyadic rights of freedom of contract. We might suppose that establishing the right of dyadic contract is a very nearly Pareto-superior move from a crude status quo in which restrictions on contract substantially suppress free exchange and even economic development. But then to establish certain collective rights that infringe the right to dyadic contracts is likely not to be even a nearly Pareto-superior move because it will enhance the power of one group at the expense of another without an offsetting

3. Arnold Toynbee, *Lectures on the Industrial Revolution* (London: Longman's, Green & Co., 1884), p. 31.

substantial impact on general economic productivity. While liber-tarians and utilitarians may agree on the establishment of the freedom of contract, they are likely to part company over the establishment of collective rights.

§26 Piecemeal versus Overall Justifications of Rights

It is not difficult to see how we might ground many rights in individual welfare. For example, my rights to own property and to enter into dyadic exchange are likely to make me better off. However, these very rights, when exercised by all, might, at least in principle, have a general effect that is detrimental to the welfare of one and all. Contrary to the implicit assumption of many rights theorists, there is no necessary implication that a system that produces individual and dyadic improve-ments in piecemeal changes results in optimal improvements for anyone overall. The logic of collective action and other barriers to what we might call collective, as opposed to dyadic, exchange suggest that we will often fail to achieve certain welfare gains if our only protected rights are for individual and dyadic voluntary moves. It is essentially an empirical claim, and a bold one, to say that such rights contribute to welfare on the whole as opposed to in a particular case of their exercise. It is an empirical claim that seems compelling for at least the era of the recent past in Western society and perhaps substantially more gener-ally, although in the darkest moments of the Industrial Revolution and of the Great Depression there were solid grounds for doubt. The issue here is whether we can justify similar claims for collective rights.

Descriptively, most rights have to do with voluntarism in choice or action: they are permissions to do certain things if one wishes to. A strong reason for concern with voluntarism is the presumption that individuals typically, even if not always, know best what contributes to their welfare. In collective contexts, however, voluntarism of *actions* is a less compelling concern and we often resort to claims of consent or contract to ground moves, such as the creation of the state, to improve individual welfare collectively. In a sense, we recur directly to concern with welfare rather than going indirectly through rights to achieve welfare. If a welfarist grounding of rights is compelling, however, it should also speak to the problem of collective welfare in those cases in which individual voluntaristic actions may be generally detrimental to welfare. Unfortunately, as I will argue, there are real difficulties in a notion of collective rights—and these difficulties suggest related difficulties in usual notions of individual rights. Of course, if the exercise of individual rights generally brought about the destruction of welfare, it would be very hard—though perhaps not impossible for certain philosophers—to defend them.

Before proceeding further, we should address a problem that might seem especially to afflict the notion of collective rights: that, incentive and knowledge problems aside, we may not be able to justify one version of such a right over another on strictly welfare grounds. Against this complaint it is easily shown that the same problem can afflict any right, whether individual, dyadic, or collective.

Suppose we were to overcome the problems of knowledge and incentive constraints against justifying various collective rights on grounds of welfare, as one might suppose we could do for, say, the affirmative action example noted earlier (§20). And suppose we establish collective rights that imply at least weak Pareto improvements, that is, the exercise of each of these rights makes the members of some group better off without harming anyone else. For any such protection there might be variant ways of securing an improvement in the welfare of the relevant group, one way being more beneficial to part of the group and another way more beneficial to another part of the group.

Now we have two plausible versions of a right, either of which would qualify as a welfare-grounded right. Exercise of one form of the right would lead to collective provision x and exercise of the other would lead to collective provision y, such that if x is provided y is no longer worth its cost and vice versa, but either is worth its cost in the strong Pareto sense of benefiting everyone in the group so long as the other is not provided. Provision of x implies an opportunity cost to those who would benefit more from the provision of y—because once x is provided y is excluded. Conflict of interest is inherent in the situation. If I prefer y and I have veto rights over the choice, I may block x. Hence, collective rights may not be unambiguously determined from specific welfare considerations. But rights cannot be sensibly defined in a generalized way for such problems—they must be defined with respect to specific welfare implications.

Note that the issue here is not simply a problem of preference revelation. I prefer y to x and would say so in a full referendum vote. There is a genuine conflict of interest. It is the usual conflict of interest over making any one of the possible moves that would get us from a Pareto suboptimal point to the Pareto frontier. Each of the possible moves will differentially benefit some at the (opportunity) cost of others. The commonplace claim that Pareto efficient moves are rationally unobjectionable is simply false for this reason.[4] If future moves face a frontier that is determined by the new status quo that results from our present move, then my future possibilities may be substantially determined by the present move. Hence, the Pareto criteria are not merely rational choice criteria: they are either heavily loaded, or they apply to drastically limited sets of alternatives, or they are virtually empty of policy import for us.

Decentralization of decision making to those who know how to and have the incentive to increase their own welfare is a strong ground for creating rights that protect individuals but not so generally for creating rights that protect large-number collectives, whose members do not have incentive to act on behalf of the collective. The possible diversity of interests within a group, even when its members share a roughly defined common interest, might seem to suggest that collective rights are even more difficult to justify than this problem of the revelation of preferences suggests. In this respect, however, collective rights do not differ from dyadic and individual protections. It is an empirical question whether interests in collective exchanges outweigh interests in dyadic exchanges. If they do, and if dyadic exchanges produce collective externalities, as many do, the protection of dyadic rights without protection of certain collective rights could actually reduce welfare rather than increase it. But this means that a welfare justification of rights must be relatively complete in its assessments of sets of rights. It cannot simply depend on piecemeal justifications of rights one by one because the welfare effects of any given right may turn on what other rights are protected.

Suppose then that we wish to assess the welfare implications of a set of rights rather than of a single right. It is likely that slight variations in the set of rights will differentially affect the welfare of members of the population being protected by the rights. Hence, for a set of individual and dyadic rights we have the problem of any collective right: there may be no set that is unambiguously Pareto preferred to every other. Indeed, as one might suppose from the Coase theorem,[5] we may virtually require that some particular property (or other) right be established in order to achieve a better outcome on the whole. Yet we may have to choose between two dramatically different rights, one that benefits Coase's rancher at the expense of his farmer and another that benefits the farmer at the expense of the rancher with, perhaps, radi-

---

4. Russell Hardin, "Difficulties in the Notion of Economic Rationality," *Social Science Information* 23 (1984): 453–467.

5. R. H. Coase, "The Problem of Social Cost." See further, §25 above.

cally different welfare results. Hence, on a strictly ordinalist account without interpersonal comparisons, we often cannot give unambiguous justifications for particular rights or sets of rights, whether these are individual, dyadic, or collective. Any system of rights has implications for *collective* welfare, not merely for individual welfare considered from act to act. Hence, a welfare justification for rights must turn on collective, not individual, welfare.

Defenses of rights often suffer from a fallacy of generalization: theorists implicitly generalize from the results of specific instances of the exercise of rights to the result of the general exercise. But the fact that each piecemeal exchange under a right of freedom of dyadic exchange is welfare enhancing does not imply that the generalized enforcement of such a right is also welfare enhancing. For the evaluation of a specific exercise, the presumptive status quo against which one could claim that the exercise yields an increase in welfare is clearly defined. For the evaluation of the generalized enforcement of the right, however, the presumptive state of affairs against which one could claim that the existence of the right is welfare enhancing is grievously ill-defined, perhaps in principle not definable. It cannot simply be some supposed state of nature for the following reason. Any one of many possible, and conflicting, rights might produce a general improvement over the state of nature. Hence, no one of these can be defended except by comparison with others. Many possible systems of rights might all be Pareto superior to the state of nature, but none of these may be Pareto comparable to any other. Each system may simply have its own distributional implications that differ from those of any other system. The claim that a particular system of rights is Pareto superior to some state of nature is not a sufficient welfare ground on which to select it over alternative rights systems.

As we have seen, there are somewhat different justifications for protecting dyadic exchange and for protecting collective exchange. The former typically does not suffer from incentive effects, so that protection need merely ensure that people be able to exchange when they wish to. The latter may suffer from incentive effects, so that protection may require more active intervention on behalf of collectives. (As the example of group representation suggests, however, collective interests need not suffer from perverse incentive effects, so that in some contexts protection may require very little intervention.) Relatively large-scale collective interests may suffer less from problems of knowledge at the level of government than do dyadic interests in particular exchanges, however, so that we might suppose intervention to protect collective interests could often be arguably justified.

Just how far might we justifiably go in such interventions? The answer depends on how much knowledge we think we have. Suppose we think we can do more than what has been supposed above: suppose we can make crude comparisons of welfare between individuals. If we assume that transferring a bit of my resources to you will do less harm to me than good to you, without any perverse incentive effects on us or others, then we may conclude, on welfare grounds, that you have a right to receive the transfer from me. The moral force of this claim would be little different from that of the welfare justification for protecting dyadic rights to exchange. It is only the knowledge claims that might differ.

This suggests that the notion of "welfare rights," meaning rights to subsistence—food, housing, and health care—is not incoherent as it is often assumed to be. There is, in the welfare justification of rights, no abstract grounding for rights of subsistence in general. Rather, such rights could be justified only in the context of the larger society's capacities to satisfy them while increasing overall welfare. One can imagine that limits of reason that often block welfare justifications of central allocations might not be severe in the case of such rights. We might confidently suppose that we can make crude comparisons of welfare adequate to conclude in favor of transfers of resources from the well-off to the poor to support modest subsistence requirements of the latter, or, in other terminology, to address their basic needs somehow defined. Moreover, we may be especially confident when it is groups rather than individuals that we are comparing, that is to say when there is a large class of people who are quite poor. In a sense, therefore, we might speak of subsistence rights as a group or collective issue.

For the "exercise" of subsistence rights there may be no incentive problems since the right can be secured by direct allocation. Whether we speak of the allocation as a right or a utilitarian act may be little more than a rhetorical matter. The claim for its being a right, however, is not on its face specious. It is fundamentally justified in welfare terms, as is the right of freedom of contract or exchange. (For this reason, I will speak of such rights as "subsistence" rights, not welfare rights—because on the present account all rights are justified in welfare terms.) There may be little gained, however, beyond rhetorical force in calling it a right because for the relevant subsistence allocations there may be no need to devolve decisions from the central to the individual level and to protect individual freedom to act in one's own interest. This is the central feature of most rights in a welfarist account: they are strategic devices for securing welfare improvements. The chief reason for setting up a system of subsistence rights might be to make relevant subsistence goods a matter of entitlement, so that those with a right to them could simply demand them and get them if qualified. This would take the burden away from central government to determine to whom to give what in any but the passive sense of responding to demand, and it might positively affect the prospects for securing the subsistence goods. But this strategic argument in support of such rights is likely to be more tenuous than that in support of, say, the dyadic right of contract.

On this account, the notion of subsistence rights is not incoherent, although it might be otiose. Such rights are not strictly collective rights: the goods to which one might be entitled under such a right go directly to individuals, not to a collective. The right of a group to representation can meaningfully be seen as collective in a much stronger sense. Many rights theorists, especially libertarian rights theorists, would bridle at the notion of subsistence rights and perhaps even at the notion of such collective rights as the right to representation, because such rights often imply taking from some to give to others. But since the welfare justification of any right is inherently subject to the same complaint, this is inadequate ground on which to reject subsistence and collective rights. Any set of rights, as compared to some alternative set, will effectively take from some to give to others.

At first one might suppose that rights whose exercise overall works against the welfare or interests of those who have them are inherently questionable.[6] But one must fill out such a claim with an account of the alternative state of affairs with respect to which the exercise works against relevant interests. If the alternative is some other system of rights, then there is not much difficulty in supposing that almost certainly some people are harmed by the general exercise of their rights relative to what they would experience under some alternative system.

No matter how we make the welfare case for rights we must finally make a collective case. And in the end we must face the objection that any particular system of rights will inherently be unfair to some to the benefit of others. Fairness claims about such systems are generally about which point on the Pareto frontier we should reach: I benefit more if we go to one point, you benefit more if we go to another. Here there arises a problem that is similar to a central issue in distributive justice: we must finally have some sense of comparative welfare between individuals or between groups before we can say much about which of two versions of a right or which of two systems of rights is to

6. Recent and increasingly commonplace claims for the miscreant's "right to punishment" therefore strike one as prima facie odd. Defense of this right would seem to require Socratic sophistry to show how such a right really does benefit miscreants.

be preferred on grounds of fairness.[7] Otherwise, we should want to claim not only that a particular system of rights is Pareto optimal but also that there is no alternative system that is similarly Pareto optimal but that benefits people differentially—but this is implausible. Hence, serious rights theorists are forced to concern themselves with distributive justice.

§27 Distributive Justice

As discussed in Chapter 2, the background structure of distributive justice is strategically a large-number analog of that of simple beneficence. In important respects, however, distributive justice is not analogous to beneficence. The latter is generally a piecemeal problem that may be a duty for an individual: I may have a duty of beneficence toward you in this fleeting moment if you, who cannot swim, have fallen into the lake before me, who can swim easily, or if you, who are impoverished and starving, come before me, who am wealthy. Concern with distributive justice, however, makes sense only at the level of institutional arrangements. I have no similarly direct duty of distributive justice, although my class or my nation may have. Distributive justice is primarily a political, not an individual moral, issue. Moreover, as discussed briefly above (§9) it may become a political duty only once there is the relevant organizational capacity to carry out redistribution.

One might object to this distinction on some such claim as that I have a duty to be fair in, say, distributing treats to the children I encounter in a park. This sounds like a duty of distribution and it is clearly only a personal, not a political, duty. But note that it need not be compelling to say in this case that I have a duty to distribute anything to the children at all. My duty here is not like the putative duty the American middle class has to give aid to those starving in the Sahel. The duty I have in the park is merely a duty of fairness in the way I distribute largesse, not of distribution per se. The issue for general discussion here is that of genuine distributive justice.

In order to make sense of the structure of a utilitarian duty of distributive justice, recall the discussion of group beneficence (§12). Again, if no interpersonal comparisons of welfare can be made, there

7. This is analogous to the argument that obligation in the law, if it is to be justified by the benefits we get from having law, cannot be law by law but rather must be to the whole system. But then it is not clear that those who are poorly served by the resultant system are so heavily obligated as those who are well served (Russell Hardin, "Sanction and Obligation," *The Monist* 68 [July 1985]: 403–418).

can be no issue of distributive justice. Suppose that we can make inter-personal comparisons but *only* ordinal comparisons. It follows that group A has a duty of beneficence to group B if it is possible in one-on-one comparisons of members of A and B to show that there is a duty of individual beneficence. It might not in principle be possible for A to carry out its beneficence to B through one-on-one beneficences—the benefit to B might come in the form of a collective good, such as a hospital or an irrigation system. It is merely the one-on-one com-parison of costs to members of A and benefits to members of B that must balance in favor of the beneficence for each pairwise comparison. In this sense, it follows that if all possible acts of dutiful individual beneficence—including those that can in principle only be carried out at the collective level—have been carried out, there can be no further duty of redistribution under a utilitarian principle of distributive justice. At the level of justification, a duty of distributive justice just is an aggre-gate duty of beneficence.

Let us spell this conclusion out in more detail to see that the reverse implication—that once full distributive justice is achieved, there is no further room for individual beneficence—may not hold. One might suppose in the abstract that, if all benefits were from a single resource that could be transferred from one person to another, then it would follow that full achievement of distributive justice and full achievement of beneficence are equivalent. But all benefits are not from a single resource. Indeed, the variety of resources that could be put to benefi-cent use may generally be far greater than that for distributive justice simply because knowledge constraints imply greater uniformity of possible judgments for distributive justice than for face-to-face benefi-cence. Hence, if all acts of distributive justice have been carried out, it may still be true that local conditions leave open the possibility for individual acts of beneficence, as in an action by the only person on the spot in a position to save someone from instant harm.

Against this account, on which distributive justice is as utilitarian as beneficence, consequentialist concern with distributive justice is com-monly believed to conflict with utilitarian prescriptions. It is plausible that much of the concern with distributive justice among critics of utilitarianism comes from a realization that things do not really add up in the simplest sense of "the greatest good." If only crude interpersonal comparisons can be made, things generally do not add up. Yet many of the examples asserted against utilitarianism by its critics assume that things do add and that the greatest sum is reached through repugnant distributions. Perhaps the most widely cited of these examples is that of William James quoted earlier (§7). Recall that James supposes that we might arrange to make millions permanently happy by consigning one miserable soul to "a life of lonely torture."[8] Joel Feinberg quotes this example and notes that it is not used by Rawls in his *A Theory of Justice*, the greatest defense of distributive justice against other claims, especially, Rawls and Feinberg suppose, the claims of utilitarianism.[9]

It is instructive that Rawls does not resort to James's criticism. By the criteria spelled out in §12 for stipulating that one group has an obligation to act beneficently toward another group, one cannot readily assert that James's bargain is utilitarian on a strictly ordinal account. By hypothesis the beneficent actor on the far-off edge of things presumably loses more from the bargain than is gained by any one of the millions who are kept permanently happy through the lost soul's leading a life of lonely torture. If we are to reach a utilitarian judgment either way for James's example, we will require comparative claims if we are to weigh the costs and benefits of the lost soul's suffering. The net of costs and benefits must be aggregated, or even additively constructed, piecemeal out of the individual contributions of all the beneficiaries of her suffering.

Rawls does not depend on supposedly cardinal, comparative welfare judgments—perhaps, indeed, because he wishes to reject the relevant utility theory. His own value theory is only crudely comparative: someone without certain basic goods is generally worse off than someone with those goods. The additional value of material goods beyond those that reasonably satisfy relatively basic needs is severely discounted.[10] Given such a value theory, Rawls can lump the population into classes whose welfare can be ordinally ranked. In a world with only gross comparisons between individual welfares, one can do little more than what Rawls does. Of course, this is still far more than what one can do in a world with no comparisons at all.

Rawls couples his crudely comparative value theory with his Difference Principle, according to which no class can be made better off at the expense of a class that is worse off. What must a utilitarian with a similarly crudely comparative welfare theory conclude? Often the util-

8. William James, "The Moral Philosopher and the Moral Life," pp. 184–215 in James, *The Will to Believe* (New York: Longmans Green, 1897; reprint, New York: Dover Publications, 1956), p. 188.

9. Joel Feinberg, "Rawls and Intuitionism," pp. 108–124 in Norman Daniels, ed., *Reading Rawls* (New York: Basic Books, n.d.), p. 113n; John Rawls, *A Theory of Justice* (Cambridge, Mass.: Harvard University Press, 1971). The example does not immediately fit into Rawls's theory, which focuses on distributions to general classes of people, not to lonely individuals.

10. This is a value theory for individuals that Epicurus might have approved (see, for example, J. M. Rist, *Epicurus: An Introduction* [Cambridge: Cambridge University Press, 1972], pp. 122–126.

itarian must agree with Rawls. Indeed, William Paley, one of the earliest utilitarians, presented a version of the Difference Principle in his defense of property. First he argued, as all defenders of property are wont to do, "that even the poorest and the worst provided in countries where the property and the consequences of property prevail, are in a better situation, with respect to food, raiment, houses, and what are called the necessaries of life, than *any* are, in places where most things remain in common."[11]

Hayek carries this view a step further. He does not merely think inequality is a concomitant of running an economy well at a given level of development. Rather, he suggests, it is more significantly necessary to economic progress: "If all had to wait for better things until they could be provided for all, that day would in many instances never come. Even the poorest today owe their relative material well-being to the results of past inequality."[12] In many theories of justice the problem seems to be in distributing what we have. Economists, Paley, Rawls, most utilitarians, and many others recognize the additional problem of producing what we distribute. Hayek emphasizes the problem of improving what we produce and how we produce it. He inverts the message of Hofmannsthal's lines:

> Many naturally must die below,
> Where the heavy oars of ships strain,
> Others live at the helm above,
> Know the flight of birds and the lands of the stars.[13]

In Hayek's view, many must have the luxury of life at the helm if others are ever to rise above the status of galley slaves. In a less dramatic statement of his problem, anyone now privileged to use a personal

---

11. William Paley, *The Principles of Moral and Political Philosophy* (London: R. Fauler, 1785; reprint, New York: Garland Publishing Company, 1978), book 3, part 1, chap. 2, p. 95; emphasis in the original. Adam Smith also puts forward a variant of the Difference Principle (Smith, *Lectures on Jurisprudence* [Oxford: Clarendon Press, 1978; notes of lectures dating from 1762–1763, not previously published], pp. 195–196. See further, Donald Winch, *Adam Smith's Politics* [Cambridge: Cambridge University Press, 1978], p. 67.)

12. F. A. Hayek, *The Constitution of Liberty* (Chicago: University of Chicago Press, 1960), p. 44.

13. My translation, which is unfair to the original:

> *Manche freilich müssen drunten sterben,*
> *Wo die schweren Ruder der Schiffe streifen,*
> *Andre wohnen bei dem Steuer droben,*
> *Kennen Vogelflug und die Länder der Sterne.*

Hugo von Hofmannsthal, "Manche freilich . . . ," p. 22 in Hofmannsthal, *Gedichte und kleine Dramen* (Frankfurt: Suhrkamp Verlag, n.d.).

computer for typing or other work will have heard and appreciated arguments for how those who go before benefit those who come after.[14] (Indeed, we are told, we suffer poorer quality at higher cost what others will eventually enjoy better for less.)

On these accounts of the value of inequality, if we want to achieve well-being in general, we are restricted in our criticism of inequality to the limited Difference Principle. This is Paley's conclusion: "Inequality of property in the degree in which it exists in most countries of Europe, abstractly considered, is an evil, which flows from those rules, concerning the acquisition and disposal of property, by which men are incited to industry, and the object of their industry is made secure and valuable. *If there be any great inequality unconnected with this origin, it ought to be corrected.*"[15] Because Paley is more often a purveyor than an originator of ideas and because his ideas do not fit together in a consistent, well-argued whole, we may wonder whether his Difference Principle is strictly deducible from utilitarian principles.[16]

How far can we go with a utilitarian deduction of the Difference Principle? If the worst-off class is more numerous than the benefactor class, then under the crudely comparative value theory (of §12), in which individual utility functions are basically similar, we may generally suppose that it is the benefactor class that should yield to the worst-off class. The utilitarian differs from Rawls only when the worst-off class is less numerous, perhaps even significantly less numerous, in which case neither class may have a duty to yield to the other. To determine a duty in such cases requires more information than Rawls typically takes into consideration, information that might generally not be available.

Rawls does not base his theory on such arguments. One can, however, make good sense of his own argument by relating it to the account here of the value theory differences between justice as order and distributive justice (recall table 2.1). On this reading, a major insight of Rawls is that prima facie cases of distributive justice as group beneficence may be seen in principle as problems of fairness in the distribution of the costs and benefits of collective action. The argument in favor of,

14. Hayek, *The Constitution of Liberty*, chap. 3 ("The Common Sense of Progress"), pp. 39–53.

15. Paley, *The Principles of Moral and Political Philosophy*, p. 95; emphasis added.

16. Trollope, with his great sense of the wisdom of his nineteenth-century world, puts a cultural variant of the Difference Principle in the mouth of the American minister, Spalding: "We haven't got the mountains, sir, but our table-lands are the highest on which the bright sun of our Almighty God has as yet shone with its illuminating splendour in this improving world of ours!" (Anthony Trollope, *He Knew He Was Right* [London: Strahan and Co., 1869; New York: Dover, 1983], 1:360).

say, a market organization of society is that it maximizes wealth or efficiency of production. But it may do so only by introducing massive inequalities of benefits from social organization, as Paley suggests. If it is nevertheless to be organized in such a way as to maximize wealth, then, in fairness, all those "cooperating" in that organization deserve fair shares of the wealth produced. Here, "fair" means simply not less than what one could have got from some other organization of the society. Hence, we must choose that organization that maximizes the position of the worst-off. Given the crudity of our value theory, this generally means the position of the worst-off class.[17]

If the distribution results from necessary arrangements for enhancing production for the benefit of all, why is fairness of the resulting distribution an issue for Rawls's argument from mutual advantage? Presumably, in part because the rewards you and I get from our arrangements are largely socially, that is, collectively produced. They are not simply the product of our own efforts. We cannot argue from desert against fairness to justify fully the anomalies of the distribution. As Mill says, "As civilization advances, every person becomes dependent, for more and more of what most nearly concerns him, not upon his own exertions, but upon the general arrangements of society."[18] Kenneth Arrow makes the same point more forcefully: "There are significant gains to social interaction above and beyond what individuals and subgroups can achieve on their own. The owners of scarce personal assets do not have substantial private use of these assets; it is only their value in a large system which makes these assets valuable."[19] Moreover, there is extensive anthropological evidence that primitive

17. Suppose we range from complete laissez-faire to complete control of our economy in the sense of redistributing income to achieve equality. And suppose it is true that market organization is the most efficient, in the sense of being the most productive, way to organize the society, with efficiency declining as we move from laissez-faire to control. Rawls's difference principle requires that we choose that level of control or redistribution that puts us at the maximum income for the worst-off class. That there is such a point on the path from no to complete control is an analog of the so-called Laffer-curve hypothesis. At complete laissez-faire, we might suppose, the worst-off would be utterly impoverished. At complete control, we might suppose, production would be so reduced as to reduce the income of each and every person below what it would be at some lower levels of control. Under these suppositions, the state of control that would maximize the position of the worst-off class would be somewhere between complete laissez-faire and complete control. Alas, even if we believe this conclusion in principle, we still may not know what level of control yields the maximum benefit for the worst-off.

18. John Stuart Mill, "Civilization," pp. 117–147 in Mill, *Essays on Politics and Society,* vol. 18 of *Collected Works of John Stuart Mill,* ed. J. M. Robson (Toronto: University of Toronto Press, 1977), p. 129.

19. Kenneth J. Arrow, "Nozick's Entitlement Theory of Justice," *Philosophia* 7 (June 1978): 265–279, quote at pp. 278–279.

state formation precedes rather than follows economic inequalities,[20] so that we may suppose that wealth of the kind that might be re-distributed in modern economies is essentially to a large extent the product of the society. It is a peculiar smugness—and lack of theory—on the part of many of the well-off in advanced societies that leads them to suppose that they somehow deserve the luxury in which they live.

To put this another way, recall that Rawls's argument is an out-growth of his earlier argument for justice as fairness.[21] This latter term is ambiguous in just the way that is relevant to the derivation of dis-tributive justice from collective action or justice as order. There are two distinct notions of "fairness": fairness of the overall distribution and fairness of the procedures by which or the way in which we reach the distribution. These are the fairness of distributive justice and, once particular institutions for it are established, of the workings of justice as order. Rawls wants to ground the former in the latter. If this move succeeds, he escapes the apparent need for the more exacting value theory for deducing duties of beneficence in the pure conflict interac-tions of distributive justice over that for deducing duties of cooperation in the Prisoner's Dilemma interactions of justice as order (see §12). Let us consider the obstacles to the success of this move.

If Rawls's grounding of his principle of distributive justice in an argument for collective action is to be compelling, it must be arguable that we could choose to organize society some other way that would not so severely penalize those worst off under the present form of organization. If the market (or other) organization happens somehow "naturally," then Rawls's position is less compelling. But revolution-ary reorganizations of numerous societies suggest that we can in fact organize ourselves differently, albeit not with fully intentional control over the nature of the final organization. Hence there is warrant for supposing, as Rawls does, that our social organization is a joint venture that might well have gone otherwise.

A major difference between the account of Rawls and the utilitarian account presented here is that Rawls in a sense assumes that the initial construction of the society is at issue whereas my discussion is generally about (utilitarian) determinations within an existing society. While focus on how one would want to structure a society de novo may help us to rethink and better understand issues in political philosophy, such utopian deliberations have little force unless their conclusions can be fitted into our understanding of how to restructure or judge existing

20. See, for example, the survey of evidence in Michael Taylor, *Community, Anarchy and Liberty* (Cambridge: Cambridge University Press, 1982) pp. 129–139.
21. John Rawls, "Justice as Fairness," *Philosophical Review* 67 (April 1958): 164–194.

societies. This, of course, is merely a variant of the dictum that ought implies can.

A potential weakness of Rawls's utopian stance is that it may yield no compelling recommendations for restructuring an actual society, so that it has no historical role in influencing action. (This is a standard criticism of utopian thinkers from conservative utilitarians such as Austin and his apparent heir, Hayek.) Yet we and Rawls are largely concerned with egalitarian distributive justice because of our place in history in the powerful sense that our concern may be a result of our success in creating institutions adequate to handle justice as order. It is only because we have these institutions that we can even suppose it possible to achieve egalitarian disributions. As already noted (§10), any redistribution we achieve or can hope to achieve is parasitic upon those institutions. In this sense, of course, any practical theory of justice that prescribes egalitarianism is inherently contingent in its prescriptions. The institutions of the state in Hume's England and Scotland could perhaps not have secured very great increases in equality other than through destruction, as opposed to redistribution, of wealth.

Any utopian theory grounded in equality of welfare, as Rawls's theory is in large part, must include in practice some way of dealing with the transition from the status quo to the ideal state of distributive justice. If the transition radically reduces the welfare of some group below that of the ideally worst-off class, it is unjust on the ideal theory. The status quo might therefore be more just than trying to achieve the statically conceived ideal state. (Recall the commonplace complaint against great social revolutions that they penalize the present generation for the benefit of future generations. At one time a standard complaint even against Stalin's continuation of the Bolshevik Revolution was that he merely indulged in "excessive" excesses.)

There is, however, a more fundamental problem with the effort to derive a principle of distributive justice from the fairness of the sharing of the gains from mutually beneficial collective action. The problem is that the analogy between the argument for fairness in small-number contexts and that in large-number contexts breaks down in part. In the two-person Prisoner's Dilemma of an exchange or exchange promise, we can typically suppose that the change from the status quo to the state in which we complete our exchange enhances the welfare of both of us. Unfortunately, the fairness of the terms of our exchange is still open for discussion. You may say that it is only fair that you get more from me than you would be willing to accept, that, say, you should get as much from me as I would be willing to yield if I had to in order to get you to exchange. Often, this is not a troubling complication simply because the terms of exchange are heavily determined for us by market conditions. And often we can know reasonably well how to balance your gains and mine simply because we know one another well.

In some large-number collective actions, we may similarly be able to ignore issues of "the terms of trade" if we are all similarly situated. But the whole issue in distributive justice is that we are not all similarly situated. If the bulk of what we enjoy is the result of collective endeavors in our society, then the bulk of what we have is up for redistribution. A utilitarian who does not countenance interpersonal comparisons can say little more than that any final distribution that makes everyone better off than in some grimmer state of affairs without such collective production is superior to that grimmer state of affairs. To go further requires interpersonal comparisons. Without such comparisons one cannot generally say, for example, that one organization of society is better than another that is significantly different.

Rawls resolves this problem with his crudely comparative value theory under which basic goods weigh very heavily in the scale of welfare while other goods are of relatively slight interest. A utilitarian could plausibly agree with this value theory, which is independent of our concern with consequences however considered. A utilitarian who agreed with this value theory might readily accept Rawls's Difference Principle as utilitarian.[22] Since it is widely supposed that Rawls opposes utilitarianism, this conclusion is striking—although it is perhaps less striking in the light of Rawls's earlier, utilitarian arguments in "Two Concepts of Rules" (as discussed in §21). It is a conclusion whose possibility Rawls acknowledges, although he says it "involves a major change in the theory" of utilitarianism.[23] In fact, to generate Rawls's distributive principle involves merely a further reconsideration of the theory of human welfare that has been undergoing change from the beginnings of articulate utilitarianism. Hence, it is chiefly the theory of human welfare that Rawls challenges in utilitarianism. It is also chiefly

22. This is also the conclusion of several philosophers and economists. See esp., Jan Narveson, "Rawls and Utilitarianism," pp. 128–143 in Harlan B. Miller and William H. Williams, eds., *The Limits of Utilitarianism* (Minneapolis: University of Minnesota Press, 1982), esp. pp. 133–136; Kenneth J. Arrow, "Some Ordinalist-Utilitarian Notes on Rawls' Theory of Justice," *Journal of Philosophy* 70, May 10, 1973, 245–263; Scott Gordon, "John Rawls's Difference Principle, Utilitarianism, and the Optimum Degree of Inequality," ibid., pp. 275–280; Partha Dasgupta, "Utilitarianism, Information and Rights," pp. 199–218 in Amartya Sen and Bernard Williams, eds., *Utilitarianism and Beyond* (Cambridge: Cambridge University Press, 1982), esp. p. 213; and several references cited in ibid. Amartya Sen criticizes Arrow's view in "Informational Bases of Alternative Welfare Approaches: Aggregation and Income Distribution," *Journal of Public Economics* 3 (1974): 387–403, esp. pp. 397–398.
23. Rawls, *A Theory of Justice*, p. 175.

the theory of human welfare that we may wish to question in Rawls's own theory. The fundamental difference between utilitarianism and Rawls's approach is in the way in which Rawls derives his value theory, ostensibly from respect for persons.

Suppose one disagrees with this value theory and thinks that, in fact, the scale of welfare does not very dramatically flatten out once we have obtained a reasonable allotment of basic goods, as Rawls supposes it does. On this alternative value theory the Difference Principle is much less compelling, although one might reach it through a fundamental intuition that it is a moral absolute or truth. One suspects that Paley's view was unreflectively grounded in such an intuition. Rawls's argument from fairness and respect for persons is especially compelling when there are negligible welfare losses from application of the Difference Principle. If, as John Harsanyi supposes from his very different value theory,[24] there were potentially huge welfare losses, the very implication of the fairness of various distributions becomes considerably cloudier.

For example, anyone who gave serious credit to Hayek's concern for progress in the condition of humanity could not easily assent to the bald intuition that the Difference Principle is a moral truth. Why? Because, at a minimum, progress may imply that all future generations will be better off than the present worst-off class only if some in the present are more unequal than a strictly current application of the Difference Principle might allow. We might suppose that we can lexicographically accommodate such inequality in the way that Rawls does: we simply allow inequalities that do not harm the worst-off but that benefit the next worst-off, and so forth. Unfortunately for his theory, it is then a contingent question whether we can redistribute the resources and production of the present generation in such a way as to raise the condition of the worst-off without radically impairing the prospects for great progress. Almost surely it is plausible, even likely, that we could achieve radical redistributions that would significantly equalize the condition of the presently worst-off class only by significantly reducing the scale of future progress. Indeed, radical land reform in many contexts may have just this long-term deleterious effect (see further, §32). While, with a value theory as limited as that of Rawls, this might present no problems for relatively wealthy societies such as modern

24. John Harsanyi, *Essays on Ethics, Social Behavior, and Scientific Explanation* (Dordrecht: D. Reidel, 1976), esp. the essays, "Cardinal Welfare, Individualistic Ethics, and Interpersonal Comparisons of Utility" (originally published 1955) and "Can the Maximin Principle Serve As a Basis for Morality? A Critique of John Rawls's Theory" (originally published 1975).

industrial states, it could be crippling for the future of anthropological and economically backward societies. Would we intuitively defend the Difference Principle even if it means poverty now and forever?

A lesser problem with Rawls's value theory is that there is little to say about what must popularly be seen as grievous inequalities among, say, the upper 80 percent of people in American society, because these inequalities in wealth and income hardly matter for the relative welfares of those 80 percent. It is only the inequality between virtually all of these people as a "class" and the remainder of the population who suffer lacks of some of Rawls's basic goods that is troubling. That is an inequality that might be eliminated without great cost to the very well-off, although absent strong and persistent political will to eliminate it we may not test this possibility.

We, unlike Hume, cannot apologize that we lack the organizational capacity to eliminate gross poverty within our own society—rather, we must admit that we collectively lack the will. Our wealth and its distribution are products of our institutional arrangements, as is our concern with distributive justice now that we have institutional capacity to effect it. Yet there is irony in Rawls's argument from mutual advantage. On this argument, redistribution of our wealth is partly justified by the fact that it is, after all, collectively and institutionally, not individually, created and that its redistribution has become technically feasible because we have developed such sophisticated institutions. Yet significant redistribution of it seems unlikely because we collectively lack the will to redistribute it through those institutions as organized.

In the face of institutional failure to deal with distributive injustice, what is the individual's duty? For example, how is the individual well-off American to respond to starvation in the Sahel? If there are no institutional arrangements at all, one can do little or nothing. One could go to render aid, but then one might be as much an additional burden as a help. To effect aid on the large scale that is of interest requires some institutional structure. This is a causal, not a moral, claim. That structure need not be a state institution—it might be an effectively organized famine relief organization. But if such an organization is lacking, the most effective action an individual can take may be the preliminary action of helping to create such an organization. In either case, where states have failed, the typical individual faces the collective action problem discussed in §12. The problem is to deal with the suffering as though it were an issue of simple beneficence.

It may seem that there lurks in the background of much of this

discussion a sense that various theories of distribution turn on considerations of desert. This is sometimes a spurious, if understandable,
association, as it is, for example, in a utilitarian account. Desert claims
generally are grounded in antecedent conditions or actions and are
therefore one of the class of antecedentalist principles. Whereas antecedent conditions and actions play a very important role in utilitarian
(and any other consequentialist) theory, they do not play a direct
justificatory role as they do in theories of desert or in Robert Nozick's
procedural theory of justice.[25] Because one's future expectations are a
major incentive to present action, antecedent conditions play a role in
utilitarianism through their causal relation to, for example, production
and consumption. In the working of utilitarian institutions of justice as
order, this role may be particularly important. It is also important in a
similar way in Rawls's theory when he allows inequalities that benefit
the worst-off class.

§28 Paternalism

The notions of autonomy, liberalism, and paternalism are tightly
intertwined and, at least since Mill, their relationships to one another
and to general utility have been confused. The confusion is not surprising because these notions are brought to bear in situations involving
severe limits to our knowledge and reasoning abilities and also involving complex strategic considerations. Philosophers and social theorists
often begin their arguments about paternalism from a principle that is
intuitively and easily grasped in some context and is then generalized
from that to other contexts to see what content of the principle sur-
vives. For example, one might think of the problem of paternalism in
the context of one's dealings with one's close associates and intuitively
perceive what ought to be limits on paternalism in that context. One
would then go on to reason whether one ought to be paternalistic in
other contexts, for example vis-à-vis children, the poor, and so forth.
When limits of reason are inadequately taken into account, however,
first principles may not generalize and may be stated with undue force.

Discussions of paternalism typically begin from examples of interventions to change the actions of a particular person under certain
circumstances. For example, Richard Arneson speaks of "forcing adult
education on a hillbilly," of coercively administered psychotherapy to
extirpate the wild Heathcliff's self-destructive passion for Catherine

25. Robert Nozick, *Anarchy, State, and Utopia* (New York: Basic Books, 1974).

Earnshaw in *Wuthering Heights,* and of B's unwanted intrusion to help A with his projected trip to the North Pole.[26] For the large class of problems of paternalism that seem to bother libertarians and many others in actual policy debates, however, such examples do not typify what is at issue. What concerns us is *what the state does systematically,* not what it does capriciously. Torquemada was in charge of an institution that sought out individuals who, contrary to their own views, supposedly needed correction by the Church for their own longer run interest. If that is what the state typically does in its supposedly paternalistic interventions, then we should be bothered by its paternalism whether our concern is with autonomy or welfare. If one imagines the usual philosopher's examples, such as those of Arneson, generalized, with the state intruding regularly, it is implausible to suppose that the institutionalized interventions would be utilitarian in any sense of welfare enhancing that would be broadly acceptable. Interestingly, Mill often seems to have kept clear the difference between institutional and ad hoc interventions. The difficult moral and political issue for state policy is whether there is a strong nonpaternalist rationale for generally prohibiting or forcing some action, a rationale that justifies state intervention in the interest of relevant people in a way that they can be supposed to accept in general.[27] The problem of such ad hoc interventions as those of typical philosophers' examples is credible only for personal, not state, intervention into the affairs of an individual (§30).

Similarly, discussions of paternalism often are plagued with unarticulated considerations. We can say with many simplistic libertarians that one should be permitted to make any commitments one voluntarily chooses to make. But the availability of certain choices may have generally bad implications, indeed coercive implications. We may often be better served by institutional prohibition of those choices in

26. Richard J. Arneson, "Mill versus Paternalism," *Ethics* 90 (July 1980): 470–489, esp. pp. 474–475.

27. Arneson himself notes that Mill goes awry in not entertaining essentially self-interested justifications for state intervention against slavery: "Neglecting the possibility of nonpaternalist rationales for prohibiting even voluntary slavery, Mill is forced to the unwelcome conclusion that there must be a paternalistic justification, which flatly contradicts his earlier assertion of principle" (ibid., p. 473). Arneson thinks Mill gets this argument wrong because he puts the case in terms of whether individuals do in fact know their own interests better than others or the state could know them (p. 485). On the contrary, Mill's error is one he sometimes does not make, as in the case of his argument for the nine-hour day: he fails to think through the strategic interactions involved in the institutionalized support of contracts for slavery and marriage in perpetuity and the question of the general welfare implications of having one system rather than another that is roughly its contrary.

order to protect ourselves against the strategic manipulation to which freedom to make those choices would subject us. Institutional prohibitions on those choices may be characterized either as limits on the freedom of choice or as limits on the power of others to manipulate us. Which characterization is relevant for discussions of paternalism depends on which state of affairs one would prefer *in general* rather than on which choice one would make in a particular instance. For example, so-called inalienable rights (as discussed in §19) are rights that limit my choices in order to protect the interests of all members of a relevant population, including myself, against perverse incentives that would undercut our interests.

It will be useful to order discussion of these issues on two dimensions. The first is defined by the degree of relevant knowledge one has about what is beneficial to the individual or the people toward whom one might act paternalistically: one may know a great deal or very little. The second dimension is defined by the extent to which a particular action is chosen in an ad hoc fashion—generally by one individual on behalf of another or a few others—or in an ongoing institutional manner. Clearly, these are dimensions of very different kinds, although both concern constraints on the plausible content of a principle of antipaternalism in the sense that they concern when it should be brought to bear. The nature of the first dimension should be evident from general discussions in this book. The second is well characterized by the distinction (in §22) between the individual level practice of promising and the institutional level practice of punishing. In passing, note that these two considerations—limits to knowledge and strategic interaction—will often run against each other. Limits to knowledge of others often recommend a high degree of autonomy while strategic interactions often recommend systematic intervention on behalf of others at the risk of seeming paternalistic.

In addition to these dimensions, one might put the possible principles of antipaternalism on a dimension from very weak to very strong. Weak principles derive concern for autonomy from considerations of welfare. Strong principles put concern for autonomy prior to concern for welfare. Unfortunately for the hope of neatness, the possible principles cannot be ordered so easily because they are more often defined by the substantive realms to which they apply than by their "strength." Despite this muddled nature of such principles, it is useful and often meaningful to rank them in crude categories from weaker to stronger. Among moderately strong principles of antipaternalism we may class the versions of John Stuart Mill, Joel Feinberg, and Gerald Dworkin, all of whom value autonomy (Mill generally speaks of liberty or freedom) enough to object to paternalist interventions except in certain cases.[28] One of the strongest versions actually articulated in the philosophical literature is that of Richard Arneson, who opposes any intervention to do for someone what the person does not want.[29] Even this latter position can be murky in some contexts. For example, as in the discussion of welfare programs below (§32), the state may choose to provide, say, housing rather than money at equal expense to the state although welfare recipients might generally prefer the money. Is that choice paternalistic? For purposes of exposition here it will be useful also to refer to a *very strong* version of antipaternalism in which *any* intrusion on behalf of others is rejected. For example, one might oppose aid even to starving residents of the Sahel on an argument that Mill proposes that recipients of aid tend to become dependent.[30] Any of these versions could be based on the generally prior value of autonomy over utility— as the actual versions of Arneson, Feinberg, and many others are.

Just as I have put forward the very strong version of antipaternalism, so one might put forward a very weak or derivative version in which concern for autonomy is derived from other concerns, particularly from utility. In the latter, the only consideration could be utilitarian and any principle of antipaternalism would be adopted only as a rule to follow, either in the sense of Rawls's institutional rules or in the evolutionary sense of Moore and Hayek. There are times when Mill seems to hold to such a version of antipaternalism and times when he seems to think considerations of liberty are overriding (perhaps because, as if by definition, the utilitarian value of liberty weighs enormously heavy in the balance). Arneson recommends that we delete Mill's hesitant passages and opt wholeheartedly for his relatively strong position: never intervene against anyone's will.[31] I will argue on the contrary that we can construct a consistently utilitarian position on antipaternalism which will be weak in the sense that the antipaternalism principle will itself be derived from the prior principle of welfare but often quite

28. Mill, *Principles of Political Economy*, book 5, chap. 11, pp. 936–971; Joel Feinberg, "Legal Paternalism," *Canadian Journal of Philosophy* 1 (1971): 105–124; Gerald Dworkin, "Paternalism," *The Monist* 56 (January 1972): 62–84.

29. Richard J. Arneson, "Mill versus Paternalism."

30. Mill says that "in all cases of helping, there are two sets of consequences to be considered; the consequences of the assistance itself, *and the consequences of relying on the assistance*. The former are generally beneficial, but the latter, for the most part, injurious; so much so, in many cases, as greatly to outweigh the value of the benefit. And this is never more likely to happen than in the very cases where the need of help is the most intense" (*Principles of Political Economy*, book 5, chap. 11, sec. 13, p. 960; emphasis added).

31. Ibid., pp. 473, 486–487.

restrictive, depending on contingent conditions, in the sense that it will recommend very limited interventions in general.

It should be clear in this account that the issue of paternalism is inherently bound up with that of rights. It is often assumed by rights theorists, particularly libertarians, that paternalism in the form of various state interventions necessarily conflicts with rights. Whereas this is plausibly true for the strongest forms of paternalism, it is not true for weaker forms. The latter, indeed, are often justified in exactly the same terms as are rights: state intervention overcomes strategic obstacles to good choices by individuals.

The first stage of the argument is briefly that considerations of limits to our knowledge and reasoning imply that autonomy can have substantial utility or can well serve welfare. This implication is contingent because the constraint of ignorance is variable. I am far less ignorant of what conduces to the welfare of those close to me than of others, and I am far less ignorant about the contribution of some things to another person's welfare than about the contribution of other things. I am nearly certain that food has great utility to the undernourished, and I doubt that public broadcasts of Bartók's wonderful quartets would have utility for most people. Hence, on utilitarian grounds intervention on behalf of others is strongly ruled out in some circumstances but not at all in others.

Let us fill out this claim somewhat more if still too briefly. In an impoverished community, ignorance is not a severe constraint in that all know what is and is not of great importance in adding to most individuals' welfare. In an affluent community ignorance is a more severe constraint—some may even want pushpin, others poetry—so that a high degree of autonomy in choosing one's own goods and pursuits is implied. Hence, with affluence we see great value in according the rights commonly associated with liberalism to anyone who wants them. It would be odd to assert, however, as is the fashion in certain philosophical circles, that these were rights more generally or absolutely—for example, even if subsistence were grievously at issue.

The second stage of the argument is that what can or cannot be done for or to a particular individual in certain realms may depend on what is done for or to some relevant class of people. This is to say that, because of strategic interaction with other outcomes, one cannot decide in the abstract whether this particular action is justified. Rather, one must decide whether the class of intervention of which it is an instance or whether the institution under which it falls is justified. Here the argument is analogous to that for the institutionalization of rights or for the institution of punishing presented earlier (§21). One cannot set up the institution in such a way as to have it work *and* to have its agents all decide independently whether to carry out their institutionally defined functions. The defense of apparently paternalistic actions by a state or other collective body is therefore not that a particular instance of the action affecting a particular individual is necessarily in that individual's interest (perhaps contrary to the individual's assertions) but that institutionalization of that action in general in relevant circumstances is best overall. The defense of apparently paternalistic actions by one individual toward another is virtually the opposite: it is that the particular action is in the relevant individual's interest in that moment.

§29 Institutionalized Interventions

Institutionalized interventions that systematically benefit definable groups of individuals have much in common with rights as legal or institutional devices to protect relevant groups, as discussed in Chapter 3. They cannot easily be tailored to fit specific individuals but must follow general patterns. To be justified, their purpose must be beneficial overall even though in a particular application of a generally justified rule for intervention we might suppose that the intervention was not beneficial, was perhaps even harmful. Many interventions can be defended on grounds that do not involve paternalistic motivations: they are directed at resolving strategic interactions that make beneficial action by individuals acting on their own difficult. As in the analysis of many rights, these interventions might be prima facie justified even without interpersonal comparison of welfare effects of the interventions. After considering such interventions, I will turn very briefly to the discussion of interventions that seem to be more directly concerned to prevent willful self-harm.

Perhaps abstract argument should here be immediately illustrated with examples. I will present three classes of examples, each class defined by a particular kind of strategic interaction. One might wish to see an exhaustive typology of such classes. As often seems true in social analyses, however, a useful typology here is not likely to be definable a priori but only to be constructed out of observed variations, as typologies in other fields are constructed. I am therefore not fully confident that I will present all important classes of strategic interactions that might justify institutional intervention into individual actions or choices. However, these three classes are conspicuously important. They are actions to intervene on behalf of others to overcome: (1) coercion by more powerful others, (2) coercion through social conventions, and (3) the failure of collective action. As should be clear either immediately or in the following discussion, these categories fit, in somewhat different order, the strategic categories of moral problems discussed in Chapter 2 (see table 2.1). Problems under (1) involve conflict of interest; problems under (2) involve conventions that may not be ideally fitted to everyone's interests; and problems under (3) involve Prisoner's Dilemma or collective action interactions.

The first of these classes—coercion by more powerful others—is, of all classes, perhaps the one that is best understood in discussions of paternalism. That certain restrictions on employers' use of labor, for example, have benefited laborers and were not paternalistic in any but perhaps the very strong sense seems to be widely agreed. This is an instance of a more general type: state intervention to equalize the terms of contract. In traditional common law, as Lord Devlin says,

> free dealing was fair dealing. So long as fraud and deceit were kept out of the ring, it was up to each party to fight for the best bargain he could get; a fair fight meant that a fair bargain would result.
>
> In business negotiations where the parties are equally matched, this is broadly true. If the Court were to interfere otherwise than as a referee to prevent fouls, or if it were to tender help to the party who appeared to be getting the worst of it, worse still if it engaged itself as an active promoter of fair dealing, sooner or later it would be telling both parties that it knew what was good for them better than they did themselves. . . . Equity, before it will redress the balance in an individual case, must be shown some inequality in status which, so to speak, rebuts the presumption of fair dealing on which the common law operates.[32]

The norms of the common law have partially been rendered obsolete by the rise of powerful economic institutions. First laborers and later consumers have required state intervention to guarantee fair dealing. Often in the latter cases the source of greater power of one of the parties is exclusive access to knowledge relevant to the other party's choosing. This is a problem which is labeled as "information asymmetry," "information impactedness," and so forth, terms that unhappily almost embody their meaning. Certain limited aspects of product regulation by modern governments are directed at instances of such imbalances of power, as is much of what the lawyer Ian Macneil calls "the new social contract" that increasingly replaces or overrides explicit contracts. The rise of the new social contract might be seen as restricting the freedom of contract or, more plausibly to many, as enhancing the individual's freedom of unfettered choice. But the restriction of choice that it typ-

32. Patrick Devlin, *The Enforcement of Morals* (London: Oxford University Press, 1965), pp. 84–90.

ically implies is not sensibly seen as paternalistic in its effects. Rather, it simply alters the balance of power between two groups.

The second class of strategic interaction—coercion through social conventions—that might justify state intervention is seldom clearly analyzed. However, many actual instances of intervention that various writers have thought to be justified involve such interaction. Because certain social conventions can be destructively coercive if they prevail, we may generally benefit from prohibiting them even though that will obviously mean prohibiting participation in them even by consenting individuals. For example, as discussed earlier (§19), because there was a residual custom of dueling to save one's "honor," Alexander Hamilton's political career could be coercively brought to an end by Aaron Burr. Hamilton evidently thought he stood to lose political face if he refused Burr's challenge to duel or if he won the duel and he stood to lose his life if he accepted the challenge but did not try to win. He apparently chose the latter risk and lost his life. Unfortunately, the right to duel can perhaps not be permitted to some, such as Burr, without coercing others to be judged by the canons of that revolting convention.

Grotesque conventions that sanction crimes of honor and passion such as murder in a duel, murder of one's spouse caught in flagrante delicto, and so forth, are relatively obvious cases for state intervention. Another case discussed in the philosophical literature is whether one should be permitted to enter a marriage in perpetuity with no future right of reconsideration. Mill puts this issue at the end of a discussion generally of contracts in perpetuity.[33] He argues against such contracts on the ground that one cannot be sufficiently knowledgeable "to decide irrevocably now what will be best for [one's] interest at some future and distant time. The presumption in favour of individual judgment is only legitimate, where the judgment is grounded on actual, and especially on present, personal experience; not where it is formed antecedently to experience, and not suffered to be reversed even after experience has condemned it."[34] While this argument is not without force, many contracts in perpetuity seem to be perfectly respectable. Universities enter contracts in perpetuity or at least until a set retirement age with many faculty members (even though the latter are not bound in perpetuity). Others, such as contracts for servitude, seem to fall under the more forceful sanction against contracts biased by an imbalance of power—as might a contract that bound a faculty member in perpetuity

33. Mill, *Principles of Political Economy*, book 5, chap. 11, par. 10, p. 954.
34. Ibid., p. 953.

to a particular university—or under the sanction against strategic incapacities of groups, as in the discussion of inalienable rights (§§19 and 23).

A contract for marriage in perpetuity would have much force only if it were backed by a strong social convention. If there is such a convention, state intervention to break it could plausibly both increase welfare and increase autonomy and might therefore not sensibly be seen as paternalistic. If there is no such convention, oddly, such contracts are likely to be binding *only if* enforced by the state—as is suggested by the history of marriage laws in Western nations under the sway of the Catholic church. In a sense, then, whether the state should intervene is a question whether the state should enforce such contracts in the first place. Do such contracts generally enhance the prospects for a form of action that would be mutually beneficial? My inclination is to agree with Mill that marriage contracts in perpetuity do not enhance such prospects in our society. But given the limits to my knowledge and reasoning ability, I am far from certain on this conclusion. Moreover, to support such a claim, we probably require relatively strong interpersonal comparisons of welfare because there are apt to be losers and winners in choosing either regime over the other.

In either case, it may be that, insofar as the state is to regulate the terms of marriage, we must have one system or the other, either permanent marriage for all who marry or the possibility of divorce for all. If contracting marriage in perpetuity is possible, very many of us might be coerced into such contracts by the forceful sanctions of social convention. Reluctance to enter the contract would unavoidably be taken to imply doubt about one's future expectations and might therefore detrimentally affect the actual marriage. If such contracting is not possible, then no marriage can be secure in perpetuity if there is not a powerful convention to support it. Hence, it might be contingently necessary for us to choose one system or the other. And either way, individual choices will necessarily be constrained by the prior systemic choice. The systemic choice, however, could be made on general utilitarian grounds without any paternalistic motivation, because there might be no alternative to choosing one or the other system.

In this latter respect, adopting one system or the other is rather like adopting an inalienable right: if it is to have its effect, it must be inalienable (as discussed in §23). A lovely example of the force of such protections is Mill's disclaimer of certain of the superior male rights under the law of marriage in England at the time of his forthcoming marriage to Harriet Taylor. In his "Statement on Marriage" he disclaimed the rights over Taylor that he was legally about to gain:

I, having no means of legally divesting myself of these odious powers (as I most assuredly would do if an engagement to that effect could be made legally binding on me), feel it my duty to put on record a formal protest against the existing law of marriage, in so far as conferring such powers; and a solemn promise never in any case or under any circumstances to use them.[35]

The record on which Mill put this disclaimer was, alas, not a public record but a manuscript that he left behind.

The rules of marriage may be largely a convention in the technical sense of Chapter 2: they bring about coordination on one kind of outcome rather than on others. Of course, split coordinations may often be workable—England has one driving convention while most of Europe has another—but often they are not. When they are backed by legal force, either positively through imposition of sanctions or negatively through lack of sanctions in cases in which they are not self-enforcing, they are likely to be inherently uniform for a given legal jurisdiction. In many nations there have been split conventions on marriage with, for example, Catholics bound by one convention and others bound by another. With the deterioration of the force of religious sanctions, however, no one can be very confident that even a supposedly Catholic marriage will survive in the context of a less severe alternative convention that is widespread and that is backed by law in many nations in a sense in which the traditional Catholic marriage vows are not.

Mill's argument against marriage in perpetuity is that I cannot know in this moment what will be best for me in the long run and therefore I cannot trust my own judgment whether to sign away certain of my liberties forever in entering into an unbreakable marriage. It is an irony in the present context that Mill argues from the ignorance *of* another than we ought to act paternalistically toward that other to protect that other from his or her ignorant actions. On the contrary, it is commonly our ignorance *about* others that recommends against paternalistic actions toward them. Moreover, if we are to argue for or against marriage in perpetuity, the argument will have to be at the level of the whole society or of the institution itself, not at the level of a given individual facing a choice. The individual may have no choice. As William James remarks, perhaps too conclusively, "What the whole community comes to believe in grasps the individual in a vise."[36]

35. John Stuart Mill, "Statement on Marriage," p. 99 in *Essays on Equality, Law, and Education,* ed. John M. Robson, vol. 21 of *Collected Works of John Stuart Mill* (Toronto: University of Toronto Press, 1984).

36. William James, "The Moral Equivalent of War," pp. 162–173, in James, *Essays in*

Finally, the third class of strategic interaction problems—the commonplace failure of desirable collective actions—is one that motivates economic theories of the state and that has recently been generalized in the logic of collective action and in the Prisoner's Dilemma. This class recalls the discussions earlier of inalienable (§§19 and 23) and group (§20) rights, which involve state intrusions that might generally fall under the censure of unsophisticated antipaternalist views. Although the distinction between two variants of the problem of collective action that I will discuss here is not ideally clear, I think it is worth maintaining. The first variant is one in which freeriding would wreck provision in cases in which the cost of provision is not altogether distinguishable from the act of provision. The second variant is one in which the relevant benefit could be provided to an individual by that individual's own action but in which collective provision is radically more efficient, indeed sufficiently so to make provision desirable even when it might not be if provision had to be individual by individual.

We can illustrate the first variant of the collective action problem with Mill's example, taken up earlier in the discussion of inalienable rights (§19), of workers who would benefit from a reduction of the workday from ten to nine hours. General understanding of the logic of collective action should convince most readers of Mill's conclusion that the workers' collectively desired benefit of a shorter workday might be obtained by no means "but by converting their supposed mutual agreement into an engagement under penalty, by consenting to have it enforced by law."[37]

More generally, in social contexts in which outcomes depend on interactions with others and not exclusively on one's own actions and choices, one may be able to effectuate one's own end only with collective intervention *even when all share an interest in achieving that end.* Systematic state intervention in such cases may be what autonomous, fully rational individuals would voluntarily choose. Hence, intervention in such cases may not be paternalistic in any but perhaps the very strongest sense.

Among the most important of all collective actions which can be secured at least some of the time only with the threat (or promise, one might prefer to say) of state coercion are contracts for mutually beneficial exchanges that cannot be carried out instantly. These collective actions are typically dyadic and therefore, in principle, among the easi-

Religion and Morality (Cambridge, Mass.: Harvard University Press, 1982; essay first published 1910), p. 171.

37. Mill, *Principles of Political Economy,* book 5, chap. 11, par. 12, p. 958.

est to regulate with spontaneous incentives. Yet without the enforcement of contracts, many exchanges would be considerably more difficult and the general loss as a result might be substantial. So long as Devlin's conditions of fairness (quoted above) are met, general state enforcement is obviously in the interest of most of us. Here, of course, we have state intervention with threatened coercion on a massive scale, and yet we would probably agree that the result is generally to increase our autonomy and our freedom of choice as well as our utility or welfare.

Now consider the second variant of state interventions that are often viewed as paternalistic but have the effect of making it possible for people to achieve their purposes more efficiently by institutionalizing the regulation of certain of their actions. For example, drug regulation by the state may be seen as a device for increasing efficiency for consumers by having specialists decide on drug quality. The efficiency gains require collective action which, again, may best be successfully achieved by having the state act as our agent just as the state is the enforcing agent in ordinary contracts between individuals. These are not easy cases for analysis in part because empowering the state to act as our agent may also be to empower it to undertake paternalistic actions, as the history of marijuana regulation in the United States suggests. But it is also too facile simply to rule that a specific action by an institutional agent is a paternalistically motivated excess. Consider the difficult case of the contemporary American prohibition of the use of so-called laetrile, an extract of apricot pits, in the treatment of cancer.

Many, including presumably Arneson,[38] would consider the ban on laetrile an utterly paternalistic action by the state. Their argument might run as follows. Against Mill's concern that users of laetrile might not have considered their actions adequately, it seems plausible to suppose that those who want to use laetrile have put as much thought into that choice as people generally ever do in any but rare circumstances. It is also reasonable to suppose that the use of laetrile would not be harmful to many of these people in any case, since many of them are terminally ill with no hope of successful treatment by standard medical practices. Hence, if ever there was an overt act of paternalism in a relatively liberal society, denying laetrile to these people would seem to count. Indeed, denial might not even be utilitarian because many of these people might genuinely have a happier existence for a while if they are taking laetrile and therefore hoping for recovery. One might

38. Arneson, "Mill versus Paternalism," esp. pp. 482–484.

doubt the rationality of those demanding laetrile, but it seems unnecessarily intrusive simply to deny them their irrational wishes.

Unfortunately, this is the way public debate over laetrile has been cast and the way it is often treated in academic discussions.[39] Against this position, note that the analysis cannot turn simply on the immediate facts of this case but must take into account the more general implications of the *kinds* of answers proposed. To allow the use of the useless and presumably harmless drug laetrile merely because people want it is not an isolated or isolatable choice. As suggested earlier in the discussion of the institutionalization of rights (§21), we cannot have a drug-regulating agency exempt laetrile from regulation without a more general policy of when to exempt. We created an agency that is justified on general principles to protect us from sloppily tested and fraudulent drugs, many of which have been massively harmful. The agency or institution uses expertise and standard procedures for reaching its regulatory decisions. We cannot then expect to have agents of that institution selectively violate the institution's rules to handle peculiar cases, such as the use of laetrile, just because popular opinion and expert opinion radically diverge. The issue turns on what set of institutions we must have if we are to regulate drugs well and what set we must have if we simply let momentary popular opinion determine outcomes. We might in such cases have recourse to democratic institutions to choose to exempt some choices from regularized control by our agency. Democratic procedures can accommodate popular demand in ways that rule-bound agencies should not be entrusted to do. The New Jersey legislature intervened to permit the eventual sale of laetrile under different rules from those that generally apply,[40] and Congress has intervened to allow the sale of saccharin (which has been shown to be carcinogenic and is therefore supposed, under the Delaney clause that governs food and drug regulation, to be banned by the Food and Drug Administration).

In one respect all of the state interventions discussed here could be viewed in part as solutions of collective action problems. If enough of us could act together to accomplish the overthrow of a dismal social convention, there would be no need of state intervention. If workers in their relative weakness in the face of corporate employers could act together to protect their interests in not being subjected to bad working conditions, they would not need the state. If consumers could act to-

39. See, for example, Amy Gutmann and Dennis Thompson, eds., *Ethics and Politics: Cases and Comments* (Chicago: Nelson-Hall, 1984), chap. 8.
40. Ibid., pp. 201–203.

gether to judge the quality of drugs, we would not need the state. There is more to the separate categories or classes of problems that provoke intervention than this, however. For example, sexual harassment in the workplace can probably not be corrected by successful collective action on the part of women because the threat by all women to pull out of certain jobs or to harass certain employers would likely not be sufficient to solve the problem. Problems in the third class, under (3) above, require state intervention merely to achieve their resolution more efficiently than they would be accomplished without state regulation, as, for example, in the regulation of drugs. But the breaking of power, either of certain individuals or groups or of conventions, might often be virtually impossible without state backing.

Are all these coercive restrictions on one's behavior antiutilitarian or somehow paradoxical for utilitarianism? Surely not. They are somewhat analogous to the Ulyssean choices of individuals to coerce themselves to do what in the larger scheme of things they would rather do despite momentary laziness or distraction that might get in the way. Ulysses knew that if he heard the sirens' song and he were free to follow his emotions, he would be seduced to his own destruction. But the experience of hearing the song was one he dearly wanted to have. Hence, he had himself bound to his ship so that he would not be free to follow his emotions and could therefore both hear the sirens and live to savor the experience. Jon Elster and Thomas Schelling have analyzed numerous analogous choices in which one coerces one's future self for good reason.[41] For example, millions of sensibly self-interested people have ingested drugs that give them a revulsive reaction to smoking or drinking. Millions more use raucous alarm clocks, sometimes set up far from bedside, to disturb themselves into productive activity. Many people, especially academics, thrive when they submit themselves to coercive deadlines. But one need not cite only such cases because the surrender of freedom implicit in them is implicit in virtually all choices. Walter Weisskopf notes that "every choice and decision entails the *sacrifice* of alternatives which have been rejected," so that "man is free mostly to renounce possibilities."[42]

Institutional restrictions on individual behavior are only partially analogous to these self-restrictions on one's own behavior. They would

41. Jon Elster, *Ulysses and the Sirens* (Cambridge: Cambridge University Press, 1979), esp. chap. 2; Thomas C. Schelling, "The Intimate Contest for Self Command," *Public Interest,* no. 60 (Summer 1980): pp. 94–118.

42. Walter A. Weisskopf, *Alienation and Economics* (New York: Dutton, 1971), pp. 22–23. A clear implication of this account is that an absolute ethic against gambling or chance taking makes life impossible for anyone who does not receive constant instruction from an omniscient adviser.

be more fully analogous if people could simply contract with each other to act for mutual benefit or if they could consent to state intervention on their behalf. Unfortunately, we know too well that neither of these is a realistic solution much of the time. In a world in which not all are utilitarians, the hope of contracting for collective benefit can be severely undercut by freerider problems. And representative government cannot seriously be expected to undertake only those specific actions for which consent has explicitly been given by all affected. Indeed, most of us may be willing—may even prefer—to delegate authority in many realms to relevant officials to decide which actions to undertake on our behalf. If division of labor and specialization make sense in our economic lives, they may well often make sense in our political lives, especially for those political decisions directed at matters of practical reason.

This conclusion may be reinforced by the realization that much of our practical knowledge is after all socially created and given to us. I do not know enough about the chemistry and biology of relevant drugs to know whether to use them in relevant circumstances. I necessarily act under the advice of others. George Stigler slyly remarks that, whereas liberals may need the state to tell them whether a car is a good buy, conservatives are smart enough to figure it out for themselves.[43] For the general point he wants to make, he is dead wrong. It is often not individuals, whether liberal or conservative, but institutions and socially defined bodies of people that know. Individuals all too often can only accept, can only agree with Wittgenstein that in large part their lives consist in accepting.[44] Moreover, most of us are too smart to want to spend our time evaluating cars and drugs in certain cases, and we are happy to delegate some power to do so on our behalf to state agencies and to privately established "authorities." Of course, this is just good Stiglerian understanding of information costs and how best to deal with them in our less than ideal world.

Much of the contemporary discussion of paternalistic intervention by the state concerns issues that are debated in terms that suggest their problem is not one of difficulties in strategic interaction such as those discussed above. The contemporary discussion focuses on such issues as whether it is right to require drivers and passengers in automobiles to wear seat belts, to require motorcyclists to wear safety helmets, and so forth. The debate over such interventions typically recalls debates over

43. George J. Stigler, *The Citizen and the State: Essays on Regulation* (Chicago: University of Chicago Press, 1975), p. 10.
44. Ludwig Wittgenstein, *On Certainty*, ed. by G. E. M. Anscombe and G. H. von Wright (Oxford: Basil Blackwell, 1969), §344.

the earlier example of the sale of laetrile to anyone who wants it. It is supposed that the state restricts individual freedom of choice merely in the interest of the individual. There are, of course, strong counterarguments in defense of requiring the use of seat belts, safety helmets, and so forth. Two are especially prominent.

First there are arguments such as those Stigler dismisses, at least for conservatives, in the sale of used cars. People may simply be misinformed about the consequences of not using safety devices. Hence, the state can take over that function, as it does for drug regulation. But in the case of drug regulation there are strong spillover effects that require a general policy: without regulation, shysters may so flood the market with variants of laetrile and even with genuinely harmful drugs that virtually everyone other than the profiteering shysters is worse off. Virtually everyone who is affected by the availability of drugs can therefore plausibly agree to the regulation of drugs. Here the state's intervention may not be paternalistic because it may be adopted at the behest of those protected. (Unfortunately, it may be prohibitively difficult to exempt Stigler from the state's regulatory scheme.) Let us similarly restrict consideration to those immediately affected in the case of regulations requiring motorcycle helmets. It appears that much, plausibly even most, of the relevant population of motorcyclists is opposed to the regulation and that those who are not opposed do not suffer significant spillover effects from lack of regulation. If these are the facts of the matter, regulating the use of motorcycle helmets is not strategically analogous to regulating the sale of medicinal drugs. In particular, one cannot get even a prima facie claim that requiring motorcycle helmets is simply a Pareto optimal move that makes virtually everyone better off or leaves them unaffected—because there is a vociferous crowd claiming that it makes them worse off.

This raises the second argument for regulation of such self-harms as taking the risks associated with not wearing motorcycle helmets. This argument is that people other than those directly at risk must suffer at least part of the costs of the consequences of taking such risks. On this argument, the issue is no longer one of paternalism but of distributive justice. And its utilitarian resolution requires interpersonal comparisons of the differential welfare effects of regulating versus not regulating. In weighing the welfare effects, one might take the views of the opponents quite seriously and count the wearing of helmets as a real cost, rather than a benefit, to some cyclists. These considerations make the issue technically interesting, perhaps, but they significantly reduce its interest for many moral philosophers. Indeed, for those motivated by issues of genuine paternalism, they make it quite uninteresting.

§30 Ad Hoc Interventions

Discussions of paternalism often focus on specific examples of what we might call ad hoc intervention to rescue a particular person from a supposed folly. When the problem of intervention is cast as an institutional problem, as discussed above (§29), the issue of ad hoc interventions makes little sense. The state will have a general policy of intervening systematically in classes of cases, such as the regulation of working hours, drug sales, marriages, and so forth, to alter behavior that would be individually chosen toward a generally more beneficial behavior. The selected behavior is generally more beneficial because it affects what a large class can do and thereby affects benefits to many others than the particular person whose behavior is regulated at a given moment. If there are ad hoc decisions to be made by the state, these will be exceptions to a standard practice of regulation or systematic intervention: the state will choose in a particular case *not* to intervene. In principle, there is no issue of choosing actively to intervene as an exception. (If there is, some official has overstepped the bounds of her office.) Hence, to argue against state intervention it generally will not do to argue, as critics painfully often do, from an example of how the state might single me out for some apparently capricious regulation against my will.

There is another class of ad hoc interventions that is often at issue in philosophical discussions of libertarianism and paternalism: interventions by individuals to force other individuals to do something directly, not collectively, in their own interest that they seemingly do not want to do. Just as Rawls supposed that practices at the individual level could be understood as the analog of norms for role holders in institutions, so one might suppose that paternalistic interventions at the individual level are analogs of interventions by the state. As is true of the morality of practices, however, paternalistic interventions by individuals are not usefully seen as mere analogs of state interventions. The knowledge conditions will often be radically different at the individual level, and when they are we cannot argue against particular interventions on grounds of lack of relevant knowledge or for general classes of interventions on grounds that we have relevant knowledge. The kinds or cases of intervention that are likely to be justifiable at the individual level are apt to be roughly the reverse of those justified at the level of the state. Hence, arguments about paternalism that do not—explicitly or implicitly—distinguish between state and individual interventions are inherently confused.

Consider Arneson's example of A and B. A has a lifetime ambition:

to go to the North Pole. She arranges to do so and then prepares a public announcement of her intentions. B "knows" that if A makes the announcement, public authorities will, "for paternalistic reasons," prevent her from taking her trip.[45] B wishes to protect A's greater aim, of fulfilling her major autonomous plan, by intervening to block her minor, even trivial, plan to announce the trip. B is essentially a consequentialist whose purpose is to maximize autonomy, infringing autonomy in small ways to enhance it in large ways. Is B morally right to intervene? It is not obviously easy to say yes or no. Indeed, it is not altogether clear what the issue is or what significance it has. Arneson's purpose is to show, by teasing out our intuitions, that we have a commitment to autonomy that is independent of our commitments to other values, such as welfare. But we may not have solid intuitions about a case that is so barren in its description, and whatever intuitions we have may not apply to any more fully described, that is, real, case.

There is one general distinction we may draw for such a case. If such intervention is *legally* at issue, then the problem becomes one of regularized institutional intervention, in which case it falls under the discussion of the foregoing section (§29). To understand the morality of legal intervention we have to consider the *class* of problems of which the instant example is merely a case. If the example is to pose an issue in its own right, then, we must assume the problem is one of what it is individually morally right to do against (or for) A, as in B's case. Surely our conclusion about what would be right must turn very heavily on information of many kinds not yet given to us in the statement of the example. If one thinks one can actually help another by acting coercively toward the other, perhaps one should. But in deciding to do so, one should be modest in one's own assumption of superior knowledge, because the very ground of the intervention must largely be that one knows better than the person on behalf of whom and against whose action one is to intervene. Arneson's example is deliberately devised to

45. Arneson, "Mill versus Paternalism," p. 475. I have changed A's gender—the power of such manipulation is one of the compelling advantages of imaginary examples—to fit a case that may have become actual. Pam Flowers, a resident of Willow, Alaska, who races dogsleds, announced her intention to be the first American and first woman to go solo to the North Pole from Resolute Bay in Canada's Northwest Territory. She expected to take about sixty days to cover the 475 miles to the pole by dogsled. Presumably the Canadian authorities would not intervene (*The Herald-Palladium,* Benton Harbor–St. Joseph, Michigan, September 27, 1986, p. 24). The first person to make such a trip was Naomi Uemura in 1978. A team of six, including one woman, made it by dogsled and a Frenchman made it solo on skis in 1986, although the latter depended on supplies flown in regularly (Will Steger, "North to the Pole," and Jean-Louis Etienne, "Skiing Alone to the Pole," *National Geographic* 170 [September 1986]: 289–317 and 318–323).

pose an internal contradiction in the achievement of A's autonomy: only by intruding in A's autonomously misguided action can B supposedly secure A's further autonomy in making her own success or failure in her greater project of going to the North Pole. Is it right or wrong in principle for me to manipulate you into securing your own well-being? Maybe, maybe not. There can be no abstract, general answer.

There is a common expression in German that one must trick or coerce someone else into her own happiness. There is a perhaps universal practice of commonly doing just that. A strong case can be made in support of the practice in relevantly restricted circumstances. These are just the circumstances that motivate Mill's discussions of individual paternalism: that one actually be in a position of having better knowledge about someone than that person has about herself. One might add to this condition that one not momentarily suffer from the akrasia or weakness of will that might hamper the other from achieving her end if left wholly to her own devices. In addition, it must generally be true that one is in a relationship—for example, a very close relationship—that secures one's motives as genuinely other-regarding and not self-interested. Hence, I would not generally be justified in intervening in your actions if I were a stranger to you with little ground for claiming to know your situation better than you do and with little reason to have your trust. If you were my very good friend, I might occasionally have reason to manipulate you to your own interest with reasonable expectation that, after the fact, you would consent to my manipulation. As with the determined moralist who follows the rule of keeping promises no matter what, however, if you are morally committed to the superior call of autonomy, I should be leery of ever manipulating you supposedly in your interest, because your particularly moralistic stance on the question of autonomy sets you up for real pain.

§31 Collective Responsibility

Clearly it is institutions and not individuals that bring about many of the most important outcomes that benefit us and serve the larger interest. And, as argued earlier (§21), individuals with roles in the institutions have their moral responsibilities defined in large part by the relationship of their roles to the institution. These facts raise a major question: Who is responsible for the institutions and their "actions"? A possible answer is: We who operate and benefit from the institutions. Moral responsibility for much of what concerns us therefore is somehow collective and not merely individual.

Collective responsibility is not a simple analog of individual responsibility. There are two complicating effects that prevent our simply aggregating from individual to collective responsibility. First, there is the problem of the logic of collective action: from the fact that doing something is in the collective interest we cannot infer that it is individually rational to contribute to the collective outcome. Second, there is the problem of the use of institutions as means for carrying out collective purposes: these institutions are created just because we cannot collectively control results through individually motivated voluntary action, but once they exist they may not "act" as intended. The chief justification of many institutions is that causal responsibility at the individual level is not consistent with collective interest or will. That is to say, institutions are a response to the logic of collective action and its moral analog.

These problems underlie all of political action and political responsibility. For example, consider the complex problem of nuclear weapons policy. It is commonly said that nuclear weapons are not democratic weapons, that is, that their control cannot be put in the hands of the people but must be concentrated in the hands of a small number of officials. This complaint addresses, and perhaps excuses, only part of contemporary policies. While actual decisions on whether to use the weapons in particular moments may not sensibly be made a matter of democratic choice, the background policies on which weapons are to be available and on how decisions concerning their use are to be made can very well be a matter of democratic policy. Hence, although the polity cannot be fully responsible for actual uses of the weapons, it can be partly responsible insofar as it accedes to arrangments that make their use possible.

Causal relations in which multiple agents bring about a particular outcome are notoriously difficult to analyze. If the agents are similar, we might suppose that we can merely divide responsibility for the outcome of their action or existence equally among them. For various relatively transparent reasons, this is not a sensible resolution of our problem in many contexts. There are three broad classes of causal relations in collective action problems that complicate the arithmetic of assigning collective responsibility back to relevant individuals:

1. A's action may be necessary but not sufficient to bring about a particular result, x.
2. A's action may be sufficient but not necessary to bring about x.
3. A's action may be necessary but not sufficient to bring about y when y is sufficient but not necessary to bring about x.

Suppose that what is necessary and sufficient to bring about x in every case is action by enough members of our group, although in cases 2 and 3 no one individual's action may be necessary. Note that cases 1 and 2 are complementary in the following sense. A's *action* is necessary but not sufficient to bring about a particular result, x, while A's *inaction* is sufficient but not necessary to bring about another result, the prevention of x. Hence, A can single-handedly prevent x but cannot single-handedly cause x. But nine other people might also be able single-handedly to prevent x. Suppose all nine join A in not acting and hence in preventing x. It might seem then that each has one-tenth of the responsibility for preventing x. But suppose A chooses not to act simply because she is aware that the other nine are not acting. Given that x would be prevented irrespective of whether she acts, does she by not acting bear any responsibility at all for preventing x? The prevention of x has multiple causes; bringing it about requires a complex set of causes. Whenever my action is sufficient but not necessary the assignment of responsibility to me is oddly asymmetric. If I do act, I alone may be responsible for the end produced. Yet, if I do not act, I may not be responsible for failure to bring about the end since someone else may act to bring it about. My action may make me culpable when my inaction would not, or vice versa.

Results that depend on multiple causes in the form of action or inaction by many people pose a problem that is the moral analog of the logic of collective action. In the logic of collective action it is not in the rational self-interest of any individual in a group to contribute to a collective good that, if it is provided, will benefit all members of the group. If bringing about a good result, x, requires action by a number of people too few of whom are going to act for my action to effectuate x, then I have no moral reason to act in the relevant way. Suppose it is reasonable to assume that no action I could undertake would effectuate x. Then I cannot be morally responsible for the failure of x to happen. But this may be true of *every* member of a particular group. The failure of all of us brings about the failure of x although no individual failure matters for the bringing about of x. The group is responsible for the failure of x but no member of the group is responsible. Yet if everybody else acted while I did not, I alone would be responsible for the failure of x.

To speak loosely for a moment, individual responsibilities do not necessarily sum to equal the collective responsibility. In a case in which ten necessary contributors to some collective outcome all fail to contribute such that no one person's action would make any difference, the sum of individual responsibilities may be said to be zero while the collective responsibility is substantial. For example, if none of the other people who must act if we are jointly to push a car out of the snow will participate, I cannot be held responsible for not contributing my share to pushing it. If many individuals can act with sufficiency, so that no one person's action is necessary, and all fail to act, we may say that each is fully responsible for the collective result so that the individual responsibilities sum to far more than the collective responsibility. For example, it is widely supposed that any one of thirty-eight people who reputedly watched Kitty Genovese's long drawn-out murder could have called the police to prevent it. Hence each of the thirty-eight is fully responsible for failure to make the single telephone call.

There is one further complication that should be mentioned. If each can contribute a clear share to a collective result independently of whether anyone else contributes, the individual responsibilities may sum to the collective responsibility. Let us say that my contribution to a disaster relief may help one family among the many who are suffering independently of whether anyone else contributes to the relief. The sum of all individual contributions may then be just the amount of relief provided. In such cases, one person's action is likely to be sufficient but not necessary. The difference between this kind of case and those under 1, 2, and 3 above is that in this kind of case we can break x down into component parts. The possibility of resolving an issue into parts can arise for all three kinds of case above. Political actions and policies by collectives often cannot be resolved into parts. They are often inherently lumpy in quality, at least to some extent: we either accomplish a general end or we do not.

On the account here, the assignment of responsibility or culpability to a particular individual may depend on what actions other individuals have taken. Hence, actions are not intrinsically evaluable (see §15). This recalls a fundamental problem in value theory: the value of something may depend on what else there is. Values can be subject to complementarity, so that x and y together may be worth more or less than the sum of each taken by itself. And they can be subject to substituion, so that x may be of no value if we already have y but of great value if we do not have y (see §33). This problem in the theory of value has its analog in causal explanations. The general problem of multiple and complex causation that afflicts explanatory theories in the social, biological, and physical sciences has been elegantly resolved in one discipline for one general problem. The problem is how to attribute to each input in production its "value" or its causal role. Economists resolved this problem by finally ignoring it and inventing price theory, under which each input has a price determined by relations of supply and demand. Inputs do not have intrinsic values, they have only contingent prices.

The assignment of joint responsibility to individuals has much of the character of the problem of evaluating inputs to production in that each individual's responsibility may depend on what others have done. But there does not appear to be an appealing analog of price theory for allocating causal responsibility. If my responsibility for producing a particular result depends in part on what others have done, moral judgment of my action or inaction may turn not on whether the result is produced but on the "fairness" of my action or inaction in the light of what others do. In failing to share in a collective burden I may not prevent the collective provision of some good but I may benefit from my inaction to the detriment of those who pick up my slack. Hence, the focus of responsibility may shift from the collectively provided good to the collective task of its provision, from a concern with, say, warfare or famine relief to a concern with fairness to my fellow providers.[46]

One way for us to overcome collective inaction when our action is jointly required for us to achieve a desired collective result is to vote to compel each of us to act. If this device is to work we must, of course, have available institutions to coerce us all to act in relevant ways once we have voted. There are at least two clear obstacles to such a resolution of our collective action problems even when we do have apparently relevant institutions available. First, there is the problem, noted by Anthony Downs,[47] that the electorate would not rationally invest to inform themselves well enough to choose policies directly. This tendency to rational ignorance recommends that we be represented to some extent by Burkean representatives. Second, for any reasonably complex policy that requires complicated organization for its implementation, we cannot expect implementing institutions to do as ordered by, for example, legislation even if the legislation seems quite clear in its mandate. To turn decisions on our behalf over to an institution is implicitly to yield a great deal of discretion over the decisions to the institution.

There is, however, one sense in which the delegation of responsibil-

46. This may explain the well-known phenomenon that large groups do not tip as much per capita as individuals and small groups do when eating in restaurants. It may be that tipping tends toward the lowest common denominator out of a notion of fairness internal to the group: I will not tip for you but will do only my share. If you are a cheapskate, I will tip less than I might otherwise have done.

47. Anthony Downs, *An Economic Theory of Democracy* (New York: Harper and Brothers, 1957).

ity to an institution can resolve the problem of assigning collective responsibility to relevant individuals. As a rule, when we have created institutions to accomplish collective purposes then it may not be hard to argue that someone is responsible individually for misdirected actions of the institutions.

§32 Welfare, Incentives, and Policies

One way to see the import of a utilitarian analysis for standard policy-making is to consider how it makes sense of certain conservative dogmas while still plausibly commending strong welfare policies. It would be surprising if it did not make some sense of both these because both the welfarist and the conservative traditions are preeminently concerned with human welfare. Their different prescriptions turn on differing social scientific beliefs about human psychology, social causation, and the nature of the value of human welfare rather than on different normative concerns.

There are conservative traditions that are grounded in authoritarian, religious, or elitist views. I will not attempt to make utilitarian sense of these. Rather, I will be concerned with the conservative tradition that typically finds its grounding in the views of Adam Smith and the Scottish Enlightenment. Despite great variation in their views, contemporary exponents of this conservatism include James M. Buchanan, F. A. Hayek, and members of the so-called Chicago School of economic theory. Despite affinities with libertarianism, this contemporary conservatism is less concerned with violations of supposed individual rights than with what its exponents consider to be paternalistic interventions into the economy for general purposes of improving some group's welfare.[48]

Central concerns of Smith and, especially, of Hayek among Smith's latter-day followers are the complexity of social relations with their unintended consequences and the wide dispersal of knowledge that cannot be centralized but that determines social outcomes. That is to say, their explanations turn on what they conceive to be substantial limits of human reason. Hence, they oppose rationalist interventions to

48. Political labels are notoriously defective in many ways. Names of actual people may serve us better than names of supposed movements or positions. An important characteristic of Smithian conservatives is that, unlike libertarians, they readily face certain apparently incorrigible facts. In particular, they are centrally motivated by the realization that states will arise and grow in power and that organized states will tend to dominate disorganized societies. Hence, they are concerned with how to live within states and to make them work well by their lights rather than with how to design utopias that might flourish without states.

remake society on the ground that no one can know or control enough to achieve predictable outcomes. Social progress comes not by plan but by unpredictable, often unnoticed, slow evolution as superior institutions and practices replace inferior ones. It does so, Hayek explicitly supposes, because individuals, like entrepreneurs in a market, have incentive to innovate and because others, like consumers in a market, have incentive to follow up beneficial innovations. No one must decide to shut down feudal estates and create industrial cities. It will simply happen through millions of individual choices not at all motivated by any general conception of how to organize society. The proper role of the state in the process is to create general institutions, procedures, and rules that will facilitate mutually beneficial interaction, not to prescribe specific outcomes.

The focus on "unintended consequences" is a focus on dynamic relationships rather than merely on static relationships. It highlights the strategic implications of actions, the secondary effects, rather than merely the intended first-order effects. Social intervention often turns perverse because it has impact at levels others than that at which it is directed. For example, one subsidizes the income of farmers only to find that they then have a strong but perverse incentive to keep their children on the land. The subsidy may have been intended to increase the welfare of farmers during a period of transition from overpopulated to efficiently populated farms, but its longer term effect is to slow the transition and to reduce the welfare of farmers' children. To follow this route to improving the welfare of farmers is to keep the problem acute and unresolved rather than to resolve it.

There is a somewhat Panglossian quality to this conservative view of society. Clearly, there is a great deal that is compelling in it.[49] But many wrong inferences are drawn from it in actual policy debates. The general inference to be drawn is that policies should be designed more to enhance incentives for productivity than to ensure or fix particular outcomes. Because, according to the psychology of contemporary Smithians, people will generally seek their own benefit, we should intervene in social relations only in ways that do not discourage them from doing so. Policies that encourage dependence on the state discourage initiative to be productive.

In much of conservative writing, the object of criticism is not welfare programs for individuals or families but policies that encourage sloth in particular industries. Companies that are given artificial monopolies by the state, for example, are likely to be less productive and

---

49. So much, indeed, that the view is shared by Mill. See n. 30 above.

less innovative than those that are forced to meet competition. Are welfare policies for individuals similarly objectionable? I think not, although some of the Smithian view may well apply even to such policies if the Smithian psychology is sufficiently important in human motivations. At the very least, we may conclude, in some variant of Rawls's Difference Principle, that equality should not go so far as to reduce production enough to make the worst-off class worse off than they would be with less equality. We may readily suppose that thoroughgoing equality achieved through radical redistribution could actually harm the worst-off class but that, with only moderately stiff progressive taxation, the condition of the worst-off class could be substantially improved far short of eliminating inequality.

This is not the place to take up this issue fully. Rather, I merely wish to illustrate how conservatives take the general complaint against state interventions to achieve specific outcomes too far in their criticisms of certain welfare programs. It is a standard argument among American economists that any state provision of goods as opposed to money is Pareto inefficient. By this they mean that some people receiving the goods might sooner have an amount of money less than the actual cost to the state of the goods. Therefore, both the welfare recipients and the state could be made better off if the state gave money instead of goods.

This, however, is a static analysis and as such it leaves out of account the strategic implications of transfers of cash versus transfers of goods. If it is not possible to set up a black market for the conversion of government-provided goods into cash, then the provision of goods will have limited effect on normal market incentives to work in order to buy other, different goods. If the government-provided goods can be converted into cash, of course, they can have powerful disincentive effects, just as straight cash transfers can. Certain goods and services can be provided by government without fear that they will be exchanged on a market. Among the most important are education and health care. These, of course, are delivered to the individual and cannot generally be passed on.

In other words, cash transfer payments are an ideal substitute for earned income to the same level. In-kind transfers involving easily marketed goods are nearly as good substitutes for earned income. Transfers of goods or services that cannot be remarketed, however, are poor substitutes for more generally useful earned income. They may therefore imply far less substantial incentive effects than do transfers of cash and marketable goods. If we wish to avoid interventions that adversely affect individual incentives, we should not readily assent to the claims for the superiority of cash transfers over provision of goods or services. Of course, in-kind transfers may be defended against cash transfers on paternalistic and even insulting grounds.[50] But there need be no paternalistic motivations in a justification of them: depending on relevant psychologies and the possibility of at least some interpersonal comparison of welfare, in-kind transfers of nonremarketable goods and services are likely to be straightforwardly utilitarian. They reduce over-all incentives to work but they leave in place at least some of the incentive to earn funds for buying goods and services other than those that are transferred.[51]

To see the apparently more dismal side of utilitarian policy analysis, consider the problem of agriculture in developing nations. This is a problem about which we know very much in the sense that we have seen several major twentieth-century efforts at intervention to affect agricultural production or to enhance the welfare of the rural popula-tion. The outlines of the problem are familiar: the rural population is large and relatively poor; many farmers are subsistence farmers who have no dealings on the market—they have no goods to sell and there-fore they can buy nothing; the whole agricultural sector is unproduc-tive in the sense that it does not adequately supply the food needs or demands of the population; and production is highly inefficient in the sense that output is small relative to gross labor and land inputs.

Hence, there are several reasons to want to intervene, reasons that may recommend different kinds of interventions. Probably the three most important reasons are to affect (1) the level of production, (2) the efficiency of production, and (3) the welfare of the agricultural popula-tion. One can affect the level of production and welfare with subsidies to farmers, but these will almost surely undermine any effort to affect efficiency. Worse, subsidies are a short-term device in the sense that to affect the level of production and the welfare of farmers in the long run

50. Pigou thinks that to suppose the state is a better judge of the needs of recipients of welfare than are those recipients themselves would be "to utter a gross libel" (Arthur C. Pigou, *The Economics of Welfare*, 4th ed. [London: Macmillan, 1932; first published 1920], p. 754).

51. This view is advocated by Pigou (ibid., part 4, chap. 9). The force of the view can be seen from a quick graph of one's indifference curve between, say, housing and all else. If the level of (nonremarketable) housing available for nothing is raised above none, the entire indifference curve for a given income must be displaced upwards from the subsi-dized level of housing. One would still trade some of everything else for additional or better housing at high enough exchange rates. The given income will now buy more of everything else per unit of housing so that one would presumably choose to buy more leisure, hence to earn less income. But the trade-off between leisure and all else but housing down to the subsidized level will not be as great as the trade-off between leisure and all else. This concern with incentive effects of transfers is clearly different from paternalist concern to transfer what is "better" for the recipient than what the recipient would buy if given cash instead of goods or services.

is likely to require the long-run continuation of subsidies. On the other hand, programs that improve efficiency in the long run may also positively affect output and welfare.

What would long-run efficiency imply? In an affluent society, a very small part of income goes for food; hence, farmers can receive only a small part of total national income, well under 10 percent. If it is to be well off, therefore, the agricultural work force must be small: in many affluent societies it is now considerably less than 5 percent of the total work force. Although one cannot say that a small agricultural work force implies efficiency of production, one can say that a large work force in the long run must imply inefficiency or relative poverty for farmers. Any government intervention that encourages people to stay on their farms is likely to encourage long-run inefficiency. Virtually any effective subsidy program will encourage people to stay on their farms and therefore will have perverse—and likely unintended—consequences. Developing rural schools or other programs that will equip and encourage the young to leave the land may have a more profound and lasting effect on agricultural efficiency and output and on farmer welfare than any equally costly program of more direct intervention in agriculture.

The grim side of this understanding is that land reform, probably the most popular of all revolutionary changes in backward societies, may be detrimental to the long-run welfare of rural populations. It risks merely securing subsistence status for the bulk of a nation's population. The commitment to being on the land that makes former peasants want land reform is a forlorn commitment. Although it may make life better for the first-generation small-farm holder, it is a preference that makes little or no sense for the interests of at least future generations. People must eventually be demoralized into leaving the land or enticed to have other preferences. Land reform and farm subsidies may give too many hope where there can be no hope for many.

Consider for a moment the case of Soviet agricultural policies. The Soviet Union is often criticized in the West for intervening too heavily on the brutal side of driving rural populations off the land and into factories, for not improving enough the lot of farm populations. The criticism may be largely backward. The agricultural population has declined less rapidly in the Soviet Union since the Bolshevik revolution than in many Western nations that have intervened very little in agriculture at similar states of development. Indeed, labor-saving mechanization was introduced relatively early in the Soviet Union. Former peasants were plausibly given more incentive to stay on the land than they would have had without the state interventions. Further-more, the state bloodied itself in its interventions by earning partial responsibility for the suffering that seems to be implicit in the low per capita income of farm workers. But if half a nation's work force is in agriculture, their incomes must be low because the value of their prod-uct is pathetically low.

5

Utilitarian Value Theory

As noted earlier, utilitarianism has two major elements: the commitment to consequentialism in some form of human welfare, and a value theory of human welfare. One can object to either or both of these elements. Much of the criticism of utilitarianism in recent times has focused on its consequentialism, often on claims that it has perverse consequences. Indeed, one of the most common forms of criticism is the often overtly silly complaint that seeking to produce good consequences is bound to produce bad consequences. Criticisms of this form generally do not stand scrutiny. Often, the criticisms are founded on unrealistic assumptions of the nature of the information or theory available to actors, often on gross misapprehensions of the nature of strategic interactions that confound simplistic views of individual agency and of the role of institutional arrangements for bringing about good results. These are the issues of the foregoing chapters.

Absent better arguments, utilitarian moral theory cannot be rejected simply on claims that, in its consequentialism, it is inconsistent or illogical. Alas, establishing this point is insufficient to make utilitarianism workable. Even if we can predict outcomes confidently, despite strategic interactions and limits to knowledge and theory, we still often face a grievous limit to our ability to judge the rightness of actions: the difficulty of assessing the values of the outcomes to those affected, including ourselves. Once our understanding of consequentialist reasoning is clear, we still want a credible, consistent value theory. This is by far the most difficult demand of utilitarianism—as it is of any serious moral theory. It is so difficult that I have no plan to try to meet it fully or even in broad outline here. Rather I wish to take up a range of issues that stand in the way of a good value theory based in human welfare. Full treatment of any of these issues would require a book, and some of them have been given strong book treatment.

If we are to develop a good value theory based in human welfare, we must be concerned with the more or less logical structure and interrelationship of welfare values (§33). Because the concern is with human welfare, we will necessarily be concerned with aggregation across individuals and even within individuals and, hence, with the nature of the person and personal commitments (§35). We will also be concerned with the sources of welfare or preferences or pleasures and, hence, with the extent to which autonomy may be overridden by social construction of individual values (§36) and the nature of our knowledge of our values (§34). After surveying these issues of the limits of welfare theory, I will conclude by relating them to the preceding discussions of utilitarianism (§37).

All of these concerns mingle our fundamental normative concern with social scientific understanding. Because this is inherently true of the subject, it should not be surprising that value theory is constantly subject to revision and improvement as social scientific understandings of psychology and social interactions advance. Richard Brandt's *A Theory of the Good and the Right,*[1] with its psychological understandings, could not have been written until relatively recently and yet it is clearly coherent with the long tradition of utilitarianism. Bentham's early efforts at explicating a consequentialist value theory based on human welfare[2] seem jejune by comparison to Brandt's or by comparison to twentieth-century economic utility theory. Similarly, Derek Parfit's *Reasons and Persons*[3] advances our understanding of the nature of the individual that, if we find his insights compelling, necessarily must affect our value theory.

My purpose here will not be to expound the ideas of Brandt, Parfit, twentieth-century economists, and other contributors to value theory, but rather to lay out a range of issues that we must address if we are concerned to enhance human welfare. Because our understanding of these problems is subject to advance from changes in social scientific understanding as well as merely from more solidly reasoned argument, we should not expect to see them finally resolved. Current understand-

---

1. Richard Brandt, *A Theory of the Good and the Right* (Oxford: Clarendon Press, 1979).

2. Jeremy Bentham, *An Introduction to the Principles of Morals and Legislation,* ed. by J. H. Burns and H. L. A. Hart (London: Athlone Press, 1970), esp. chaps. 4 ("Value of a Lot of Pleasure or Pain, How to Be Measured") and 5 ("Pleasures and Pains, Their Kinds").

3. Derek Parfit, *Reasons and Persons* (Oxford: Clarendon Press, 1984). See further, the symposium on Parfit's book, *Ethics* 96 (July 1986): 703–872, ed. Brian Barry.

ings of these problems cannot provide conclusive evidence against our developing a good value theory. Pending changes in our understanding of these problems, knock-down refutations of utilitarianism that turn on any particular theory of human welfare are not compelling. On the other hand, even a bit of understanding of the nature of the structure of the value theory that must underlie a notion of human welfare can clarify many supposed difficulties in utilitarianism.

Here we face one of the oddities of normative theory more generally. We commonly assert with Hume, and rightly so, that values are not objective (T3.1.1, pp. 467–470). Yet, our understanding of any particular notion of value and its content may well turn on objective facts. Any notion of human welfare, for example, depends on objective understandings of the nature of humans and their pleasures and pains. Any notion of virtue may depend similarly on understandings of the functional relationship between particular candidate virtues and human well-being or flourishing. Only a purely rationalist, deductive notion of value or one that is authoritatively given not to be questioned can be well understood without consideration of numerous social scientific, perhaps especially psychological, facts. Whether human welfare is a value to be sought is not subject to objective answer. What its content must be, however, is in large part an objective matter.

Much of what has gone before in this book has concerned the substantive content of utilitarianism, as in the discussions of rights (Chap. 3) and institutional arrangements more generally (Chap. 4). Clearly, the substantive content of any consequentialist moral theory turns on its value theory. If the latter changes, the former may also change. For example, as noted especially in the discussion of distributive justice (§27), Rawls's theory of justice depends very heavily on his value theory, so much so that the utilitarians whose views he claims to reject must accept his theory of justice if they share his theory of value or of human welfare. The chief difference between Bentham's utilitarianism and any credible utilitarianism today is that no theory today can plausibly be based on additive, interpersonally comparable, cardinal utility without radical revision of the best present understanding of such a utility theory.

§33 Utility Theory

The most articulated and sophisticated effort to deal with the theory of human welfare and even of value theory in general has been the development of utility theory in economics from roughly the time of

Bentham to the present. Any effort to understand human welfare should take account of the issues in that utility theory—or perhaps one should speak of many utility theories. There are three very general and fundamental issues that I wish to discuss here: these are what we may call the interpersonal comparability, the scale, and the scope of utility measures. These issues turn on, respectively, the differences between interpersonally noncomparable and interpersonally comparable utility or welfare, ordinal and cardinal utility, and marginal and holistic utility assessments. The first two of these have come up frequently in earlier chapters, and the last will be of interest below in the discussion of personal identity (§35). After first dealing with two conceptual matters, on which there should be no disagreement,[4] I will turn to these three issues, on which there is great and ongoing disagreement.

A common misperception is that utility is inherent in objects or states of affairs, that it is somehow objective. While there are obviously objective correlates of most claims for utility, utility is a coherent notion only at a subjective level. It is utility to you or to me that interests us. The adze that was wonderfully utilitarian to one of our ancestors may be of no direct, usable interest to us. If it has utility to us, it is as a collector's item that has a market value or that somehow sparks our curious interest as it hangs permanently on the wall, unused, giving us pleasure or instruction merely by its visible presence.

One way to make this understanding undeniably clear is to show the changing relationship of value to use in various contexts, either over time or in relation to contingent facts. The example of the adze above fits both of these. But consider a starker example. The island of Manhattan was sold by the Manahatta Indians to the first European settlers there for a collection of baubles. The building in which the Tiffany and Company jewelry store on Fifth Avenue is housed occupies a tiny fraction of Manhattan. Part of the "unexpended air rights" over that building was sold for $5 million in 1979 to Donald Trump for his Trump Tower. Trump acquired an option to purchase the building itself, including the land on which it stands, at an additional $1.2 mil-

---

4. At a very fundamental level, of course, there is horrendous disagreement. Kant asserts that "everything empirical is not only quite unsuitable as a contribution to the principle of morality, but is even highly detrimental to the purity of morals. For the proper and inestimable worth of an absolutely good will consists precisely in the fact that the principle of action is free of all influences from contingent grounds, which only experience can furnish" (Immanuel Kant, *Grounding for the Metaphysics of Morals,* in Kant, *Ethical Philosophy,* trans. James W. Ellington [Indianapolis: Hackett, 1983; originally published in German in 1785], p. 34; Akademie ed., p. 426). Hence, on this account utility theory is no part of Kantian moral theory—and one may wonder about human welfare.

lion.[5] The value of the land on which Tiffany's stands today has no doubt been affected by the general shortage of land in such a location in a society of greatly increased population and wealth. Demand and supply relationships change drastically not only over the centuries but even over a few years. In the light of such experiences, one cannot sensibly suppose that value is strictly inherent in particular objects. Rather, it is a contingent function of the uses that can be made of them and of the demand of people for those uses.

A more perverse problem with the notion of utility is that the utility of any object can vary enormously for a given individual as a function of the availability of other objects. As late as 1869 the great English economist W. Stanley Jevons proposed, as an advance in understanding, that we write the utility function of an individual as the sum of the utilities of all objects the individual consumes. This way of viewing utility was shared by other great late nineteenth-century economists, such as Léon Walras and perhaps Alfred Marshall.[6] With F. Y. Edgeworth's formal recognition, in *Mathematical Psychics*,[7] that our valuations of goods interact, this simplistic view formally lost its credit, although informally it may still prevail in many circles. The view is incoherent because valuations interact in two ways: goods can be substitutes or complements. To take a trivial example, the value of a car to me is a function both of whether there are available substitutes in public transportation for getting where I want to go and of what complementary goods, such as roads, fuel, and services, are available. (As will be noted below, the problems of substitutability and complementarity play a significant role in the understanding of ordinal utility.)

With this brief background let us turn to the three major issues of comparability, scale, and scope. The first distinction that affects the power of utilitarian prescriptions is whether we can compare the welfares of different individuals. If we cannot, we are severely restricted in the range of choice situations we can resolve even partially on utilitarian moral grounds. The significance of interpersonal comparability should have been suggested by various discussions of substantive moral issues

5. *New York Times,* February 7, 1979, p. B.3.
6. Paul Anthony Samuelson, *Foundations of Economic Analysis* (Cambridge, Mass.: Harvard University Press, 1947), p. 93.
7. F. Y. Edgeworth, *Mathematical Psychics: An Essay on the Application of Mathematics to the Moral Sciences* (London: C. Kegan Paul, 1881), esp. pp. 104–110. Pareto speaks tolerantly of those who made the wrong but simpler assumption: "We cannot blame them, because, briefly, questions must be resolved one after the other, and it is always better not to hurry" (Vilfredo Pareto, *Manual of Political Economy* [New York: Kelley, 1971; translation of 1927 French ed.], chap. 4, sec. 11, pp. 183–184).

in earlier chapters. Without it, pure conflict interactions and the conflictual aspects of mixed-motive interactions are outside our purview. Utilitarianism reduces to a recommendation to coordinate when coordination is mutually beneficial. More generally, utilitarianism can do no more than recommend ranking any outcome over all those to which it is Pareto superior.

This is a more devastating conclusion than it may at first appear to be. Reduction of our criterion to the Pareto criterion may mean it usually gives us *no* advice. We may have no criterion for choosing among the many Pareto superior future states to which we could move because a choice between these would involve conflict: if we are choosing between future states A and B, you may be better off in, say, A than in B, and I may be better off in B than in A. There might be specific static comparisons for which there is one alternative state that is superior to all others under consideration.[8] But if we take the long view and consider a further range of future states we might move to, we cannot expect to find any one state that is uniquely superior to all other possibilities. Hence, in our world, a utilitarianism with no interpersonal comparisons would be empty unless, because of limits to information, theory, and time, we can suppose many choices are virtually decoupled from the longer run future.

The second distinction is how strong any comparisons we can make are. If they are merely ordinal, we are more restricted than if they are cardinal. (This does not exhaust the realm of possibilities, of course, because we can make variously refined comparisons from fully additive to purely ordinal, but let us focus on the extremes.) As already noted, if comparisons are merely ordinal, they will often be very hard to aggregate. This is not to say that we will never be able to make aggregate prescriptions of the form that group p should act on behalf of group q. But such prescriptions will have to be based on one-on-one comparisons, which will often be indecisive in the sense that they can recommend neither action by p for q nor action by q for p. If we had a highly refined interpersonally comparative cardinal measure and we faced no obstacles of limits to information and so forth, we could generally add up benefits and costs, as Bentham and many other utilitarians and critics suppose we can, to each group, compare the sums, and recommend specific action.

There are fundamental difficulties with both ordinal and cardinal utility theories even as applied strictly to a single individual without any

---

8. See further, Russell Hardin, "Difficulties in the Notion of Economic Rationality," *Social Science Information* 23 (1984): 453–467, esp. pp. 454–459.

concern for comparison between individuals. Given that various other goods or services or whatever opportunities may be complementary to or substitutable with some of the things in two states of affairs we are ordinally comparing, we must implicitly make such a comparison ceteris paribus. But this means that ordinal comparisons are implicitly of whole states of affairs fully determined. Intellectually, this is a severe demand.[9] If we suppose we suffer from ordinary limits of reason, then surely we cannot sensibly suppose we generally or ever base our choices on comparisons of whole states of affairs. But any cardinal utility theory should be reducible to an ordinal theory; hence, any cardinal theory has the same problem of intellectual unrealism in addition to its own severe problems in assuming that anyone could meaningfully store or generate the fine evaluations implied by a cardinal weighting of all states of affairs.[10]

A cardinal theory has a further difficulty that is of special consequence if we suppose welfare to be additive across individuals. To suppose that we have a complete, continuous cardinal ordering over all possible states of affairs is to suppose that statements such as the following are meaningful and credible:

> The welfare difference between a state of poverty, A, in which you have nothing but a single small bowl of beans each day and that state, B, in which you have two bowls each day is equivalent to the welfare difference between a state of general wealth, P, in which you have a mansion and manifold other goods and that state, Q, in which you have all of this plus, say, a diamond bracelet; and furthermore that the welfare difference between states A and P is equivalent to that between states B and Q.[11]

9. Proust remarks that "the absence of one part from a whole is not only that, it is not simply a partial omission, it is a disturbance of all the other parts, a new state which it was impossible to foresee from the old" (Marcel Proust, *Remembrance of Things Past* [New York: Random House, 1934], 1:234). William James makes the same point. Our issue is, he says, "not a question of this good or that good simply taken, but of the two total universes with which these goods respectively belong" (James, "The Moral Philosopher and the Moral Life," pp. 184–215 in James, *The Will to Believe and Other Essays on Popular Philosophy* [New York: Longmans, Green, 1897; essay first published 1891], pp. 209–210).

10. For further discussion of these and related difficulties in contemporary ordinal and cardinal utility theories, see Russell Hardin, "Rational Choice Theories," pp. 67–91 in Terence Ball, ed., *Idioms of Inquiry: Critique and Renewal in Political Science* (Albany, N.Y.: SUNY Press, 1987).

11. This is essentially Martin Shubik's "crossover property" (Shubik, *Game Theory in the Social Sciences: Concepts and Solutions* [Cambridge, Mass.: MIT Press, 1982], p. 421). Compare Pareto's hostile view of the assumptions of this property. He says that "if we were to ask a peasant woman who has never had any diamonds, 'if you were a millionaire, how many diamonds would you buy at such and such a given price?', we would get a reply made at random and without any value" (Pareto, *Manual of Political Economy*, chap. 4, sec. 26, p. 188).

It is not belligerence to the enterprise of choice theory that makes me think I do not know what this massive claim means. Indeed, the difficulty of crediting this claim with serious meaning is similar to the difficulty that moves Rawls to adopt his seemingly peculiar value theory. How can comparison of welfares of individuals in different states vaguely like those at P and Q on the one hand and like those at A and B on the other plausibly commend taking away the extra bowl of beans from those in an impoverished group in order to give those in a wealthy group the extra bauble?

The final distinction that governs the power of utilitarianism is that our comparisons can be of quite different kinds: those that involve whole reckonings of the well-being of various individuals and those that involve only reckonings of the effects of certain changes on them. Let us label these reckonings "holistic" and "marginal," respectively. In general, it would be odd to have a theory of distributive justice that focused only on marginal comparisons, that ignored the larger background of overall welfare, or the larger range of resources and consumptions of the parties involved. This is the essential shortcoming of viewing the problem of social or distributive justice as merely a problem in fair division in the technical sense of the large bargaining literature on problems of fair division.[12] Distributive justice will not be achieved if we ignore my wealth and your extreme poverty as we now decide on how to divide the increment of income to us from a sudden small windfall.

Concern for egalitarianism and distributive justice tends to be associated with concern with holistic welfare and the nature of the status quo. Procedural theories of justice tend to start from the status quo somehow defined and to address only marginal changes in welfare and how these are achieved. A utilitarian who has a relevant value theory would have to be concerned with holistic welfare. To some extent, the scope of our value theory will depend on our understanding of personal identity, as discussed below (§35). If lives are not well connected over time, the range of holistic welfare theories will be reduced. The scope will also turn on what we conceive to be the nature of welfare. For example, if welfare is merely the sum of momentary pleasures over one's life, as in Edgeworth's view,[13] the notion of holistic welfare loses its force.

Let us back up for a moment to survey these issues in welfare theory. In schematic terms, welfare can be conceived as interpersonally com-

12. See further, Brian Barry, *Theories of Social Justice* (Berkeley: University of California Press, forthcoming), esp. early chaps.
13. Edgeworth, *Mathematical Psychics*, passim, for example, p. 8.

parable or not comparable, as ordinal or cardinal, and as holistic or marginal. In principle, none of these dimensions depends on either of the others, so that we have eight possibilities, ranging in power or completeness from holistic, interpersonally comparable, cardinal welfare to marginal, interpersonally noncomparable, ordinal welfare.[14] If we are restricted to the latter, which is the weakest of the possibilities in this range, utilitarianism has very little scope: it essentially recommends that we make any available unique Pareto improvements in the status quo. When, as will typically be true, there are mutually exclusive changes that would be Pareto improvements, it makes no compelling recommendation about which of these to attempt. In political theory, such a welfare theory can recommend little more than the nature of institutions we should have for making marginal changes in the status quo.

If we have a slightly stronger theory that is holistic, interpersonally noncomparable, and ordinal, we may be able to go slightly further to say something about the superiority of different whole arrangements of our society over others. If we have the strongest of welfare theories here, we may be able in principle to go very far and to decide all organizational and distributive issues. For example, if we have a theory and measure of interpersonally additive welfare and all of us are utilitarian, then, as Donald Regan argues, all interactions would be effectively reduced to coordination interactions: we merely represent each outcome as the sum of its values to all of us and coordinate on selecting that outcome with the highest sum of values.[15] To the extent we do not have such a value theory and to the extent we cannot all know enough about the welfares of all others involved, we cannot reduce all

14. It might seem that whether welfare can be represented as cardinal for each individual separately is of no concern for social and moral choice unless the measures can then be compared across individuals. (For example, see Amartya Sen, "Informational Bases of Alternative Welfare Approaches: Aggregation and Income Distribution," *Journal of Public Economics* 3 [1974]: 387–403, esp. pp. 390–392.) In practice this is not strictly correct. Suppose my ranking of several mutually exclusive outcomes is $x > y > z$ and yours is $z > y > x$. Further, suppose in our cardinal measures the difference between x and y for me is trivially small while that between y and z is very large, and the difference between z and y for you is trivially small while that between y and x is very large. In this case, even if we are narrowly self-interested and not at all utilitarian in our motivations, we might readily agree that the way to treat our interaction is as though it is a coordination game in which the mutually best outcome is y. Neither of us would sensibly suppose it worthwhile to invest any significant effort in obtaining our slightly more preferred outcomes x and z, respectively. Hence, the addition of cardinal information that is not interpersonally comparable to the ordinal rankings helps us resolve our interaction to mutual benefit. See further, n. 11 above, Pareto's discussion of the poor woman and diamonds.

15. Donald H. Regan, *Utilitarianism and Co-operation* (Oxford: Charendon Press, 1980).

our interactions to easily resolved coordination interactions, although some of them may happen to be such interactions. If we had the most powerful of these welfare theories, if we faced no information constraints, and if we were all utilitarian, then the strategic distinctions drawn out in Chapter 2 would be of no interest; we could simply treat all choices as one big choice over the best of all states of affairs and then coordinate on achieving that best state or one of the equally best states. Moral theory is interesting and difficult because none of these conditions is met. Yet it is of greater scope and greater interest than it would be if we had only the weakest of welfare theories.

For most of social life, these are crucial constraints: we often do not have an adequate value theory, and we generally do not have adequate knowledge to make it obvious what is the utilitarian thing to do. Indeed, in far too many contexts, it seems that the best utilitarian advice can be little more than to say that many very different kinds of actions, perhaps benefiting many different parties, are acceptable. This does not mean that we are in principle indifferent between the outcomes of these various actions but that we are in fact ignorant of how to rank them on a utilitarian scale, perhaps fundamentally ignorant. The power of our utilitarianism depends heavily in principle on the power of our welfare theory—and, of course, on the extent to which we can overcome limits of reason in assessing facts and causal relations.

To make full holistic cardinal comparisons, we require a unique cardinal welfare scale that has the same zero point and the same unit interval for all persons. To make marginal cardinal comparisons, we require a cardinal welfare scale that has the same unit interval for all persons. The inherent difficulties of such notions, as discussed above, suggest that our cardinalism cannot go so far as this even though it seems wrong to suppose, with Pareto[16] and many other economists, that we can make no comparisons at all.

Many of the advances or innovations in utility theory have been motivated by demands of convenience or theoretical simplification. For example, the analysis of risk proceeds easily if we assume that individuals have cardinal utility functions. The reduction of individual utility theory to strictly ordinal rankings is appealing because the analysis of market equilibrium requires nothing more than this, so that the successive simplification of assumptions in equilibrium theory leads to ordinal utility. Sometimes, the innovations are recommended by their apparent realism, as in Pareto's jettisoning of cardinality and of interpersonal comparisons. Paul Samuelson thinks the convenience that

16. Pareto, *Manual of Political Economy,* chap. 4, sec. 32, p. 192.

motivated the development of Neumann-Morgenstern cardinal utility theory—which was needed for many results in game theory—is an insufficient ground for commending it more generally.[17] Oskar Morgenstern thinks on the contrary that the theory "will surely in the long run completely replace conventional indifference curve analysis."[18] Surely Samuelson is right. Martin Shubik turns concern for convenience into an epistemological argument for cardinal utility. He says that, because a strictly ordinal theory will not suffice, "the need for solutions to bilateral bargaining situations provides a strong . . . argument for cardinal utility."[19] One might sooner conclude that there may simply be no solutions to such problems.

The most we are likely to be able to agree on is a very crudely comparative welfare theory not unlike that adopted by Rawls. We may speak of rough levels of welfare ranging from subsistence or worse to opulence. One could give up a lot of resources in a relatively high level of welfare without radically affecting one's well-being. If those resources were transferred effectively to people in much lower levels of welfare, those people could be substantially affected, could even be lifted into a higher rough level of welfare. Rawls effectively assumes several levels, most of which are below some level of satisfaction of what might be called "basic needs," and one of which is above the level of satisfaction of those needs. Under his Difference Principle he supposes that distributive justice is enhanced when goods or resources are taken from those in the highest of these levels and transferred to those below.

As Samuelson notes, "The concept of utility [in economics] may be said to have been undergoing throughout its entire history a purging of objectionable, and sometimes unnecessary, connotations."[20] The same is true more generally of our understanding of utilitarian value theory. It may also be that to some extent—for example, for the power of its implications—the result of changes in the more general value theory is similar to that of the economic utility theory: "The result has been a much less objectionable doctrine, but also a less interesting one."[21] Shubik notes slyly of the change from complete cardinal to marginal, ordinal utility theory that we have become "not only ordinalists but

17. Paul A. Samuelson, "St. Petersburg Paradoxes: Defanged, Dissected, and Historically Described," *Journal of Economic Literature* 15 (March 1977): 24–55, p. 49.
18. Oskar Morgenstern, "The Collaboration between Oskar Morgenstern and John von Neumann on the Theory of Games," *Journal of Economic Literature* 14 (September 1976): 805–816, p. 814.
19. Shubik, *Game Theory in the Social Sciences: Concepts and Solutions,* p. 103.
20. Samuelson, *Foundations of Economic Analysis,* p. 90.
21. Ibid.

relativists, able to discern better from worse but not good from bad."[22] Again, he thinks this change undercuts our hope of constructing a good choice theory in bargaining contexts. Yet, Kenneth Arrow's effort to found a theory of social choice on strictly ordinal rankings without interpersonal comparisons is in some ways the beginning of modern social choice theory.[23] Indeed, because of its nearly minimalist value theory it has been an important stimulus to the rejoining of moral and political theory.

On a simplistic Benthamite value theory, but for constraints of information, we could have determined what was the single best state or set of best states out of all possible states of affairs. On any sensible contemporary understanding of the possibilities of a theory of welfare, the notion of a best state of affairs is generally a chimera.[24] The continued discussion of utilitarianism as though such a state of affairs were plausibly its goal is an anachronism. A goal of utilitarian theorists must be to make realistic sense of the notion of human welfare and then to derive consequentialist implications from that notion.

§34 Intuitions in Moral Theory

The narrator of Edgar Allan Poe's "The Sphinx" relates his pompous opinion in an argument: "I contending that a popular sentiment arising with absolute spontaneity—that is to say, without apparent traces of suggestion—had in itself the unmistakable elements of truth, and was entitled to much respect."[25] Alas, he was speaking in defense of omens. The moral of the tale is that the narrator misperceives a small moth crawling down a spider's thread in his host's country cottage for a raging monster charging down the hill toward him, a misperception so powerfully felt that he faints and then lives in terror until the truth is shown him by his host. The difference between the nearly certain sensation of fact of Poe's narrator and many similarly nearly certain views of many moral theorists is that the narrator's misperception was of an objective fact. He could be shown the error of his strongly held

22. Shubik, *Game Theory in the Social Sciences: Concepts and Solutions*, p. 122.

23. Kenneth J. Arrow, *Social Choice and Individual Values* (New Haven, Conn.: Yale University Press, 1951; 2d ed. 1963).

24. Pareto notes of a theory that prevailed at one time that "facts subsequently materializing took it upon themselves to refute it." This is roughly the story of our endeavor (Vilfredo Pareto, *The Mind and Society*, vol. 4, trans. Andrew Bongiorno and Arthur Livingston [New York: Harcourt, Brace, 1935], §2316, p. 1667 n. 12).

25. Edgar Allan Poe, "The Sphinx," pp. 65–69 in Poe, *Tales of Mystery and Imagination* (London: Dent, Everyman's Library, 1908), p. 66.

view. Moral theory seems necessarily grounded in intuitions of truths or values that cannot be objectively demonstrated or disproved.

It is commonly argued that this is the major difference between moral theory, or value theories in general, and objective theories in the sciences.[26] The claim is compelling but perhaps not fully apt. The chief difference is not that there are ungrounded assumptions from which flow our deductions of the effectiveness or rightness of actions. Against this view, when we push back the claims that seem to be well grounded in any realm, objective or moral, we find them grounded eventually in claims that are at best intuited, that are merely accepted but not adequately tested or demonstrated. As Wittgenstein says, "At the foundation of well-founded belief lies belief that is not founded."[27] This is as true of our belief that Mont Blanc is roughly 4000 meters tall as that right actions are welfare enhancing. At some point, despite the firmness of my belief that Mont Blanc is roughly that tall, I would be incapable of demonstrating its truth in a fully grounded sequence of factual claims, none of which was based on mere faith or authority. (Of course, I would not even begin to try—I am quite content with the truth of the belief.)

What clearly distinguishes many hard factual claims from virtually all value claims (that are other than functional or indirectly factual assertions) is that almost everyone is content with stopping the quest for final grounding of the factual claims and that those who push furthest in that quest generally agree on the truth or falsity of the initial claims. The chain of reasoning back to prior assumptions or "truths" in moral discourse is generally shorter, and there is remarkable disagreement on conclusions, especially among those who push the quest most assiduously. Apart from religious believers, few people disagree more vehemently about the rightness of various moral views, especially foundationalist views, than do professional moral theorists. There are philosophers who assert essentially that utilitarianism is so far from being a moral theory that it is evil. Others assert that supposedly rationalist groundings of such theories as those of Kant and Alan Gewirth are vacuous, that the Aristotelian concern with virtue is roughly the philosophical equivalent of callously fiddling while Rome burns, that commonsense morality is little more than a collection of prejudices. There is often venom in these assertions and, it seems, surprise or contempt that anyone could hold any but roughly one's own views.

26. Gilbert Harman, *The Nature of Morality: An Introduction to Ethics* (New York: Oxford University Press, 1977), esp. chap. 1.
27. Ludwig Wittgenstein, *On Certainty* (Oxford: Basil Blackwell, 1969), §253.

Despite the profundity of disagreement, remarkably much of the debate in moral theory turns on assertions of what we intuit to be true or right or good. It is when debate stops at intuitions that strong assertions take over. I wish briefly to discuss the role of intuitions in moral theory. It is an important topic not merely because intuitions have played such a large and often silly part in moral theory and debate but more significantly because moral theory cannot proceed at all without some intuition or intuitions. If it is to proceed well, the place of intuitions must be kept self-consciously clear so that we may know what is the nature and source of many of our strongest disagreements.

First, I will discuss in a cursory way the nature of intuitions in general, or of that limited class of intuitions that we may call "pragmatic intuitions," and then I will turn to their role in moral theory. A solid understanding of the nature of pragmatic intuitions in general would depend on substantial progress in our understandings of cognition and of the organization of knowledge in the mind. This is hotly contested terrain and I do not wish to pin discussion on specific theories of the day that are essentially speculative, although real progress can only come through attempts to apply such theories. It is a difficult fact of consequentialist moral theory that it demands far greater intellectual breadth and depth than any one person is apt to be able to master.

That supposedly individual thoughts are more nearly social in origin and content is a claim that applies to pragmatic thinking in general, not merely to moral thinking. Ludwik Fleck's statement of this problem in the sciences is a part of our contemporary understanding (which is itself, no doubt, highly conventional): "Cognition is . . . not an individual process of any theoretical 'particular consciousness.' Rather it is the result of a social activity, since the existing stock of knowledge exceeds the range available to any one individual."[28]

A constructive account of how we build up an actual picture or structure of reality of which we come to be relatively certain would no doubt be long, complex, and difficult. It might even be sufficiently complex not to be transparent so that it would not finally be compelling to most of us. Hence, of a particularly implausible belief, Anscombe writes, "It is easiest to tell what transubstantiation is by saying this: little children should be taught about it as early as possible."[29]

28. Ludwik Fleck, *Genesis and Development of a Scientific Fact* (Chicago: University of Chicago Press, 1979), p. 38.

29. G. E. M. Anscombe, "On Transubstantiation," pp. 107–112 in Anscombe, *Ethics, Religion and Politics* (Minneapolis: University of Minnesota Press, 1981; originally published as a pamphlet by the Catholic Truth Society, London, 1974), p. 107. This

Oddly, however, a destructive account might be relatively easy and perhaps even convincing. By a destructive account I mean an account of how the sense of confidence in some part of one's picture of reality might be shattered and what consequences its shattering might have. Although other examples might serve as well here, consider a plausible account of the intellectual or psychological reaction of grief at the loss of a particularly close associate—a spouse, parent, or child—one with whom one has been so heavily involved as to have defined large parts of one's picture of reality in terms of that person's role in it.

In a quasi-biological account of a kind that has become too easily popularized, Colin Murray Parkes suggests that the tendency to look for the departed may be an evolved trait which survived because it would have kept a parent looking for a lost child.[30] On such an account, it is plausible that the grief reaction might not have evolved. On an account of how the mind organizes its grasp of reality, however, it is hard to imagine how the duration of the grief reaction and many of its manifestations could plausibly not be vaguely as they are. One may suddenly expect the departed person to appear simply because so many associations recorded in the mind have not automatically been erased or laid over with the knowledge of that person's death. One may have full knowledge and belief of the death somewhere in the mind, knowledge that is readily available, even foremost in consciousness. Nevertheless, that knowledge does not reorganize other knowledge and beliefs that are also readily available. The recurrent sense of loss that defines grief might be the result of the need to correct associations of various thoughts with the presence of the loved one. As these associations are provoked, one by one, they must be informed with the fact of the loved one's death. In this respect, the complex system of knowledge that one has of a close loved one may resemble other complex systems of knowledge that one has. That is what is at stake here: systems of knowledge, not particular facts. The death is almost a single fact; the life was a systematically interrelated set of facts.

In John Updike's story, "The Music School," the protagonist says,

> This morning I read in the newspaper that an acquaintance of mine had been murdered. . . . My acquaintance with him was slight. He has become the only victim of murder I have known, and for such a role anyone seems drastically miscast, though in the end each life wears its events

---

might sound more like a recommendation for how to manipulate belief than for how to encourage understanding.

30. Colin Murray Parkes, *Bereavement: Studies of Grief in Adult Life* (New York: International Universities Press, 1972), pp. 40–41.

with a geological inevitability. It is impossible, today, to imagine him alive.[31]

The problem with richer acquaintances is that it is impossible *not* to imagine them alive. Geological inevitability takes longer than a day for richer relationships. It is that longer period that helps make for certain manifestations of grief.

Now turn to distinctively moral intuitions, especially substantive intuitions, such as that it is wrong to lie, to break a promise, or to kill a person. We have already discussed some of the difficulties in the view that promise keeping is somehow a priori apprehensible as right. Because the value of promising, and therefore also presumably the fact of it, turns on the contingent facts of our condition, it would be odd to suppose it to be right independently of such facts.

What of more urgent substantive moral principles? Hume supposes that even parricide is not objectively wrong. Rather, Hume (T3.1.1, pp. 467–470) argues, our moral judgment of a parricide requires that we add to the facts of the case "certain passions, motives, volitions and thoughts." Julius Kovesi disagrees and counters that these latter "do not just colour certain hard facts but are new material elements out of which our reason forms moral notions as other aspects of the world are material elements out of which our reason forms other notions."[32] He therefore thinks disapproval of the parricide is rational "because it is part of the formation and use of the notion of parricide. . . . The moral agent is not a lonely observer contemplating other human beings. The relevant sense of feelings, etc., is the one in which these are everyone's feelings, including those of the murderer, the murdered and the observer."[33]

On an analogous account the view of almost all Europeans in 1492 that the world was flat was similarly rational—as indeed it surely was. But it was possible eventually to test that view and to find it wrong in the light of its inconsistency with other strongly held beliefs. It is a distinctive quality of many moral judgments that they seem to be grounded only in social conventions and, to some extent, logical or other intuitions independent of these conventions. It will not do to test them for rightness by showing their fit with the conventions any more than it would to settle the question of the flatness of the earth by testing it against conventional European understandings in 1492. Hence,

31. John Updike, "The Music School," pp. 138–143 in Updike, *The Music School* (Greenwich, Conn.: Fawcett Publications, 1967), p. 138.
32. Julius Kovesi, *Moral Notions* (London: Routledge and Kegan Paul, 1967), p. 71.
33. Ibid., p. 72.

Kovesi has a valid disagreement with Hume only if his claim that "these are anyone's feelings" does not turn on their being the conventional feelings. We would pull the ladder that Kovesi says he wishes to climb out from under him if we showed that these feelings originate in social conventions. Short of showing that, we may establish a plausible case that we have a strong sense of certainty about our moral views because we associate them in part with factual claims, of which we are often certain, and in part with analytical and quasi-analytical claims, such as instincts for form, of which we are commonly certain. Such instincts as those for symmetry, form, and so forth are relatively free of content and are therefore not particularly moral.

First, consider how we learn facts and how we learn moral views. What is the general moral practice comes to be what we know to be true, just as what are our relationships with others and with the world at large comes to be what we know. The comparable certainty with which we assert factual and moral claims may result partly from the way in which we learn to assert facts and to make moral judgments. When children learn what are chairs or tables and what is right or wrong, as Wittgenstein notes of the learning of facts, "there isn't any question of certainty or uncertainty yet in their language-game. Remember: they are learning to *do* something."[34] Moreover, teaching children moral rules is often less a moral than a pragmatic concern. Consider lying and truth telling. Most of us probably discounted the future far more heavily as children than we do as adults. If the value of any time beyond the present hour is discounted nearly to nothing, the rational incentive not to lie will generally be slight or nil. To impress on a child the importance of not lying is therefore largely to impress on the child the importance of future consequences, hence the importance of the future.

Where can the moral judgments have originated if we have merely learned them? Some of them may be typically conventional not only in the commonplace sense of that word but also in the strong technical sense of Chapter 2 (especially §11): they are coordination points in complex, repeated interactions of various forms. If we had come to coordinate on other principles, we might often be as well served. But once we have reached a given convention we may not easily be able to switch to another.[35] Some of them may be coordinations of an easier

34. Ludwig Wittgenstein, *Remarks on the Philosophy of Psychology*, vol. 2 (Chicago: University of Chicago Press, 1980), §341.

35. Russell Hardin, "Rationality, Irrationality, and Functionalist Explanation," *Social Science Information* 19 (1980): 755–772.

kind: they may be the best imaginable principles for human existence as we know it. In either case, they seem inherently contingent.

Historical and anthropological evidence substantially supports the claim that some of the most fundamental moral principles of extant societies came into being as conventions in the technical sense of Chapter 2. Lon Fuller supposes that laws, even the most plausibly moral laws such as laws against murder, initially served a coordination function and only later, "as the result of legal and moral progress," came to be seen as simple prohibitions of what is wrong.[36]

That certain moral principles are conventions in this sense does not mean they are therefore necessarily less moral. Indeed, the strongest argument for the rightness of certain principles for action must be that they are conventions. Why else should one be morally bound to drive on the right in North America?[37] However, more must be at stake in the defense because, clearly, there could be a convention in the ordinary sense—or even a convention in the technical sense of §11 that was based in wrong understanding of causal effects—that was harmful to those who followed it and associated with it might be strong moral views of its rightness.[38] Nevertheless, one might suppose that to violate that convention would generally be beneficial, in which case one would be hard pressed to say that the violation was wrong. If our moral intuitions are grounded in the experience of conventional practices, they therefore cannot in principle be compelling *as intuitions*.

Nevertheless, we are likely to conflate our socially constructed principles with our supposedly intuitive sense of what is right. For example, a sociologist of knowledge, trying to understand the issue of abortion in contemporary Western ethics, would probably find certain historical facts of overwhelming importance: official Catholic doctrine on the issue has repeatedly changed in dramatic ways over the centuries. For example, the bull *Effraenatam* of Sixtus V, issued in 1588, declared that all abortion and all contraception were to be treated as murder. John T. Noonan, Jr., suggests that the explanation for this harshest of Catholic doctrines on these issues is to be found "almost wholly in the personality of Sixtus V." Gregory XIV repealed all

36. Lon L. Fuller, "Human Interaction and the Law," pp. 212–246 in Fuller, *The Principles of Social Order* (Durham, N.C.: Duke University Press, 1981; originally published 1969), pp. 231–232.

37. Russell Hardin, "Does Might Make Right?" pp. 201–217 in J. Roland Pennock and John W. Chapman, eds., *Nomos 29: Authority Revisited* (New York: New York University Press, 1987).

38. C. D. Broad presents a succinct, lucid account of how such moral conventions might arise and prevail despite their disutility (*Ethics*, ed. C. Lewy [Dordrecht: Martinus Nijhoff, 1985], pp. 201–203.

Effraenatam's penalties "except those applying to abortion of an en-
souled, forty-day-old fetus." The decree of Sixtus V was "to be in this
part as if it had never been issued."[39] Even non-Catholics in relatively
secular Western societies must have difficulty factoring out the influence of Catholic doctrine on their intuitions. Yet a reading of the work
of many moral theorists on abortion suggests that the history of this
doctrine plays little conscious role in their effort to understand the
morality of abortion.

Consider another example. Wittgenstein says, "The sentence, 'I
believe it and it isn't true,' *can after all be the truth*. Namely when I believe
it and this belief turns out to be wrong."[40] There is another way in
which it can plausibly be true in a virtually intended sense. Some beliefs, such as the belief that one will be punished for wrongdoing, are
associated with powerful emotions that may even motivate actions.
Yet one can come to believe false what one earlier believed true while
failing to exorcise the emotional associations of the earlier belief and,
therefore, while continuing to act on the earlier belief. When we are
concerned to work out a set of moral principles, we may easily enough
overcome an unexorcized emotional tie to a formerly held principle.
But, as with the grief reaction, we are likely to find it harder to factor
that tie out of our sense of the rightness of other, related principles. For
example, we may come to believe that our sexuality is not wrong by
overcoming, at least consciously, the contrary moral sense induced by
rebukes for our childhood sexuality and curiosity. We may nevertheless continue to judge extramarital sex wrong largely because we
once judged sexuality in general wrong. Hence, we might judge cheating a spouse, say, on financial matters less harshly than cheating on
sexual relations. There may be reasons for such a judgment but our
early, emotionally scarred dealings with sex should not reflexively
prejudice the issue.

It seems likely that conventional understandings, with their common assimilation to the character of objective facts, cannot determine
the whole of a moral code within at least any thoughtful individual
mind. For example, outright contradictions might be hard to accept, as
individuals in the South of the United States often have found conventional views of individual equality and racial discrimination contradictory and finally untenable at once. Hence, the possible content of a

39. John T. Noonan, Jr., *Contraception: A History of Its Treatment by the Catholic
Theologians and Canonists* (Cambridge, Mass.: Harvard University Press, 1965, enlarged
ed. 1986), pp. 362–363.
40. Wittgenstein, *Remarks of the Philosophy of Psychology,* vol. 2, §418.

moral code might be substantially constrained by extramoral principles or canons, as is commonly argued.

Consider how this may work even for concerns other than logical contradiction in Gilbert Ryle's discussion of scrupulousness. Ryle notes that his conscience is provoked only by his own actions or thoughts and not by others', whereas he has moral convictions about both himself and others. Hence moral convictions and conscience, though related, are distinct.[41] This is not merely a matter of superior knowledge of self than of others because an omniscient god would not feel pangs of conscience over my immoral actions (although in all fairness an om-ni*potent* god should). He concludes that "there seems to be a sense in which *real* acceptance of a principle (does not lead to, but) *is* being disposed to behave in accordance with it. . . . A man's party manners show whether he 'knows' the rules of etiquette; his ability to *cite* 'Etiquette for Gentlemen' does not."[42] Further, "we use the word 'conscience' for those moral convictions which issue not in verdicts but in behaving or trying to behave."[43] For Ryle, "Qualms of conscience can occur only when I am both disposed to act in one way and disposed to act in another and when one of these dispositions is an operative moral principle."[44]

Immediately one notes that there are strongly held convictions of conduct other than moral ones. They should involve similar syndromes. "Is this so?" Ryle asks, and then he presents three other rule systems: prudence (as in not overdrinking or staying up too late, knowing what must follow), rules of etiquette, and rules of arithmetic. He suggests that scrupulousness, having scruples, though of different sorts, "is common to all cases where *real* acceptance of rules or principles is the being disposed to behave in a certain way, but where this disposition is balked of its normal actualization by some special temptation or interruption."[45]

Though he is aware that there are important differences in the scruples associated with different codes or systems of rules for behavior, Ryle is not concerned to discuss them. Clearly the differences could be substantial, as are the differences in the codes. The scruples one feels to get proofs right may be largely a response to an a priori code. Con-

41. Gilbert Ryle, "Conscience and Moral Convictions," pp. 185–193 in Ryle, *Collected Essays 1929–1968*, vol. 2 of *Collected Papers* (New York: Barnes and Noble, 1971; essay first published 1940).
42. Ibid., p. 187.
43. Ibid., p. 188.
44. Ibid., p. 189.
45. Ibid., p. 191.

science in particular is more than merely one of a class of urges for scupulousness because it behaves differently from the others in important respects. As for table manners, the most meticulous intelligent person might, despite a bit of initial squeamishness, find it easy enough to follow the elliptical injunction, "When in Rome." Conscience is not so readily adaptable. Despite their avaricious crudeness, Cortés and his men were, we can believe, profoundly appalled at that part of Aztec morals that condoned human sacrifice.[46] The difference between conscience and other members of the scrupulous class is not merely a difference in the way we use words. It is a radical difference in the earnestness with which we hold those principles regulated by moral principles and those regulated by, say, a social code of table manners.

Scrupulousness, then, may be an instinctual urge that works itself out in various realms of behavior and thought. How it works itself out varies considerably, and when it is coupled with ethical concern it gives extraordinary force to conscience. Urges for such values as harmony, scrupulousness, and symmetry may all be instinctual in part. What any of them implies for ethical conduct or being, however, is not strictly instinctual because it requires conscious processes in its articulation and because it is brought to bear on conventionally determined intuitions. Perhaps the chief role of the extramoral considerations is to structure conscious notions such as universalizability or impersonality.[47]

In sum, then, our moral intuitions may get their apparent certainty from our early confusion of moral principles or rules with matters of fact. If, given our substantive moral intuitions, we take the moral point of view, we may then restructure our conventional principles to fit instincts for form, some of which may seem to have a quasi-analytic character. To the extent our intuitions run afoul of simple logic, we may even consciously reject some of them. Unfortunately for our mental capacities, the whole system of relevant intuitions and extramoral constraints may be too large and complex for us to grasp it whole or to work out all its incoherencies. The principal incoherencies may be pragmatic rather than simply logical: they turn on our larger understanding of the world in which we act for better or for worse.

As argued above, we work with two general classes of intuitions: those that have substantive moral content and those that do not. For anyone not foolishly convinced of the elemental rightness of his or her direct intuitions of substantive moral "facts," as H. A. Prichard often

46. Bernard Williams, *Morality* (New York: Harper, 1972), pp. 24–25.
47. See Keith Dowling, "Consistency, Impartiality, and Universalizability," *South African Journal of Philosophy* 5 (1986): 53–55.

seems to be, intuitions always play a questionable role. We rely on them but we test them against each other and against theory. We may especially test different kinds of intuitions against each other. For example, we may suppose that human welfare is our chief concern in moral theory and also that lying is directly wrong. The first of these is a notion of the good, and the second a notion of the right. If these two come into conflict, we may think we have reached an impasse, as W. D. Ross seems to think we often must, or we may reconsider our intuitions. Similarly, we may have intuitions of what is good or right that come into conflict with our instincts for form, especially for impartiality.

Prichard, Ross and others give reasoning from direct, substantive intuitions a bad name. Prichard supposes that, if ever we doubt whether one would have an obligation to do A in a particular circumstance B, "the remedy lies not in any process of general thinking, but in getting face to face with a particular instance of the situation B, and then directly appreciating the obligation to originate A in that situation." How do we reach the relevant conclusion? By "letting our moral capacities of thinking do their work."[48] Kant would have detested this view. "To appeal to common sense," he writes, "this is one of the subtle discoveries of modern times, by means of which the most superficial ranter can safely enter the lists with the most thorough thinker, and hold his own."[49]

The use of such intuitions in moral theory has come back into favor through the more modest and sophisticated form of reasoning that Rawls calls "the method of reflective equilibrium." In this method, one tests intuitions against principles that are often deduced from simpler, less doubted intuitions and tests principles against relatively direct intuitions.[50] To a large extent, this method is little more than common sense in moral reasoning because we have no choice but to rely in part on intuitions. For example, at base, utilitarianism is founded on a substantive moral intuition: that the good is constituted in human welfare somehow conceived. We can justify various utilitarian claims by reference to this intuition but there seem to be no prior principles from which to justify this intuition itself. Most serious moral theorists, other

48. H. A. Prichard, "Does Moral Philosophy Rest on a Mistake?" pp. 1–17 in Prichard, *Moral Obligation and Duty and Interest* (London: Oxford University Press, 1968; first published 1912), p. 17.

49. Immanuel Kant, *Prolegomena to Any Future Metaphysics,* trans. Paul Carus (La Salle, Ill.: Open Court, 1902), p. 6.

50. John Rawls, *A Theory of Justice* (Cambridge, Mass.: Harvard University Press, 1971), pp. 20–21 and elsewhere.

than rationalists and believers in revelation, would grant that their own theories are similarly grounded in one or more substantive intuitions. It is this necessarily intuitive grounding that rules out complete objectivity in morals. It is, of course, not the use of just any intuition but the use of substantive moral intuitions—that there are natural rights, that promise breaking is wrong, that human welfare is the good—that blocks objectivity because these intuitions cannot be tested. The intuitions at issue in the present discussion, unlike those in much of argumentative moral theory, are relatively systematic: they inform whole moral theories. They are not about specific claims of rightness or goodness in this or that specific momentary application. They are subject to criticism from within relevant theories and are not merely intruded from without to refute a particular theory.

In addition to testing our intuitions against our theories, however, we should also strive to understand the sociological or psychological source of many of our supposed intuitions. For moral philosophers, ironically, one of these is our very theorizing. Our intuitions, if they were ever somehow autonomous or real, cannot be any longer after we have theorized enough to be doing moral philosophy. We are like those linguists who test grammaticality against native speakers' instincts. The linguist immersed in theory begins to have highly educated, not "natural," instincts and often cannot perform credible tests of grammaticality through introspective inquiry. Moral theorists should grant that *their* substantive intuitions may similarly be discredited by immersion in theory. Extended visits in the state of reflective equilibrium must eventually tilt the balance toward theory and away from "native" intuitions.

Finally, we should be alert to a peculiar problem of comprehending pragmatic claims. Mathematical proofs that cannot be surveyed whole have a logical development from one stage to the next so that piecewise intuition seems to be sufficient for us to grasp them and to judge their validity. Pragmatic conclusions may require parallel considerations of varied kinds that must be weighed together, not sequentially. If these cannot be surveyed whole and together, they cannot confidently be forced to yield credible conclusions. Yet we commonly assert intuitive resolutions of pragmatic problems as though we had surveyed all of the considerations at issue. Recall one of the earlier criticisms of William James's refutation of utilitarianism with his example of the woeful soul tortured for the benefit of millions of others (§7). Much of our understanding of the world is grounded in intuitions that have withstood the test of experience. Intuitions that fail that test are more likely to be purged from our systematic views. If we now import a startlingly contrary assumption about how the world works, we cannot readily trust our instant intuitions about that radically changed world—they cannot yet be backed by the test of surviving experience.[51]

Among the general constraints on our possible moral principles or systems is that our education in decision theory comes from the context of our lives and, again, that our knowledge and intuitions are socially derived. This does not distinguish pragmatic moral intuitions from scientific facts because the latter are commonly constructed from more parts than any individual can have grasped. But there is a conspicuous difference in the ways scientific theories and moral principles are tested. The latter are tested largely by thought experiments in which intuitions are given free rein. Just as no one may grasp all of the theories and practices that go into establishing the height of Mont Blanc, so no moral theorist may be able to grasp all relevant considerations while performing one of the thought experiments that litter the pages of moral theory and, more generally, of decision theory. A crucial test between different theories or of different principles may be virtually hopeless.

It is commonly asserted, for example, that utilitarianism is wrong because it runs afoul of our intuitions with all their sense of certainty. It seems likely that our intuitions more often run afoul of utilitarian considerations in actual life. That is, we generally can act without calculation or even serious consideration. Occasionally, however, we suspect that unreflective action from intuitive principles might be poor action. These occasions are likely to be occasions when utilitarian considerations will be seen to override unreflective, intuitive reaction, as for example when we break a promise because the general benefit from doing so is substantial.

To the extent that their origins are social, reliance on substantive moral intuitions may be no better than the traditionalist's reliance on extant institutions. The justification in both cases is at best the justification of Moore for conservative acceptance of ordinary morality and of Hayek for conservative (or eighteenth-century liberal) defense of capitalist arrangements: they have survived the social test (see further, §5). If one could believe in a sanguine version of functionalism, one might share Moore's and Hayek's views. The irony is that intuitionist arguments for various moral principles are more nearly an unconscious version of such conservative, functionalist utilitarianism than an alternative to it.

What intuitions does utilitarianism require? Sidgwick says that it

---

51. Recall Wittgenstein's remark, n. 55, chap. 1, above.

requires the fundamental intuition that, in essence, the good is human welfare.[52] This is a very general substantive intuition. And it seems to require some intuitions of general form, in particular, of impartiality. To go very far, however, the theory also requires many intuitions about what constitutes welfare and how it is enhanced. This is not as parsimonious a list as one might like in a simple, largely deductive theory. Still, with the possible exception of certain strictly rationalist theories, no serious contender among moral theories requires less reliance on intuition than does a utilitarianism fitted to the limits of our reason.

How does this list compare to those of other moral theories? Virtually all serious contenders require such basic, if different, intuitions as utilitarianism's two very general classes of intuitions that the good is human welfare and that our principles must universalize. The far larger class of intuitions about what constitutes human welfare is a collection of substantive intuitions like those required for rational choice as well. These intuitions are about very different kinds of things from those that chiefly figure in the intuitionist theories of Ross, Prichard, and many other moral theorists. A utilitarian claims no intuition about the "truth" of moral principles, duties, or whatever. Rather, my own preferences or, better, my own values are intuitively apprehended *by me,* yours by you, and so forth. In acting on your behalf I must attempt to grasp what your values or interests are. I can do this with some confidence for certain values by generalization or projection. For others, I must have more direct information from you. While I may make mistakes in such intuitions, there need be no supposition that my mind is somehow naturally endowed with substantive knowledge. We should firmly reject the traditional intuitionist's nagging residue of Descartes's belief that god could not deceive us by putting clear but false ideas into our heads, so that "everything we conceive very clearly and very distinctly is true,"[53] as Poe's narrator thought and as remarkably many moral theorists often seem to think, at least of *their* clear and distinct intuitions.

§35 Personal Identity and Weakness of Will

For any theory of human welfare, a fundamental issue is the nature of the individual human person. This may lead to a concern with various

52. Henry Sidgwick, *The Methods of Ethics,* 7th ed. (London: Macmillan, 1907), pp. 386–387 and 406–407.

53. René Descartes, *Discourse on the Method,* pp. 111–151 in John Cottingham, Robert Stoothoff, and Dugald Murdoch, eds., *Philosophical Writings of Descartes* (Cambridge:

causal issues, such as all of the issues that generally interest those who think morality consists in virtue, the essentially functionalist issues of what produces human flourishing. Even more fundamentally it leads to a concern with how an individual experiences welfare. As is utility, welfare is essentially a subjective notion and experience. Hence in a welfare theory we must be concerned with the subjective nature of the individual.[54] This is not to say there are no objective correlates of welfare—there are—but that the value of the objective contributions to welfare is in their subjective experience.

An understanding of the subjectivity of experience raises questions of the subjective identification of the individual over time. There is a large philosophical literature on the more general problem of identity, of inanimate objects as well as of persons, that focuses on objective identity or continuity.[55] This is the traditional problem of the ship that is slowly reconstituted, plank by plank, as rot sets in, so that in the end there is no part of it that was originally there. Is it then the "same" ship? Similarly, identity for a person would be a matter of the constancy of personal character and preferences in the face of constantly renewed molecular structure and, more interestingly, of slowly changing experience. In large part, although perhaps not exclusively, identity of persons is a matter of external manifestations of character, personality, behavior, and so forth. One might, with Parfit, separate identity into objective and subjective considerations.

In moral theory, a more urgent concern than the correlates and logic of identity is the following: Should I now be concerned with the experiences and welfare of that person who will bear my objective, legal, or whatever identity ten years from now or of that similarly related person of ten years ago whose identity I now bear? And should that future person be responsible for my present actions? To answer such questions, we must consider the *subjective commitments* of the individual, not merely the subjective nature of personal psychology. Insofar as ethical choice is a matter of going against self-interest, this point is especially

---

Cambridge University Press, 1985; *Discourse* first published in French in 1637), part 4, p. 130.

54. As Samuelson notes, "If one were looking for a single criterion by which to distinguish modern economic theory from its classical precursors, he would probably decide that this is to be found in the introduction of the so-called subjective theory of value into economic theory" (Samuelson, *Foundations of Economic Analysis,* p. 90).

55. For example, Robert Nozick's discussion of personal identity (in his "closest continuer theory") is typical of most in focusing on objective identity (Robert Nozick, *Philosophical Explanations* [Cambridge, Mass.: Harvard University Press, 1981], pp. 27–114).

clear. Hence, I will here use 'identification' to refer to commitment or what Parfit calls "concern."[56] If such identification with the self over time is very tenuous, then identity ceases to be a concern in our evaluations over time (even though it may still be a major factor in our causal explanations).

Weak identification may follow simply from weak identity, but it can also be independently associated with strong identity. Indeed, one of the correlates that could characterize one's strong identity over time is that one consistently displays very weak identification with future selves. We may salvage a connection between identification and identity only by locating an objective core of the person to which subjective commitments are to attach. Alas, whatever makes a person a particular person seems to be shorn away to get at the core that is identical. Twang, the Thai heroine of *The Sinking of the Odradek Stadium,* writes in her creative English: "I learn from Origen that on the Lost Judgment the blessed souls will roll into heaven, for they will be resuscitate in perfection, as spheres."[57] Metaphysicians may be motivated by concern for their spherical souls; others must wonder what difference our concern can make to such a blessed soul. Twang combines Buddhist and early Catholic views to reach the relevant understanding of how to find the core of one's identity. She says that "things must disappear, and even so consciousness of them. Therefore, contemplating the consciousness as well as any thing . . . , you are to think of it impermanent not permanent, miserable not happiness, impersonal not a personality—you are to feel aversion to it; take no pleasure from it; detach yourself of it; give it up."[58] There may be moral theories that still have content for persons with so little content or capacity for welfare, but utilitarianism is not one of them.

Perhaps the chief way in which concern for identification as opposed to identity comes into moral theory is through concern with akrasia or weakness of will. We all know the feeling that we can enjoy something this moment only at significant cost to ourselves in the future (recall Ryle's concern with scrupulousness over such prudential matters as

---

56. Parfit, *Reasons and Persons,* passim, for example, p. 313. This subjective sense of one's commitment to one's futures motivates Thomas Nagel's discussion in *The Possibility of Altruism* (Oxford: Clarendon Press, 1970).

57. Harry Mathews, *The Sinking of the Odradek Stadium and Other Novels* (New York: Harper & Row, 1975), p. 519.

58. Ibid., p. 520. One may be reminded of Kant's stipulation that "the inclinations themselves, being sources of needs, are so far from having an absolute value such as to render them desirable for their own sake that the universal wish of every rational being must be, rather, to be wholly free from them" (Kant, *Grounding for the Metaphysics of Morals,* p. 35; Akademie ed., p. 428).

overdrinking and staying up too late, §34). And most of us know all too well the tendency to succumb to attractions of the moment despite future costs that might seem substantially to outweigh the momentary pleasures. Proust's alter ego, Marcel, who has dedicated his life to the creation of a literary masterpiece, puts off his writing with the observation, quite compelling in the moment, that it "would be puerile, on the part of one who had waited now for years, not to put up with a postponement of two or three days."[59] By a process of steady addition, two or three days can turn into decades. The problem of akrasia, however, is not sensibly seen as merely a problem of tenuous identification over time, even though these two problems may get intertwined in our accounts of actions and choices over time.

Consider certain respects in which we may view the problem of akrasia as analogous to certain problems of conflicting interests over time. You do something for me today on the strength of my promise to reciprocate tomorrow. When tomorrow comes it may not be in my interest then to reciprocate. But it was generally in my interest overall to exchange your favor today for mine tomorrow. It is from this larger perspective of my overall interest that we can meaningfully say that it is in my interest to be able to bind myself against my fleeting, particular interest of the moment when tomorrow I must reciprocate. Analogously, we may say of certain actions that they are akratic, that is, that they reduce one's overall welfare and are therefore against one's overall interest even though they may seem straightforwardly to enhance one's welfare in a particular moment.

Suppose we conclude against this analogy and assert that our understanding of interpersonal exchange over time is different from that of akrasia over present and future consumptions. It is different just because we somehow suppose that the present and future selves of a person are essentially the same whereas the two people in the promising relationship are distinctively different. This is inherently a moral judgment, not merely a logical claim, because it implies that one ought to be concerned with one's future self even if one is not.

There is still another way in which we might speak of akrasia, one that is especially prevalent in discussions of ethics. We might say that one does now what one now knows is contrary to one's very nearly present interests. For example, I may start drinking in this moment with the knowledge that I will suffer almost immediate ill consequences. Instantly one may retort, "Ah, but that is just alcoholism and its perverse, uncontrollable nature." But I need not be an alcoholic to

---

59. Proust, *Remembrance of Things Past*, 1:419).

succumb to an afternoon's (self-) destruction. Yet it would be odd to suppose that the person is so fractured into momentary selves as to be different from minute to minute. Even one who is very weakly attached to the future of next year or next decade is unlikely to be weakly attached to the next hour or minute.

This second problem, of what, for emphasis, we may call *momentary akrasia,* seems to have a different etiology or basis than the earlier problem of weak identification over longer periods of time. Indeed, one might suppose that I could suffer from momentary akrasia even though I do not generally have difficulty taking my more distant future selves into account in my present actions and commitments.

Unless it is merely an error to opt for the minor pleasure at major cost, whether in the next moment or in the more distant future, we apparently have two ways to make sense of inconsistent actions or choices that might seem akratic. First, one may be a conflicting jumble of urges, instincts, reasons, and so forth, as for example in Freud's complex theory of the mind. On such an account one's personal identity is a motley jumble from which we should expect conflicting choices. This model of the self would readily fit problems of momentary akrasia. Second, one may simply not care as much about the future as about the present quite apart from objective grounds for discounting future values.[60] On such an account one's personal identification is weak over time even though one's identity is not necessarily confused in this moment. This model would fit longer term subjective commitments.

The opposite of the former view is to suppose that the person is very highly integrated, as though there were something like Freud's superego governing the relationship between different instincts, desires, and so forth. The opposite of the latter would be to suppose that one has a strong attachment to one's future selves, so strong perhaps as to make one indifferent between present and future consumptions apart from objective considerations of uncertainty about futures.

Hence there are two ways of making sense of inconsistent commitments: commitments may falter synchronically or diachronically, that is, in any given moment, as in the motley view of our interests, or over time, as in the view that one has ever weaker attachments to farther future selves. These two aspects of our problem may be overlaid, so

60. Trollope remarks of Thomas Gibson's somewhat loose definition of that future in which he might marry Camilla French, his formally announced fiancée: "A bill at three months sits easier on a man than one at sixty days; and a bill at six months is almost as little of a burden as no bill at all" (Anthony Trollope, *He Knew He Was Right* [London: Strahan and Co., 1869; reprint, New York: Dover, 1983], 2:7). In Gibson's case one might suspect very loose commitments to future selves rather than mere discounting.

that we may suppose that what are commonly labeled instances of weakness of will follow sometimes from the motley quality of the person and sometimes from the person's weak attachment to future selves. To keep these categories or dimensions straight, let us speak of the *integrated* and the *motley identity* views, and of the *weak* and the *strong identification* views.

On the strong identification view, my interests are always the same: to maximize my consumptions overall, subject to objective grounds for discounting future consumptions. If I am not a motley self, then on the strong identification view to say that I suffer from akrasia in any given moment is to say that somehow my reason nods and lets me act in a way that does not maximize my consumptions overall. On this account, akrasia is merely an error. On a weak identification view, again if I am not a motley self, to say that I suffer from akrasia is similarly odd. At most it is a confusing way to say I make mistakes in judgment. Otherwise, again, it implies that it is inherently wrong to have weak identification with distant selves.

To speak of weakness of will, as we commonly do, instead of akrasia, highlights the motley identity view, as for example in the Freudian conception of the compartmentalized mind with a superego concerned with consumptions or well-being overall and bits of the id competing for pleasures or other urges of the moment in disregard of the future. It is not simply that I make an error but that the "wrong" part of my motley identity gains momentary control. To make such a claim stick, to say that there is something wrong or weak about my action, we must have a theory of value for the person that morally differentiates consumptions that feed different parts of the motley self.

Alternatively, if I wish to criticize you for your supposedly akratic commitments to your future selves on the claim that they are as much you as is your present self, while you feel subjectively only weakly tied to those future selves, I should as well criticize you for your weak commitments to others in this moment.[61] To say, on the ground that it will reduce other opportunities later, that one ought not now do what one enjoys doing now will force us inexorably into valuing not the person as we typically know a person but the person's whole life, as we might once it has taken on an aspect of Updike's geological inevitability (as in the discussion of grief in §34). If we do parcel our identity over time while insisting that it is still all one, then any supervenient claims we make about what actions benefit and what actions harm us will be inescapably paternalistic.

61. This is the inverse of Nagel's argument in *The Possibility of Altruism*.

We cannot occupy the position of a whole life in order to overlook actions or consumptions within it to say which contribute more or less to the life. For suppose, as must happen if akrasia is a serious issue, that one's momentary, partial self disagrees with any supervenient claims about what one ought to do in this moment. What person or part of a person is to arbitrate the dispute? And if we have an answer to this question,[62] how is the dispute to be arbitrated? A coalescence of all our partial interests and valued consumptions into one overarching utility function or welfare index suggests the quality of the utility theory in Arrow's impossibility theorem.[63] In that utility theory it is whole states of affairs, not marginal contributions to whole states of affairs, that must be compared.[64] On a strong identification theory it is variant whole lives, not variant consumptions per se, that must be compared.

A view that couples genuinely strong identification and integrated identity seems finally inconsistent with experience: while some of one's motley urges, values, and desires may remain remarkably constant over time, some of them surely cannot, if only for biological reasons, so that it seems implausible that one could integrate them in an unchanging function over time. At the very least, on a view that couples strong identification and integrated identity the notion of akrasia reduces to the trivial notion of carelessness or nodding reason. Moreover, it seems implausible that our subjective concern with our pleasures or consumptions over time could be unrelated to the moment from which we view them. For example, it is surely not symmetric with respect to time. I may be keenly moved by consideration of what may happen to me in one or ten years but no longer seriously moved by what did happen to me one or ten years ago.[65] Indeed, I might now think that ten years ago it would have been better that x happen and yet be glad now that y happened because if x had happened I would not have become the person I now am. It is in more than one sense, therefore, that I cannot identify with Malcolm Roland Schlette, who, for thirty-one years, harbored a grudge against the man who prosecuted him in a trial that sent him to jail for twenty years and who, at age seventy-two, fulfilled

---

62. J. C. Flugel supposes Freud has an answer in the superego (Flugel, *Man, Morals and Society* [New York: International Universities Press, 1945]).

63. Arrow, *Social Choice and Individual Values*.

64. As already noted (§33), this utility theory makes impossible demands on our reason. See further, Russell Hardin, "Rational Choice Theories."

65. Of course, as in the grief reaction, §34, I might suffer from sudden moments of intense feeling through Proustian involuntary recall of past events. This, however, is a matter of objective identity insofar as it suggests how the mind is neurologically organized rather than what one's general commitments are.

his threat of thirty-one years earlier by shooting the former prosecutor dead.[66]

The interesting questions therefore arise for a view of identification that is at most moderately strong. Such a view automatically brings in some degree of discounting of future consumptions for reasons of weakened identification over time. It then raises questions of distributive justice or of fairness as between present and future selves. It may also make it less incoherent to view the person as a motley whose overall well-being, considered in the moderately short run, makes sense.

In sum, our view of personal identification inherently infects our value theory. If we think identification is highly consistent over time we are forced to consider "whole life" values rather than marginal consumption values. The implication of some degree of weakness of personal identification over time may be even more far-reaching. It is that choices about the present versus various futures are inherently moral choices that involve trading off well-being as though for "one person" against that for "others." Hence, as Thomas Nagel argues, rational choice for one individual over time is morally analogous to choosing over outcomes for many individuals in any given moment.[67]

We might escape the first of these conclusions—the consideration of whole life values—if we hold a value theory like that of Edgeworth and, apparently, Bentham. Edgeworth supposes that welfare is measurable in interpersonally comparable units of pleasure and pain that are some function of duration and intensity of pleasure.[68] (With the proper linear scale of intensity, the function would be simply the product of duration and intensity.) With this value theory, we can measure total welfare for a population independently of concern for their identities or identifications over time. It is interesting that Mill and Rawls opt for considering whole life values, as is suggested by their concern with "life plans." It is plausible that Mill is confused on this point and that he opts both for whole life values and for an interpersonally additive notion of utility in a form that would seem to be additive intertemporally for a given person as well.[69]

If our view of personal identity infects our value theory it must

66. *New York Times*, November 20, 1986.
67. Nagel, *The Possibility of Altruism.*
68. Edgeworth, *Mathematical Psychics*, p. 8.
69. It is also Mill—the same Mill?—who argues against marriage in perpetuity on the ground that "the presumption in favour of individual judgment is only legitimate, where the judgment is grounded on actual, *and especially on present,* personal experience" (Mill, *Principles of Political Economy*, book 5, chap. 11, par. 10, p. 953). See further, §29 above.

presumably also infect many of our substantive utilitarian conclusions. For example, note how it may radically affect the terms of debate over supposed instances of paternalism by the state (as generally discussed in §29). Many paternalistic laws that enforce one's better behavior may clearly have originated in paternalistic action by some people to control others in the supposed best interests of those others. Such laws, however, might also be enacted at the behest of those who wish to control themselves by imposing external discipline on their actions or by having the state do for them what they know they would not do well for themselves. If one supposes that the problems of personal identity and identification are particularly severe, so that one cannot meaningfully speak of akrasia but only of effectively different identities, one might suppose all such laws are not paternalistic but rather are invidiously redistributive: they impose costs on some selves in order to benefit others. But if one supposes that the greater problem of personal identity is one of gradual change or of a multiplicity of conflicting urges, character traits, self-images, values, and so forth, inadequately governed by an organizing superego, one might readily think our collective action to get the state to intervene against us in our own behalf is fundamentally rational and self-interested.

Examples of legislative acts that are often characterized as paternalistic but that may more fruitfully be seen as either self-serving or beneficent acts to deal with akrasia or weak personal identification include laws on social security, restrictions on access to one's private pension funds before retirement, bar-closing hours, the fluoridation of drinking water (although this is primarily beneficial for children, for whom state paternalism is not generally found objectionable), and many regulatory issues. Thomas Schelling's example of hockey players' machismo in not wearing helmets[70] is an elegant case of akrasia that is collectively reinforced, so that it may not easily be overcome by individuals imposing constraints on themselves but might very nearly require an authoritative imposition. Similarly, although they might have originated from generally paternalistic motives, contemporary bar-closing hours might well be supported by most of those frequently forced to leave bars at evening's end. They might support the laws as a device for blocking collective reinforcement of akratic tendencies to linger against their greater interests. In many of these cases severe costs to later selves may follow from very modest levels of akrasia—hence,

70. Thomas C. Schelling, "Hockey Helmets, Concealed Weapons, and Daylight Savings," *Journal of Conflict Resolution* 17 (September 1973): 381–428.

only slight constraints need be imposed to achieve quite beneficial outcomes.

On this account, momentary akrasia is partly analogous to certain limits to rational decision making. We choose with inadequate information because gaining better information would be too costly. And we act from relatively weak character because developing a stronger character would be unrewarding. In many cases we would rather turn over to others the task of making more informed decisions for us or of controlling ourselves in weaker moments. On a very weak view of personal identification, however, laws controlling momentary selves are inherently redistributive: they impose on one set of individuals this moment to benefit "another" set in a farther future.

One of the most remarkable aspects of long-term akrasia and of personal identity and identification over time is that they force attention to the distinction between one's consumptions and one's interests. In much of ethics and in much of state action, as in Chapters 3 and 4, we can run these two categories together and simply focus on interests. If we maximize one's interests we maximize one's consumptions. There is no independent reason for concern with interests per se. Rather, we are concerned with them as means to achieving well-being through relevant consumptions. It is in my interest to increase my resources, with which I accomplish certain consumptions. If we focus exclusively on consumptions, we need face no difficult problems of conceptual coherence when we note that one consumption may trade off with another. We complicate matters somewhat if we bring interests into our value theory and say that our consumptions trade off with our interests. If this move is seen as letting interests stand as proxy for alternative consumptions, it should cause no confusion.

Unfortunately, we cannot easily do without concern with interests rather than simply with consumptions. We do not know enough about another or even about ourselves to try to bring all of, say, our own consumptions, potential or actual, into a full evaluation of various ways we might go. We virtually require the notion of interests as a proxy for as yet undetermined and even unconsidered consumptions to be traded off against present consumptions. If identification is very weak, we do not need such a proxy because we can speak directly of immediate consumption alternatives. If identification is even moderately strong, we must have such a proxy. Without it, the mind, our reason, boggles.

Interests are a useful proxy for alternative consumptions just because they comprise a far less manifold category than do consumptions. Certain resources, almost reducible to money in certain highly articulated societies, and health are plausibly the chief constituents of the category of interests.

It is not meaningless to speak of interests on the weak identification view, but it is not necessary to do so. Someone who finds it virtually necessary to invoke the notion of interests in the discussion of an individual's actions implicitly holds a stronger identification view. At the collective level, however, we often find it necessary to speak of interests rather than of consumptions just because we are concerned with the consumptions of many people rather than of only one. (Hence, as noted in §12, there is some ground for the concern with resources rather than welfare in some discussions of distributive justice. The reason for this, again, is that we need resources or interests as a proxy for welfare in the face of grievous constraints of information.) This would still be true even if we held a very weak identification view. This conclusion would most obviously follow if we were, as we typically would be, concerned with consumptions of the many over time. But it also follows even if we are concerned with very short-term consumptions of the many—simply because we need a proxy for the unmanageably manifold category of consumptions.

In sum, if we are concerned with an individual and if we hold a very weak identification view, we need speak only of consumptions, of direct notions of welfare. If we are concerned with an individual and we hold a strong identification view or if we are concerned with a collective and we hold either a weak or a strong identification view, we must generally also speak of interests as a proxy for consumptions or welfare.

§36 Endogeneity of Preferences and Individual Autonomy

Perhaps the most difficult issue in a welfare theory of the good is that what satisfies individuals varies from individual to individual in ways that seem to be accidental in a potentially important sense. In particular, what satisfies me is often largely a function of where I happen to be and where I happen to have grown up. Does this accidental nature of what satisfies me matter in judging that getting it is good? In some contexts it seems to. Recall especially Marx's concern with false consciousness and his consequent dismissal of concern for specific—subjective—preferences. This is not a single, neatly defined issue but a collection of diverse, messy issues. I have no intention or hope of resolving them here, but I wish to note them as issues that may undercut our understanding of the notion of human welfare as well as of many other value theories.

The concern with the source of our judgments of welfare and preferences comes under various terms, including endogeneity of preferences, false consciousness, relativism, and, in some of its uses, autonomy. An obvious problem for a welfarist theory is to judge whether apparent satisfactions are eo ipso good and whether they are as satisfactory as alternatives that might be "learned." It is often supposed that the chief problem for certain other moral theories, such as Kantian theory, is whether individual choices and values are autonomously adopted. Clearly these problems are related. They suggest that various moral theories face similar and similarly difficult problems. Perhaps the most radical difference between utilitarian theories and Kantian theories is that the latter typically claim to count autonomy as good in itself whereas utilitarian theories typically do not. Yet if the notion of autonomy is not coherent we may find ourselves wondering why we should value mere pleasures or satisfactions. Indeed, we may even wonder what can be the coherence of a notion of individual welfare.

Briefly stated, the problem with autonomy is that, as many have concluded, the notion is substantively empty. This fact, Gerald Dworkin notes, "raises the question why the development, preservation and encouragement of autonomy is desirable."[71] A radically autonomous person must be like Twang's spherical souls (§34), and hollow to boot. There is nothing to grasp and no content. To get from spherical hollowness one must generate ideas and values spontaneously or one must be somewhat like Proust's young Marcel, whose mind absorbed the opinion of another "at one draught, like a dry lawn when water is poured on it."[72]

Similarly, one may suppose that a concern to satisfy preferences *tout court* lacks substantive grounding unless we unpack the preferences themselves and justify them. But if they are accidentally formed and could as well have been radically different, it seems hard to justify them. One answer to the question of how to deal with accidentally formed preferences and values is to stipulate simply that the satisfaction of what people want is, with corrections for misunderstandings and akratic tendencies that run against their interests, good. This may seem to threaten our moral theory with a sociological variant of the fallacy of evolutionary ethics that supposes that what has evolved is what should be, as though survival of the fittest were a normative rather than merely a descriptive or causal principle. In this move, one seems directly to derive an 'ought' from an 'is' in supposing that what is is good.

71. Gerald Dworkin, "The Concept of Autonomy," *Grazer Philosophische Studien* 12 (1981): 203–213, p. 213.
72. Proust, *Remembrance of Things Past,* 1:368.

Yet it would be wrong to suppose that preferences that are somehow accidentally formed are prima facie rejectable for that reason. Some preferences are easily "interchangeable" for others in principle even though one person or group may strongly hold one while another person or group holds another, as for example is true of tastes for food. We may reasonably suppose that the welfare or pleasure derived from satisfying either preference would be good and that it need not matter *which* preference one has. This claim is roughly analogous to the claim that in certain coordination games *the way in which* a good result is achieved does not matter—what matters is *that* a good result is achieved. *De gustibus non est disputandum* is, in this context, both a factual and a normative claim. Sappho puts the case well, if only fragmentarily:

> As for him who finds
> fault, may silliness
> and sorrow take him![73]

For the most part I am inclined to agree with Sappho, which is to say that most of the issue in the apparently random element in the formation of particular tastes is merely analogous to the choice of possible coordination points, each of which is as good as any other. Unlike the fallacious reason for deeming an outcome good in evolutionary ethics, however, this claim is not definitive irrespective of other considerations. What considerations are relevant and what truth this claim has at all depend on the nature of human welfare.

There are at least two kinds of problems with the formation of values. First, there is the problem of their source. My values may depend on experience or on the values of others and society. Second, there is the problem of their object. To varying degrees my values may reflect something about the outside world or about my inner state.

The first problem, which is related to that of intuitions discussed earlier (§34), is very well studied and extensively discussed from at least Descartes and Locke forward, although it would still be false to say we have a good understanding of its real significance for value theory. On the side of experience, Proust reports a familiar instance: "I had already drunk a good deal of port wine, and if I now asked for more it was not so much with a view to the comfort which the additional glasses would bring me as an effect of the comfort produced by the glasses that had gone before."[74] At a less physiological level, we all develop tastes for

---

73. The fragment is no. 2 in Mary Barnard, ed. and trans., *Sappho: A New Translation* (Berkeley: University of California Press, 1958). Barnard entitles the fragment, "We shall enjoy it."

74. Proust, *Remembrance of Things Past*, 1:612.

doing what we have done. That we do not develop tastes for doing *all* that we have done gives some ground for supposing there is more to our tastes than merely habit or Pavlovian learning. Perhaps the role of learning or experience is essentially to select that one of many possible tastes on which we might have coordinated, all of which are plausibly on a par. Social "imposition" of tastes is a tougher case to fit to individual autonomy, but we might suppose that many possible tastes are really quite generally acceptable and that social narrowing of the field to coordinate us all on particular tastes is not completely destructive of our autonomy, so that our socially adapted tastes have merit enough to deserve satisfaction.

These two phenomena—experience and social adaptation—may come together in many tastes, as in the peculiar taste of the Japanese for the high-risk consumption of fugu, a raw-fish delicacy made from the puffer fish, as celebrated in the elegant traditional verse:

> Last night he and I ate fugu
> Today, I help carry his coffin.[75]

If the flesh of the fish is tainted even slightly by certain parts, including the liver, ovaries, and intestines, it is deadly. One cannot imagine the cultivation of a taste for fugu outside a certain organized milieu, and yet it is plausibly also true that once the taste is cultivated it is real and its satisfaction is worthy of at least some risk.[76]

The second problem—sometimes described as mental state versus objective state preference satisfaction—is less extensively discussed and possibly more troubling. Again, Proust captures the problem well: "I had guessed long ago . . . that when we are in love with a woman we simply project into her a state of our own soul, that the important thing is, therefore, not the worth of the woman but the depth of the state."[77] It may be especially troubling when it is coupled with deliberate learning, as one might suppose it was in the case of Proust himself or of Oscar Wilde or, at an opposite extreme, of certain Stoics and religious hermits. It typically raises a specter for utilitarianism in the guise of

75. Quoted in Noel D. Vietmeyer, "The Preposterous Puffer," *National Geographic* 166, no. 2 (August 1984): 260–270, p. 261.
76. One who has not developed the taste may doubt it is worth the risk: nearly 200 lives were lost to fugu in a recent decade in Japan. But the risk to moneyed consumers may be slight because they can afford to eat fugu prepared by highly skilled licensed master fugu chefs; it is those who scrimp on costs and prepare the fish at home who are the chief losers in the game of high stakes (ibid., p. 264). Perhaps the taste for fugu is in large part a taste for defying risk, always easier to do when the risks can be brought down to a lower level.
77. Proust, *Remembrance of Things Past,* 1:627.

drug-induced mental states of great pleasure that have virtually no objective correlates outside the persons in the relevant states. Within limits one may still suppose that whatever enjoyments come from mental states that are only weakly determined by objective correlates are still good except insofar as they may detrimentally affect longer run interests. At some point, however, drug-induced and other extraordinary states may raise problems more fundamental even than those in evaluating welfare; they may raise questions about what counts as a state of consciousness and as a person, a rational being, or even merely a conscious being. Such inquiries may help to determine the boundaries of the application of ethics but they are not so clearly a part of ethics, and they are surely not at the center of ethics.

§37 Utilitarianism and the Limits of Welfare Theory

As noted at the outset of this book, utilitarianism can most instructively be viewed as a program, not as a definitive theory. It is not merely what, for example, Bentham said but what makes sense of what he said that matters to us. What makes sense is open to change as we think and write about issues that the program has brought up. It seems clear that what is most open to change in our understanding of utilitarianism at the moment is the value theory of human welfare. Beyond its initial base in the fundamental intuition that the good is human welfare, utilitarianism requires a value theory that itself is likely to have further intuitionist elements. As discussed in §33, however, it has a further problem in that the likely structure of its value theory may be fraught with logical difficulties. Alas, the same seems likely true of any value theory complex enough to be taken seriously for moral theory.

What are the problems that most plague a utilitarian value theory? At the least, the problems of the preceding four sections: the lack of a fully acceptable welfare theory; the burden of intuitionist reasoning at certain points; the nature of the person who is the subject of welfare; and the bases of an individual's preferences, whose satisfaction is at issue in the enhancement of welfare. These problems interact in many ways, some of which have been noted. For example, if my commitment to my future selves is extremely weak, then it may not seem to matter that my preferences are endogenously formed and not really my own. They must be not really my own if my present self did not even exist until very recently and is merely the recipient of tastes, habits, and abilities developed by my former selves.

Nevertheless, we can say very much even while we are limited in our theory. G. E. Moore, commenting on the basic issue of utilitarian value theory, says that "it is impossible that, till the answer to [the question what is good] be known, any one should know *what is the evidence* for any ethical judgment whatsoever."[78] Moore is notorious for the confusions he has raised for the notion of what it means to "know" anything at all and perhaps that is the central issue with his claim here. One suspects, however, that many philosophers would simply disagree with his apparent implication here. We are quite sure that the foundations of our knowledge of anything at all are dubious and, when pushed back far enough, finally "unknown." Yet we are often quite confident of our judgments.

We are like Hume, confident at higher levels of knowledge but doubtful of our foundations. As in our discussion (§33) of utility theory, in acknowledging that our notion of rationality may be orderly only at the margin, we echo Hume's confidence in much of his practical reasoning in the face of skepticism about its foundations. "Nothing is more certain," Hume writes, "than that men are, in a great measure, govern'd by interest" (T3.2.7, p. 534). The same Hume writes, "I am uneasy to think I approve of one object, and disapprove of another; call one thing beautiful, and another deform'd; decide concerning truth and falsehood, reason and folly, without knowing upon what principles I proceed" (T1.4.7, p. 271).

Given the inherent limits of reason discussed in this book, we can only sympathize with Hume. But we can also be relatively confident that some actions will tend to enhance welfare while others will tend to detract from it. Even the limited welfare theory in which interpersonal comparisons are not allowed is sufficient to recommend many actions and institutional structures. Hence, we can construct systems of government protections that may not be ideal but that may be very good in the context of our limited reason. In particular, they may tend to produce results that are far better than what would follow from other protections or from none at all. The more demanding we are in the precision of our results, the less satisfied we can be, unless we can surmount the problems of our welfare theory.

The difficulties in our value theory may exacerbate some of the difficulties of other limits of reason. For example, our best understanding of strategic interaction is probably from game theory. But the strongest results of game theory depend on very strong value theory assumptions, stronger assumptions than we can find credible for the more general social interactions we might wish to regulate with moral norms and political institutions. Even with its very strongest value

78. G. E. Moore, *Principia Ethica* (Cambridge: At the University Press, 1903), p. 6.

theory assumptions, however, in game theory there are commonly no determinate solutions to relatively simple problems of choice. It would be surprising if the addition of the broader utilitarian concern for the interests of all, rather than merely the interests of oneself, did not reduce the indeterminacy for such games. This follows because the payoffs in each cell in a game between utilitarians must appear to be the same for all participants unless someone is in error. (Recall the earlier discussion of Regan's game theoretic account of utilitarian choice, §33).

What we need for many choice contexts, however, is an ordinal game theory without interpersonal transferability of utility. Such a theory may add to the indeterminacy of cardinal game theory in some ways even while the utilitarian principle of considering the benefits and costs of all, rather than merely the self, reduces it. We should probably not expect generally determinate results from a game theory with these two modifications. Hence, we should not expect determinacy in social choice whether it is moral or purely self-interested. Those who are uncomfortable with an indeterminate theory may think its indeterminacy is a ground for rejecting utilitarianism. That would be an odd conclusion: if indeterminacy is in the nature of things, we should expect good theories to be indeterminate. Determinacy is not a distinctively moral criterion and we should not reject moral theories on it. Indeed, any theory that is not substantially indeterminate should be doubted at the outset because it can achieve determinacy only by covering most actions and choices we make under an umbrella of moral indifference.

In conclusion, I think it clear that we can separate the two parts of utilitarian moral theory and deal with them to a large extent as though they were separable. We can proceed on the analysis of structural issues without first constructing a fully adequate welfare theory. And we can proceed with the analysis of welfare theories, such as economic utility theory, independently of their use in utilitarianism. Again, I think that the second of these projects is more in need of hard work than is the first. We have come relatively far in the understanding of the strategic structure of interaction and of cognitive limits of reason and their relevance to individual choice and institutional design. What we now need more urgently is a better understanding of the nature of the person whose welfare is of interest and a conceptually more coherent and compelling welfare theory. We could also benefit from a richer understanding of the workings of intuition in moral reasoning and of the ways in which our tastes, preferences, and other values are formed.

References

Anscombe, G. E. M. "Modern Moral Philosophy." Pp. 26–42 in Anscombe, *Ethics, Religion and Politics,* vol. 3 of *Collected Philosophical Papers.* Minneapolis: University of Minnesota Press, 1981.

———. "On Transubstantiation." Pp. 107–112 in Anscombe, *Ethics, Religion and Politics,* vol. 3 of *Collected Philosophical Papers.* Minneapolis: University of Minnesota Press, 1981; originally published as a pamphlet by the Catholic Truth Society, London, 1974.

Arneson, Richard J. "Mill versus Paternalism." *Ethics* 90 (July 1980): 470–489.

Arrow, Kenneth J. "Nozick's Entitlement Theory of Justice." *Philosophia* 7 (June 1978): 265–279.

———. *Social Choice and Individual Values.* New Haven, Conn.: Yale University Press, 1951; 2d ed. 1963.

———. "Some Ordinalist-Utilitarian Notes on Rawls' Theory of Justice." *Journal of Philosophy* 70 (May 10, 1973): 245–263.

P. S. Atiyah. *Promises, Morals and Law.* Oxford: Clarendon Press, 1981.

———. *The Rise and Fall of Freedom of Contract.* Oxford: Clarendon Press, 1979.

Austin, John. *The Province of Jurisprudence Determined,* ed. H. L. A. Hart. New York: Noonday, 1954; first published 1832.

Barry, Brian. "Don't Shoot the Trumpeter—He's Doing His Best." *Theory and Decision* 11 (1979): 153–180.

———, ed. Symposium on Derek Parfit's *Reasons and Persons, Ethics* 96 (July 1986): 703–872.

———. *Theories of Social Justice.* Berkeley: University of California Press, forthcoming.

Barry, Norman P. *Hayek's Social and Economic Philosophy.* Atlantic Highlands, N.J.: Humanities Press, 1979.

Baumol, William J. *Welfare Economics and the Theory of the State.* Cambridge, Mass.: Harvard University Press, 1952.

Beale, Hugh, and Tony Dugdale. "Contracts between Businessmen: Planning and the Use of Contractual Remedies." *British Journal of Law and Society* 2 (Summer 1975): 45–60.

Bentham, Jeremy. *An Introduction to the Principles of Morals and Legislation,* ed. J. H. Burns and H. L. A. Hart. London: Athlone Press, 1970.

Berkeley, George. "Passive Obedience: Upon the Principles of the Law of Nature." Pp. 101–135 in Alexander Campbell Fraser, ed., *The Works of George Berkeley,* vol. 4. Oxford: Clarendon Press, 1891; essay first published 1712.

Blackstone, William. *Commentaries on the Laws of England.* Chicago: University of Chicago Press, 1979; 4-vol. facsimile of lst ed. of 1765–1769.

Blom, John J. *Descartes: His Moral Philosophy and Psychology.* New York: New York University Press, 1978.

Bok, Sissela. *Secrets: On the Ethics of Concealment and Revelation.* New York: Pantheon, 1983.

Braithwaite, R. B. *Theory of Games as a Tool for the Moral Philosopher.* Cambridge: At the University Press, 1955.

Brandt, Richard. *A Theory of the Good and the Right.* Oxford: Clarendon Press, 1979.

Braybrooke, David. "The Choice between Utilitarianisms." *American Philosophical Quarterly* 4 (1967): 28–38.

Broad, C. D. "The Doctrine of Consequences in Ethics." *International Journal of Ethics* 24 (April 1914): 293–320.

———. *Ethics,* ed. C. Lewy. Dordrecht: Martinus Nijhoff, 1985.

———. "On the Function of False Hypotheses in Ethics." *International Journal of Ethics* 26 (April 1916): 377–397.

Brock, Dan W. "Recent Work in Utilitarianism." *American Philosophical Quarterly* 10 (October 1973): 241–276.

Carritt, E. F. *Ethical and Political Thinking.* Oxford: Clarendon Press, 1947.

Coase, R. H. "The Problem of Social Cost." *Journal of Law and Economics* 3 (1960): 1–44.

Cooper, Wesley E., Kai Nielsen, and Steven C. Patten, eds. *Canadian Journal of Philosophy,* supp. vol. 5, *New Essays on John Stuart Mill and Utilitarianism.* Guelph, Ontario: Canadian Association for Publishing in Philosophy, 1979.

Dasgupta, Partha. "Utilitarianism, Information and Rights." Pp. 199–218 in Amartya Sen and Bernard Williams, eds., *Utilitarianism and Beyond.* Cambridge: Cambridge University Press, 1982.

David, Paul A. "Clio and the Economics of QWERTY." *American Economic Review Papers and Proceedings* 75 (May 1985): 332–337.

Dawson, John P. *Gifts and Promises: Continental and American Law Compared.* New Haven, Conn.: Yale University Press, 1980.

Descartes, René. *Discourse on the Method.* Pp. 111–151 in John Cottingham, Robert Stoothoff, and Dugald Murdoch, eds., *The Philosophical Works of Descartes.* Cambridge: Cambridge University Press, 1985; *Discourse* first published in French in 1637.

———. Letter to Elisabeth, January 1646. Pp. 632–637 in Descartes, *Oeuvres Philosophiques,* vol. 3, ed. Ferdinand Alquié. Paris: Garnier Frères, 1973.

Devlin, Patrick. *The Enforcement of Morals*. Oxford: Oxford University Press, 1965.

Donagan, Alan. "Is There a Credible Form of Utilitarianism?" Pp. 187–202 in Michael D. Bayles, ed., *Contemporary Utilitarianism*. Garden City, N.Y.: Doubleday, 1968.

―――. *The Theory of Morality*. Chicago: University of Chicago Press, 1977.

Dorman, Neil A. "The Refutation of the Generalization Argument." *Ethics* 74 (January 1964): 150–154.

Dostoevsky, Fyodor. *The Brothers Karamazov*. Harmondsworth, Middlesex: Penguin, 1958.

Dowling, Keith. "Consistency, Impartiality, and Universalizability." *South African Journal of Philosophy* 5 (1986): 53–58.

Downs, Anthony. *An Economic Theory of Democracy*. New York: Harper and Brothers, 1957.

Doyle, Arthur Conan. "The Adventure of the Abbey Grange." Pp. 491–507 in *The Annotated Sherlock Holmes*, vol. 2, ed. William S. Baring-Gould. New York: Clarkson N. Potter, 1967. 2 vols.

Dworkin, Gerald. "The Concept of Autonomy." *Grazer Philosophische Studien* 12 (1981): 203–213.

―――. "Is More Choice Better Than Less?" Pp. 47–62 in Peter A. French, Theodore E. Uehling, Jr., and Howard K. Wettstein, eds., *Social and Political Philosophy*, vol. 7 of *Midwest Studies in Philosophy*. Minneapolis: University of Minnesota Press, 1982.

―――. "The Journal of Mathematical Ethics: A Proposal." *Philosophical Forum* 13 (Summer 1982): 413–415.

―――. "Paternalism." *The Monist* 56 (January 1972): 62–84.

Dworkin, Ronald. "What Is Equality? Part I: Equality of Welfare." *Philosophy and Public Affairs* 10 (Summer 1981): 185–246.

―――. "What Is Equality? Part II: Equality of Resources." *Philosophy and Public Affairs* 10 (Fall 1981): 283–345.

Edgeworth, F. Y. *Mathematical Psychics: An Essay on the Application of Mathematics to the Moral Sciences*. London: C. Kegan Paul, 1881.

Elster, Jon. *Ulysses and the Sirens*. Cambridge: Cambridge University Press, 1979.

Etienne, Jean-Louis. "Skiing Alone to the Pole." *National Geographic* 170 (September 1986): 318–323.

Feinberg, Joel. "Duty and Obligation in the Non-Ideal World." *Journal of Philosophy* 70 (May 10, 1973): 263–275.

―――. "The Forms and Limits of Utilitarianism." *Philosophical Review* 76 (July 1967): 368–381.

―――. "Legal Paternalism." *Canadian Journal of Philosophy* 1 (1971): 105–124.

―――. "Rawls and Intuitionism." Pp. 108–124 in Norman Daniels, ed., *Reading Rawls*. New York: Basic Books, n.d.

Findlay, J. N. *Plato and Platonism*. New York: Times Books, 1978.

Fleck, Ludwik. *Genesis and Development of a Scientific Fact*. Chicago: University of Chicago Press, 1979.

Flew, Antony. *An Introduction to Western Philosophy*. Indianapolis: Bobbs-Merrill, 1971.

Flugel, J. C. *Man, Morals and Society*. New York: International Universities Press, 1945.

Friedlander, Paul J. C. "H-Day Is Coming in Sweden." *New York Times*, August 20, 1967, sec. 10, pp. 1 and 31.

Frost, Robert. "Mending Wall." Pp. 47–48 in Frost, *Complete Poems of Robert Frost*. New York: Holt, Rinehart and Winston, 1949.

Fuller, Lon L. "Human Interaction and the Law." Pp. 212–246 in Fuller, *The Principles of Social Order*, ed. Kenneth I. Winston. Durham, N.C.: Duke University Press, 1981; essay originally published 1969.

Gärdenfors, Peter. "Rights, Games and Social Choice." *Nous* 15 (1981): 341–356.

Gewirth, Alan. "Can Utilitarianism Justify Any Moral Rights?" Pp. 143–162 in Gewirth, *Human Rights: Essays on Justification and Applications*. Chicago: University of Chicago Press, 1982.

Gompers, Samuel. "Discussion at Rochester, N.Y., on the Open Shop— 'The Union Shop Is Right'—It Naturally Follows Organization." *American Federationist* 4 (April 1905): 221–223.

Gordon, Scott. "John Rawls's Difference Principle, Utilitarianism, and the Optimum Degree of Inequality." *Journal of Philosophy* 70 (May 10, 1973): 275–280.

Green, T. H. "Liberal Legislation and Freedom of Contract." Pp. 43–74 in Green, *Political Theory*, ed. John R. Rodman. New York: Appleton-Century-Crofts, 1964.

Gutmann, Amy, and Dennis Thompson, eds. *Ethics and Politics: Cases and Comments*. Chicago: Nelson-Hall, 1984.

Hamilton, Allan McLane. *The Intimate Life of Alexander Hamilton*. New York: Charles Scribner's Sons, 1910.

Hardin, Russell. *Collective Action*. (Baltimore: Johns Hopkins University Press for Resources for the Future, 1982.

———. "Difficulties in the Notion of Economic Rationality." *Social Science Information* 23 (1984): 453–467.

———. "Does Might Make Right?" Pp. 201–217 in J. Roland Pennock and John W. Chapman, eds., *Nomos 29: Authority Revisited*. New York: New York University Press, 1987.

———. "The Emergence of Norms." *Ethics* 90 (July 1980): 575–587.

———. "Exchange Theory on Strategic Bases." *Social Science Information* 21 (1982): 251–272.

———. "Rational Choice Theories." Pp. 67–91 in Terence Ball, ed., *Idioms of Inquiry: Critique and Renewal in Political Science*. Albany, N.Y.: SUNY Press, 1987.

———. "Rationality, Irrationality, and Functionalist Explanation." *Social Science Information* 19 (1980): 755–772.

———. "Sanction and Obligation." *The Monist* 68 (July 1985): 403–418.

Harman, Gilbert. *The Nature of Morality: An Introduction to Ethics.* New York: Oxford University Press, 1977.

Harrison, Jonathan. *Hume's Theory of Justice.* Oxford: Clarendon Press, 1981.

Harsanyi, John. *Essays on Ethics, Social Behavior, and Scientific Explanation.* Dordrecht: D. Reidel, 1976.

Hart, H. L. A. "Rawls on Liberty and Its Priority." *University of Chicago Law Review* 40 (1973): 534–555.

Hayek, F. A. *The Constitution of Liberty.* Chicago: University of Chicago Press, 1960.

———. *The Mirage of Social Justice,* vol. 2 of *Law, Legislation, and Liberty.* Chicago: University of Chicago Press, 1976.

Heath, Anthony. *Rational Choice and Social Exchange.* Cambridge: Cambridge University Press, 1976.

Hodgson, D. H. *Consequences of Utilitarianism.* Oxford: Oxford University Press, 1967.

Hofmannsthal, Hugo von. "Manche freilich . . ." P. 22 in Hofmannsthal, *Gedichte und kleine Dramen.* Frankfurt: Suhrkamp Verlag, n.d.

Hume, David. *An Enquiry Concerning the Principles of Morals,* in Hume, *Enquiries,* 3d ed., ed. L. A. Selby-Bigge and P. H. Nidditch. Oxford: Clarendon Press, 1975; *Enquiry* first published 1751.

———. *A Treatise of Human Nature,* 2d ed., ed. L. A. Selby-Bigge and P. H. Nidditch. Oxford: Clarendon Press, 1978; *Treatise* first published 1739–40.

Hutcheson, Frances. *Inquiry into the Original of Our Ideas of Beauty and Virtue.* London, 1725.

James, William. "The Moral Equivalent of War." Pp. 162–173 in James, *Essays in Religion and Morality.* Cambridge, Mass.: Harvard University Press, 1982; essay first published 1910.

———. "The Moral Philosopher and the Moral Life." Pp. 184–215 in James, *The Will to Believe.* New York: Longmans Green, 1897; reprint, New York: Dover Publications, 1956.

———. *The Principles of Psychology.* Cambridge, Mass.: Harvard University Press, 1981; first published 1890.

Kadish, Mortimer R., and Sanford H. Kadish. *Discretion to Disobey: A Study of Lawful Departures from Legal Rules.* Stanford, Calif.: Stanford University Press, 1973.

Kant, Immanuel. *Grounding for the Metaphysics of Morals.* In Kant, *Ethical Philosophy,* trans. James W. Ellington. Indianapolis: Hackett, 1983; originally published in German in 1785.

———. *Prolegomena to Any Future Metaphysics,* trans. Paul Carus. La Salle, Ill.: Open Court, 1902.

Knight, Frank. "The Role of Principles in Economics and Politics." Pp. 251–281 in Knight, *On the History and Method of Economics.* Chicago: University of Chicago Press, 1956.

Kovesi, Julius. *Moral Notions.* London: Routledge and Kegan Paul, 1967.

Leveen, Steven. "Tangled Typing." *Science 81* (May 1981): 84–86.

Lewis, C. I. *An Analysis of Knowledge and Valuation*. La Salle, Ill.: Open Court, 1946.

Lewis, David K. *Convention*. Cambridge, Mass.: Harvard University Press, 1969.

Lindsay, A. D. *The Modern Democratic State*. New York and London: Oxford University Press, 1947.

Locke, John. *An Essay Concerning Human Understanding,* ed. Peter H. Nidditch. Oxford: Clarendon Press, 1975; *Essay* first published 1689.

Luce, R. Duncan and Howard Raiffa. *Games and Decisions*. New York: Wiley, 1957.

Lyons, David. *The Forms and Limits of Utilitarianism*. Oxford: Oxford University Press, 1965.

———. "Utility and Rights." Pp. 107–138 in J. Roland Pennock and John W. Chapman, eds., *Nomos 24: Ethics, Economics, and the Law*. New York: New York University Press, 1982.

Macauley, Stewart. "Non-contractual Relations in Business." *American Sociological Review* 28 (1963): 55–66.

MacCallum, Gerald C., Jr. "Negative and Positive Freedom." *Philosophical Review* 76 (July 1967): 312–334.

Mackie, J. L. "The Disutility of Act-Utilitarianism." *Philosophical Quarterly* 23 (October 1973): 289–300.

Macneil, Ian. *The New Social Contract*. New Haven, Conn.: Yale University Press, 1980.

March, James G., and Herbert Simon. *Organizations*. New York: Wiley, 1958.

Martial. *The Epigrams of Martial,* trans. James Michie. London: Hart-Davis, MacGibbon, 1973.

Mathews, Harry. *The Sinking of the Odradek Stadium and Other Novels*. New York: Harper & Row, 1975.

Mill, John Stuart. "Austin on Jurisprudence." Pp. 165–205 in Mill, *Essays on Equality, Law, and Education,* ed. John M. Robson, vol. 21 of *Collected Works of John Stuart Mill*. Toronto: University of Toronto Press, 1984.

———. "Civilization." Pp. 117–147 in Mill, *Essays on Politics and Society,* ed. John M. Robson, vol. 18 of *Collected Works of John Stuart Mill*. Toronto: University of Toronto Press, 1977.

———. "On Liberty." Pp. 209–310 in Mill, *Essays on Politics and Society,* ed. John M. Robson, vol. 18 of *Collected Works of John Stuart Mill*. Toronto: University of Toronto Press, 1977.

———. *Principles of Political Economy,* ed. J. M. Robson, vols. 2 and 3 of *Collected Works of John Stuart Mill*. Toronto: University of Toronto Press, 1965.

———. "Statement on Marriage." P. 99 in *Essays on Equality, Law, and Education,* ed. John M. Robson, vol. 21 of *Collected Works of John Stuart Mill*. Toronto: University of Toronto Press, 1984.

———. "Utilitarianism." Pp. 203–259 in Mill, *Essays on Ethics, Religion and Society,* vol. 10 of *Collected Works of John Stuart Mill*. Toronto: University of Toronto Press, 1969; essay first published 1861.

Moore, G. E. *Principia Ethica*. Cambridge: At the University Press, 1903.

Morgenstern, Oskar. "The Collaboration between Oskar Morgenstern and John von Neumann on the Theory of Games." *Journal of Economic Literature* 14 (September 1976): 805–816.

Mulholland, Leslie A. "Rights, Utilitarianism, and the Conflation of Persons." *Journal of Philosophy* 83 (June 1986): 323–340.

Nagel, Thomas. *The Possibility of Altruism*. Oxford: Clarendon Press, 1970.

Narveson, Jan. "Promising, Expecting, and Utility." *Canadian Journal of Philosophy* 1 (December 1971): 207–233.

———. "Rawls and Utilitarianism." Pp. 128–143 in Harlan B. Miller and William H. Williams, eds., *The Limits of Utilitarianism*. Minneapolis: University of Minnesota Press, 1982.

Neumann, John von, and Oskar Morgenstern. *Theory of Games and Economic Behavior*, 3d ed. Princeton: Princeton University Press, 1953; first published 1944.

Nicholas, Barry. *An Introduction to Roman Law*. Oxford: Clarendon Press, 1962.

Noonan, John T., Jr. *Contraception: A History of Its Treatment by the Catholic Theologians and Canonists*, enlarged ed. Cambridge, Mass.: Harvard University Press, 1986; first ed. 1965.

Nozick, Robert. *Anarchy, State, and Utopia*. New York: Basic Books, 1974.

———. *Philosophical Explanations*. Cambridge, Mass.: Harvard University Press, 1981.

Oates, Whitney J., ed. *The Stoic and Epicurean Philosophers*. New York: Modern Library, 1940.

Olson, Mancur, Jr. *The Logic of Collective Action*. Cambridge, Mass.: Harvard University Press, 1965.

Paley, William. *The Principles of Moral and Political Philosophy*. London: R. Fauler, 1785; reprint, New York: Garland Publishing Company, 1978.

Pareto, Vilfredo. *Manual of Political Economy*. New York: Kelley, 1971; trans. of 1927 French ed.

———. *The Mind and Society*, 4 vols., trans. Andrew Bongiorno and Arthur Livingston. New York: Harcourt, Brace, 1935.

Parfit, Derek. *Reasons and Persons*. Oxford: Clarendon Press, 1984.

Parkes, Colin Murray. *Bereavement: Studies of Grief in Adult Life*. New York: International Universities Press, 1972.

Perry, Ralph Barton. *The Thought and Character of William James*. Boston: Little, Brown, 1935.

Pigou, Arthur C. *The Economics of Welfare*, 4th ed. London: Macmillan, 1932; first published 1920.

Plato. *The Republic*.

Poe, Edgar Allan. "The Sphinx." Pp. 65–69 in Poe, *Tales of Mystery and Imagination*. London: Dent, Everyman's Library, 1908.

Pretz, Vera. "Promises and Threats." *Mind* 86 (October 1977): 578–581.

Prichard, H. A. "Does Moral Philosophy Rest on a Mistake?" Pp. 1–17 in Prichard, *Moral Obligation and Duty and Interest*. London: Oxford University Press, 1968; essay first published 1912.

Proust, Marcel. *Remembrance of Things Past,* vol. 1. New York: Random House, 1934. 2 vols.

Quinton, Anthony. "Utilitarian Ethics." Pp. 1–118 in W. D. Hudson, ed., *New Studies in Ethics,* vol. 2. New York: St. Martin's, 1974.

Raphael, D. D. *British Moralists, 1650–1800*. Oxford: Oxford University Press, 1969. 2 vols.

Rapoport, Anatol, Melvin J. Guyer, and David G. Gordon. *The 2 × 2 Game.* Ann Arbor: University of Michigan Press, 1976.

Rawls, John. "Justice as Fairness." *Philosophical Review* 67 (April 1958): 164–194.

———. *A Theory of Justice.* Cambridge, Mass.: Harvard University Press, 1971.

———. "Two Concepts of Rules." *Philosophical Review* 64 (1955): 3–32.

Regan, Donald H. *Utilitarianism and Co-operation.* Oxford: Clarendon Press, 1980.

Rist, J. M. *Epicurus: An Introduction.* Cambridge: Cambridge University Press, 1972.

Robbins, Lionel. *An Essay on the Nature and Significance of Economic Science.* London: Macmillan, 1937; first published 1932.

———. "Bentham in the Twentieth Century." Pp. 73–84 in Robbins, *The Evolution of Modern Economic Theory and Other Papers on the History of Economic Thought.* Chicago: Aldine, 1970.

Roberts, T. A. *The Concept of Benevolence.* London: Macmillan, 1973.

Ryan, Alan. *Property and Political Theory.* Oxford: Basil Blackwell, 1984.

Ryle, Gilbert. "Conscience and Moral Convictions." Pp. 185–193 in Ryle, *Collected Essays 1929–1968,* vol. 2 of *Collected Papers.* New York: Barnes and Noble, 1971; essay first published 1940.

Samuelson, Paul A. *Foundations of Economic Analysis.* Cambridge, Mass.: Harvard University Press, 1947.

———. "St. Petersburg Paradoxes: Defanged, Dissected, and Historically Described." *Journal of Economic Literature* 15 (March 1977): 24–55.

Sappho. "We shall enjoy it." Fragment no. 2 in Mary Barnard, ed. and trans., *Sappho: A New Translation.* Berkeley: University of California Press, 1958. (The title of the fragment is Barnard's.)

Schachner, Nathan. *Alexander Hamilton.* New York: A. S. Barnes, 1946.

Scheffler, Samuel. *The Rejection of Consequentialism: A Philosophical Investigation of the Considerations Underlying Rival Moral Conceptions.* Oxford: Clarendon Press, 1982.

Schelling, Thomas C. "Hockey Helmets, Concealed Weapons, and Daylight Savings." *Journal of Conflict Resolution* 17 (September 1973): 381–428.

———. "The Intimate Contest for Self Command." *Public Interest,* no. 60 (Summer 1980): 94–118.

————. *The Strategy of Conflict*. Cambridge, Mass.: Harvard University Press, 1960.

Schwartz, Alan. "Products Liability and Judicial Wealth Redistributions." *Indiana Law Journal* 51 (Spring 1976): 558–589.

Sen, Amartya. "The Impossibility of a Paretian Liberal." *Journal of Political Economy* 78 (1970): 152–157.

————. "Informational Bases of Alternative Welfare Approaches: Aggregation and Income Distribution." *Journal of Public Economics* 3 (1974): 387–403.

————. "Liberty As Control: An Appraisal." Pp. 207–221 in Peter A. French, Theodore E. Uehling, Jr., Howard K. Wettstein, eds., *Social and Political Philosophy*, vol. 7 of *Midwest Studies in Philosophy*. Minneapolis: University of Minnesota Press, 1982.

————. "Liberty, Unanimity and Rights." *Economica* 43 (1976): 217–245.

————. "Personal Utilities and Public Judgments: Or What's Wrong with Welfare Economics?" *Economic Journal* 89 (September 1979): 537–558.

Shubik, Martin. *Game Theory in the Social Sciences: Concepts and Solutions*. Cambridge, Mass.: MIT Press, 1982.

Sidgwick, Henry. *Methods of Ethics*, 7th ed. London: Macmillan, 1907; first ed. 1874.

Silver, Charles. "Utilitarian Participation." *Social Science Information* 23 (1984): 701–729.

Singer, Marcus George. *Generalization in Ethics*. New York: Alfred A. Knopf, 1961.

Smith, Adam. *Lectures on Jurisprudence*, vol. 5 of *The Glasgow Edition of the Works and Correspondence of Adam Smith*. Oxford: Oxford University Press, 1978; notes of lectures dating from 1762–1764.

————. *Lectures on Rhetoric and Belles Lettres*, vol. 4 of *The Glasgow Edition of the Works and Correspondence of Adam Smith*. Oxford: Oxford University Press, 1983. From recently discovered student notes.

Steger, Will. "North to the Pole." *National Geographic* 170 (September 1986): 289–317.

Stewart, Dugald. "Account of the Life and Writings of Adam Smith, LL.D." Pp. 269–351 in Adam Smith, *Essays on Philosophical Subjects*, vol. 3 of *The Glasgow Edition of the Works and Correspondence of Adam Smith*. Oxford: Oxford University Press, 1980; Indianapolis, Ind.: Liberty Press, 1982.

Stigler, George J. *The Citizen and the State: Essays on Regulation*. Chicago: University of Chicago Press, 1975.

Taylor, Michael. *Community, Anarchy and Liberty*. Cambridge: Cambridge University Press, 1982.

Toynbee, Arnold. *Lectures on the Industrial Revolution*. London: Longman's, Green & Co., 1884.

Trollope, Anthony. *The Duke's Children*. Oxford: Oxford University Press, 1973; originally published 1879–1880.

————. *He Knew He Was Right*. London: Strahan and Co., 1869; reprint, New York: Dover, 1983. 2 vols.

Ullmann-Margalit, Edna. *The Emergence of Norms*. Oxford: Oxford University Press, 1977.

Updike, John. "The Music School." Pp. 138–143 in Updike, *The Music School*. Greenwich, Conn.: Fawcett Publications, 1967.

Urmson, J. O. "The Interpretation of the Moral Philosophy of J. S. Mill." *Philosophical Quarterly* 3 (1953): 33–39.

Vietmeyer, Noel D. "The Preposterous Puffer." *National Geographic* 166 (August 1984): 260–270.

Warnock, G. J. *The Object of Morality*. London: Methuen, 1971.

Warshow, Robert Irving. *Alexander Hamilton: First American Business Man*. New York: Greenberg, 1931.

Weisskopf, Walter A. *Alienation and Economics*. New York: Dutton, 1971.

Whitehead, A. N. *Introduction to Mathematics*. London: Williams and Norgate, 1911.

Williams, Bernard. "A Critique of Utilitarianism." Pp. 76–150 in J. J. C. Smart and Bernard Williams, *Utilitarianism: For and Against*. Cambridge: Cambridge University Press, 1973.

———. *Morality*. New York: Harper, 1972.

Winch, Donald. *Adam Smith's Politics*. Cambridge: Cambridge University Press, 1978.

Wittgenstein, Ludwig. *On Certainty*, ed. G. E. M. Anscombe and G. H. von Wright. Oxford: Basil Blackwell, 1969.

———. *Remarks on the Philosophy of Psychology*, ed. G. E. M. Anscombe and G. H. von Wright. Chicago: University of Chicago Press, 1980. 2 vols.

———. *Zettel*, trans. G. E. M. Anscombe. Oxford: Basil Blackwell, 1967.

Wood, Alan. *Bertrand Russell: The Passionate Skeptic*. New York: Simon and Schuster, 1958.

Index